Across Boundaries

TON VOSLOO

Across Boundaries

A life in the media in a time of change

Jonathan Ball Publishers
Johannesburg & Cape Town

All rights reserved.
No part of this publication may be reproduced or
transmitted, in any form or by any means, without written
permission from the publisher or copyright holders.

© Text: Ton Vosloo, 2018
© Photos: Ton Vosloo & Media24
© Published edition: Jonathan Ball Publishers, 2018

Published in 2018 by
JONATHAN BALL PUBLISHERS
A division of Media24 (Pty) Ltd
PO Box 33977
Jeppestown
2043

ISBN 978-1-86842-888-5
ebook 978-1-86842-889-2

Twitter: www.twitter.com/JonathanBallPub
Facebook: www.facebook.com/Jonathan-Ball-Publishers
Blog: http://jonathanball.bookslive.co.za/

Translated by Linde Dietrich
Design and typesetting by Triple M Design, Johannesburg
Set in 11/15 pt Minion Pro

The publication of this book was made possible by a generous
grant from the LW Hiemstra Trust – established by Riekie
Hiemstra in remembrance of Ludwig Wybren (Louis) Hiemstra.

△ LW Hiemstra Trust

Printed by *paarlmedia*, a division of Novus Holdings

The day I started working on my memoirs, my wife Anet offered me a Chinese fortune cookie. I cracked it open, and it read:

Confucius say:
If you think you're going to sum up your whole life
on this little bit of paper,
you're crazy.

So I just carried on with the craziness anyway!

Contents

Foreword ix

1   Childhood and first years in journalism 1
2   The metamorphosis of Naspers 23
3   A global giant 39
4   Tencent, the colossus in the stable 46
5   Koos Bekker, the talisman 60
6   The press and politics: Vanguard thinking and paving the way 72
7   Invasion of the North 87
8   A tectonic shift 101
9   Connecting with our black compatriots 120
10   Leadership 128
11   *Broedertwis* 138
12   Turbulence at Nasionale Pers 154
13   Shock waves, a tsunami and ongoing ripples 166
14   Presidential tempers 181
15   Hit the big story hard! 195
16   Verwoerd sinks our sport 207
17   St Nelson and me 215
18   Robert Mugabe and John Vorster 223
19   Entry into a wider world 231

20 Does Naspers still have a soul? 242
21 Afrikaans in decline 251
22 Lighter moments 262
23 The future of Naspers in South Africa 273

Notes 279
Prizes, awards and honours 283
Books by the author and contributions to books 284
Acknowledgements 285
Index 287

FOREWORD

When Ton Vosloo retired in 2015 after a 59-year career in publishing, the most successful combination of chair and chief executive that South Africa has ever seen came to an end. Shortly after his appointment as managing director of Nasionale Pers in 1984 – before the group changed its name to Naspers in 1998 – Ton and Koos Bekker's idea for a pay-television channel in South Africa became a reality. As they say, the rest is history.

Ton was not only a CEO who encouraged transformative talent, but also, eventually, a wise chair who supported a visionary chief executive – and thereby, between 1984 and 2015, created wealth of R905 billion for Naspers shareholders.

While competition between a chair and a CEO is commonplace nowadays, the Naspers example tells a story of complementarity, symbiosis and co-operation that produced incredible results.

The Ton/Koos story is one of people who gave each other space and support, but also one of people who knew Darwin was right when he said it is not necessarily the strongest that survive, but those that are the most flexible and adaptive to change. Ton allowed Koos to build one of the world's most flexible media businesses – which is today one of the leading Internet companies. It was a leadership combination many businesses can only dream of.

Hendrik du Toit, CEO of Investec Asset Management, London, 2017
Du Toit has been a non-executive director of Naspers from 2017

CHAPTER 1

Childhood and first years in journalism

On 3 January 1955, Hester Vosloo put her only surviving son – I, Theunissen, just 17 – on the train to Pretoria at the station in Uitenhage. With a one-way ticket in my pocket, I set off to start my employment as junior clerk in the Department of Forestry's long corridors, in Hamilton Street's V Building, on 5 January.

My career in journalism, therefore, started in a roundabout way. Since my youth, I had wanted to become a journalist.

From the age of 14, nicknamed Ton by my friends, I had written stories covering school sports for two local English-language weeklies, the *Uitenhage Times* and the *Uitenhage Chronicle*.

After an initial detour via Forestry in Pretoria, my life's journey would soon start heading in the direction of my desired career.

My mother, Hester Jacoba Combrinck Pienaar, commonly known as Hetta, was born in the Karoo town of Middelburg in 1906. She was married to Jacobus Johannes Vermaak Vosloo, born in 1902.

Vossie, as my dad was known, came from a big family of poor subsistence farmers and woodcutters in the Witels forestry area of the Humansdorp district, in the heart of the beautiful Tsitsikamma region. His birthplace, Robbehoek, has become a thriving dairy-farming area since the impoverished farmers' sour grass was ploughed up and replaced with sweet grass.

In 2003, I published a family history of the Vosloos titled *Nuttige Burgers*

(Useful Citizens). Genealogist Daniel Malan Jacobs had done thorough research. In my preface, I write that the Vosloos 'harbour a good deal of individualism in their genes. A common trait is that of practical people who are inspired by far-off vistas. They could and did do things, mostly constructive. Useful citizens!'

The earliest known document that contains a reference to the Vosslöhs (the German spelling) is dated 20 April 1413. The first mention of the progenitor Jan Vosloo at the Cape, in a resolution of the council of policy of the Dutch East India Company, bears the date 22 October 1689.

My father was the youngest of eight children born of my grandfather's first marriage. Oupa Jan later married for a second time, and four more children were born.

After leaving school with a Standard 6 (today's Grade 8) my father became a mounted policeman in the South African Police (SAP). Pa was a neat man and a proud police officer. Photos attest to his shiny leather gaiters and the spick-and-span state of his uniform.

From Middelburg, Hetta Pienaar went to the Denneoord teachers' training college in Stellenbosch and became a primary-school teacher. She played hockey at Stellenbosch. There was a fair amount of sport in her veins: her only brother, Wynand (Bunny) Pienaar, played first-league rugby in the Eastern Province and later coached the Olympics club's first team.

Hetta went to teach at farm schools in the north-eastern Cape Province, including the one on the Southeys' farm Hillmoor in the Steynsburg district. She was related to the Combrincks from Bethulie in the southern Free State, hence 'Combrinck' was one of her baptismal names. She became engaged to a distant cousin, Flip Combrinck, but he died tragically before their marriage after apparently having ingested snails hidden in lettuce. Hetta subsequently became acquainted with the friendly officer from the police station on Hillmoor, and married him in 1928.

Their first child, Wynand Frederick – Freddie for short – was born in Colesberg in 1934. The family moved to Uitenhage when Constable Vosloo was transferred. I arrived in 1937, and Joan (Joanna Jacoba) seven years later, in 1944.

Freddie and I kicked rugby balls made of stuffed tobacco bags around in the street in front of our house at 85 Graaff Reinet Road, Uitenhage. There was no shortage of playmates: next door were the eight or nine Van Antwerpens, further down the street the numerous Strydom brothers, and in the same neighbourhood the Knoetze and Crouse boys – not to mention the Carlettis of Italian descent on the corner.

We were a horde of boys who roughed one another up, played '*aspaai*' and 'dokkie-dokkie', with stones flying around us, shot with catapults, and trapped birds with home-made glue that we called by its English name, birdlime. 'Dokkie-dokkie' was a game in which round river stones were piled on top of one another. Each player got a turn to rebuild the pile while the others pelted both him and the target with stones. Bruises were commonplace, as were direct hits to the head.

Pa Vosloo was a constable at Uitenhage, and had a new three-bedroomed house built, a modern one for those days. It had a garage and an outside toilet built of bricks. The bathroom had a copper geyser that Freddie and I stoked with tomato-box planks at bath time.

Pa would go out into the district on patrol, sometimes bringing home delicious oranges or sweet melons from the irrigated farms around Kirkwood. In the winter, he would go on hunting trips with his friends. On his return, we would feast on venison, sausage and biltong made from the kudu, bushbuck and duikers they had shot.

In the early 1940s, Uitenhage got a modern police station, as well as a block of flats for police personnel, where I befriended the sons of the English-speaking Chief Constable Winer, Paul and Trevor. They would later become an academic and a computer boffin respectively, overseas.

On Saturdays, Ma and Pa played tennis at the Police Club, where they would slake their thirst with beer from big, brown bottles. Freddie and I would run around with the other police kids, and I would sometimes play in the sandpit. In the storeroom for the tennis equipment, I once came across a beer bottle and took a swig. Big drama – the bottle contained not beer, but Jeyes Fluid, a disinfectant. I must have screamed blue murder, because Hetta immediately forced some or other oil down my throat in the mess hall. Theunissen was not one to pass up the chance of a drink, then!

I survived the Jeyes Fluid, as I had the disaster a year or two earlier when, on a visit to family in Colesberg, I had picked prickly pears by hand in Oupa Jim Norval's back yard. I was, of course, covered in thousands of tiny thorns that Ma and my aunts had to remove with great effort and many handfuls of fat and butter.

On Sundays, Freddie and I would walk for miles in the heat to the Sunday school at the Dutch Reformed Moederkerk (Mother Church). Afterwards, we would go for a swim in the municipal pool. Sometimes, our family would drive out of town to The Springs, a holiday resort built around a number of bubbling artesian springs from which Uitenhage pumped a portion of its drinking water. There, we would eat watermelon in summer, smear one another with the sticky rinds and cavort in the swimming pool with hundreds of other playmates.

As an aside, I reported much later for *Die Oosterlig* on a speech by the English-speaking mayor of Uitenhage, Gerald Smith. He referred to The Springs as Die Springe (the jumps)! At least he had tried to be bilingual.

And then, the world turned dark: the Second World War broke out. Pa, along with nearly all the other men at the police station, joined the South Africa Police Brigade in 1941; there was pressure on those in uniform to participate in the war. Pa was not anti-war. I later found out that he had been a Freemason from as far back as his Karoo days. In those days, the leadership structure of the SAP was pro-English, and many young Afrikaners in the police became Freemasons.

With Pa gone, Hetta had to raise me and Freddie. Dark blinds were installed in the windows of our house to prevent the enemy from spotting us. Uitenhage was 35 kilometres from Port Elizabeth and the sea; why the Germans would want to attack it was a mystery to us. Perhaps it was because Uitenhage's big railway workshop had been converted into a munitions factory where bayonets, among other things, were produced. Along with other women, my mom went to work there, sharpening bayonets. It was here, presumably, that she learnt to smoke.

Pa went to Egypt and Libya with the Police Brigade. In 1943, one of his legs was badly burned when boiling water spilled on it. He was treated at the field hospital at the then-famous Shepheard's Hotel in Cairo. After being

CHILDHOOD AND FIRST YEARS IN JOURNALISM

discharged, he resumed his career in 1943 with the police in Uitenhage.

I cannot remember much about him. Once, when I was about five years old, James, the son of our domestic worker Sarah Steenekamp, and I were playing around the Willys car Pa was working on. Presumably, he was getting the car ready for use; it had stood on blocks in the garage during the war. James and I had a disagreement and started fighting. The tears flowed, and Pa flew out from under the car, grabbed a few planks that were lying around and gave both of us a good hiding. This was the only hiding I recall getting from him. Later, Hetta would beat me and Freddie with Pa's leather belt when we were naughty.

And then came our truly dark days. It was 28 January 1944, a sweltering summer's day in Uitenhage. While patrolling the streets on a bicycle, Constable Vosloo raced after a suspected pickpocket. He became nauseous and suffered a seizure in the street. Someone ferried him to hospital, where he was treated by Dr Solly Ofsowitz, but it was too late.

That afternoon, Hetta was visited by Chief Constable Winer, and then by a clergyman, and suddenly we were fatherless. Hetta was five months pregnant and had two boys to care for. What I remember of the funeral service in the Moederkerk is the pungent scent of the large bunch of white St Joseph's lilies. The police squad fired a salute over our heads at the graveside.

The primary school Freddie attended was Laerskool Jordan. The name was later changed to Laerskool Handhaaf, which upset me. Eventually, I joined him there. We walked to and from school every day – a helluva distance, barefoot, but the soles of our feet were rock hard.

To make ends meet, Ma took in a newlywed detective and his wife as lodgers: Sergeant Grobler and his friendly wife Dixie. She was an English-speaking woman from Cradock, of Irish descent, whose maiden name was Mann. I remember the nice detective only as 'Uncle'.

On 9 May 1944, Hetta gave birth to our little sister Joan. We were now a household of three children.

In 1946, however, Hetta was hit by another calamity. Freddie was a crack athlete, but one afternoon he tripped over a hurdle during a race and broke his arm. Teacher Johnny van der Merwe came to break the news to Hetta.

Freddie became increasingly listless, and was no longer the spirited boy he had been before the accident. Examinations and, finally, a visit to a specialist in Port Elizabeth led to a cruel diagnosis: a brain tumour. Freddie had to be operated on by Dr Krynauw in the Johannesburg General Hospital. At the time, Dr Krynauw was the only surgeon in the country who performed operations of this kind.

It was December 1946. With Joan in her arms, Hetta, the sick Freddie and I travelled by train, with her sister Anna Beetge, via Colesberg to Johannesburg. At Colesberg, Joan and I, along with Aunt Anna, were deposited in the waiting arms of Oom Luther Norval and his wife Martie, my mom's sister and Anna's twin. The train then departed with Hetta and Freddie; the tears flowed. We would stay with the Norvals for the long summer holiday until Freddie was able to leave the hospital.

Freddie's operation was performed towards the end of December. Hetta was accommodated by the Spies family, who lived in Hillbrow, close to the hospital. That family's mother was Ada Winer's sister, Chief Constable Winer's Afrikaans wife. This was typical of the way in which everyone supported one another. Freddie was getting better, the telegram read. It was his thirteenth birthday on 4 January 1947.

But on 7 January, another message arrived: the operation had not succeeded. Freddie was dead.

Freddie was buried next to Pa in Uitenhage. I have a photo of Hetta dressed in black, the toddler Joan in white in her arms, and me, standing next to Pa's Willys.

Ma's brother Oom Bunny Pienaar and his five sons took me under their wing, and I visited them in Despatch. My uncle took us to the bioscope in Uitenhage for a matinee show of *King Kong*. But I was overcome with grief about my brother and cried right through the film. To this day, I have avoided movies that feature King Kong.

Hetta rented out the house in Uitenhage and we moved to a cheaper home, a flat next to a café in Church Street. My mom, a trained teacher but now out of practice and underqualified, took a job as an assistant in the hospital's cafeteria.

Our home was now closer to the well-stocked municipal library to which Hetta had taken me from the time I could walk. I devoured English books, as there were no Afrikaans books. The Winer brothers also lent me some of their books, such as Biggles's war stories, and the adventures of the mischievous Just William, in Richmal Crompton's series about daring fun in English grammar schools.

To me, reading was, and still is, indispensable. It is part of my existence, like life-giving oxygen. Hence, I owe the biggest debt of gratitude to my mother, who introduced me to the library as a toddler.

Probably the most convincing argument in favour of reading is the one penned by the famous German-born Swiss writer Hermann Hesse. In 1930, this winner of the Nobel Prize for Literature wrote an essay titled 'The Magic of the Book'. An apposite excerpt reads:

> Among the many worlds that man did not receive as a gift from nature but created out of his own mind, the world of books is the greatest ... Without the word, without the writing of books, there is no history, there is no concept of humanity. And if anyone wants to try to enclose in a small space, in a single house or single room, the history of the human spirit and to make it his own, he can only do this in the form of a collection of books.

During the day, Joan and I were in the care of Sarah Steenekamp. In 1951, I was in Standard 7 (today's Grade 9) at Hoërskool Brandwag. There was no career guidance to speak of, and I chose the wrong subjects – for example, no third language or mathematics, subjects that would have helped me had I been able to go to university. I loved geography and broadened my knowledge by studying atlases.

In 1954 I passed matric after a multifaceted school career. In the final exams, I obtained distinctions in English and geography. I was rugby and cricket captain, played tennis for the school, and experienced puppy love in three or four relationships that went no further than passionate kisses. I learnt no social graces from my mom. All my life, I have been clumsy on the dance floor and lacking in charm in the company of women.

But my big interest from my early youth was newspapers and magazines. Hetta took out a subscription for me to *Die Jongspan*, a delightful magazine for Afrikaans children, published by Nasionale Pers Limited. We also sporadically read *Die Oosterlig*, published twice weekly in Port Elizabeth.

I became friends with Basil Ferreira. He had a stand next to Uitenhage's old railway station from where he sold *Die Oosterlig*. In those days, it was an afternoon paper; Basil would intercept the workers who came streaming out when the late-afternoon train arrived from PE. I found myself a selling spot opposite the station in Market Street, in front of Anderson's bakery. People had to buy bread, I reasoned, so that was where I sold my quota of copies of *Die Oosterlig*, which cost three pennies apiece. I think I got a penny per copy – precious pocket money.

In addition to selling newspapers, I used to work as a messenger at the law firm Conradie, Campher and Pieterse during the holidays. My job was to duplicate documents on the old Gestetner machine and deliver the mail. One afternoon, I was riding down Church Street on my bike, the metal basket on the front filled with letters, when a bee flew into the front of my shirt. I slapped wildly at it, screaming, and the bike fell over. Letters spilled all over the street. I had to scurry like mad to collect all the letters, the bee sting forgotten.

Partner Conradie's first name was Frans. He later became a member of the Provincial Council for Uitenhage and a Cape member of the Executive Committee. Frans was a cultivated person and, as I would find out later, a prominent member of the Afrikaner Broederbond. His son Leo started his career at *Die Burger* and subsequently became a diplomat in France. He was married to a journalist colleague, Renée Rautenbach.

Partner Giep Pieterse played a big role in my entry into the newspaper industry. I elaborate on this later in this chapter.

When I was in about Standard 8 (now Grade 10), I read about journalism as a career in a career-guidance magazine. The monthly salary of an editor could be as high as £240 – an astronomical sum. I went to see the owner of the *Uitenhage Times*, Mr John Hultzer, and asked whether I could contribute reports about school sports. He accepted the proposal. I did the same at *The Chronicle*. And so I started writing reports – by hand,

CHILDHOOD AND FIRST YEARS IN JOURNALISM

naturally, at the time.

I wrote about rugby and athletics, and had my first experience of a conflict between my reporting and the claims to my loyalty of the party that was the subject of my report. Our school played a rugby match against our arch-rival, Muir College. I was in Standard 8, and already in the first team. We lost narrowly: 8–5. The *Uitenhage Times* published my report with the headline 'Muir triumphs over Brandwag'.

At the first rugby practice after the report's publication, coach Attie van Aswegen blew his whistle, called all of us players together, held the newspaper with the headline aloft, and scolded me: where had I got the idea that Muir had triumphed? We had only lost by a measly three points! Needless to say, I could not advance the excuse that I had not written the headline.

The rebuke was like water off a duck's back, however. A journalist's first loyalty is to his craft. Later in my newspaper career, I was often slapped down in this way, notably by politicians – but by then my skin had thickened considerably.

At school, we were compelled to attend meetings of the Christelike Studentevereniging (CSV), an Afrikaans Christian student association. I filled a diary with puppy-love stories and religious anxieties. How pious we were in my schooldays. I blushed when I recently dug up this nonsense again.

My flirtations with impiety at least also exposed me to some other things. Next to the church hall was a block of flats that belonged to the Dutch Reformed Church. An Afrikaans Leeskamer (reading room) was opened on the bottom floor. I started reading Afrikaans and became besotted with the adventures of Rooi Jan.

My reading matter also included the first so-called controversial Afrikaans sex novel, *Meng My Wyn* (Mix My Wine) by HA van der Merwe. There was some superficial sex in the book, and I deemed it advisable to hide it under my mattress. One Saturday, Hetta and Sarah were changing the sheets on my bed and turned the mattress over. *Meng my wyn* was exposed. Hetta said to me: and this? I shook my head. No reprimand followed. I was, after all, starting to mature.

Later, I would discover that the Leeskamer had been established under the influence of the FAK, the federation of Afrikaans cultural societies. Under the protective hand of the Broederbond, the Afrikaans leaders of the town had embarked on self-empowerment initiatives of this nature. In 1948, Uitenhage, a United Party (UP) stronghold, swung to the National Party. The Nationalists even built their own hall for meetings in the town.

After the war, the economy grew; first Goodyear, and then Studebaker and Volkswagen, established themselves in our town, along with Fine Wools and other supporting industries, such as the big railway workshop. Despatch prospered and workers flocked into the town from all quarters, the whites virtually all Nationalist. Despatch's hostility towards the 'Sap' (UP) opposition even led to it being nicknamed Hitler's Halt.

The black people started to become more attuned to their own nationalism. Amid blistering fights the town council swung from 'Sap' to Nat, and the bank accounts from Standard and Barclays to Volkskas.

My own Afrikaner sentiments were fairly tepid. In primary school, I joined the Voortrekkers for the sole purpose of attending the youth camps opposite Humewood beach in Port Elizabeth, then promptly resigned. Our teachers at Brandwag were mostly Nationalist, some more ardently than others. We were the first generation to be educated under the Afrikaner-nationalist banner after the 1948 Nat victory.

In our world, black people existed somewhere far off. Although black political pressure was building, whites generally viewed black activists as agitators. No one in the white community agitated for better housing or wages for black or coloured workers.

In our home, Sarah Steenekamp was regarded as a member of the family. Yet everyone knew this side was our place, and that side was hers. It was no different in white English-speaking households. In the early 1950s, whites were blissfully asleep in a Rip Van Winkle world.

With school behind me, and no noteworthy career guidance, I followed up on a talk we had been given on forestry with three friends from matric. We were fascinated by the images of plantations, dense greenery and wonderful scenic beauty. So the four of us went to see the regional head of the Department of Forestry in Port Elizabeth. I guess he nearly fell off his chair with surprise at these four new recruits. The result was that I secured a position as clerk, grade III, in Pretoria – plus a train ticket – and had to report for duty on 5 January 1955.

I left Uitenhage, and a tearful mother on the station platform, only to find myself back there after 18 months – unbeknown to me, on my way to the top in the media industry.

In 1955, Pretoria was a tranquil capital city, with the statue of Oom Paul having just been moved from the station square to Church Square. The city had celebrated its centenary under the leadership of the mayor, Dr Hilgard Muller, later minister of Foreign Affairs, a classicist and a refined gentleman if ever there was one.

I installed myself in the Springbok boarding house in Proes Street. Out of my salary of £23, I had to pay £10 for board and lodging. Out of the £13 that was left, I paid something like £1,50 for a set of encyclopaedias an agent had sold me, and £3 for a Sanlam policy. You soon discovered that the Afrikaans-oriented civil service had informants everywhere who provided book peddlers and Sanlam with tips, on which they earned commission. Pretoria was Sanlam world by then – the company was getting its turn after Old Mutual's dominance before the political transition of 1948.

I tried to enrol at Tukkies (the University of Pretoria), but was admitted only on condition that I study a German matric-level course at the Pretoria Technical College after hours. I did so with waning enthusiasm. I played cricket for Tuks (second league at the time) and rugby for Pretoria Club (close to my boarding house), the latter against four players who would later become famous. Frik du Preez was then at Garnisoen, the defence-force club. Louis Schmidt, a busy flanker, was the fiery captain of the Tuks under-19 team. Tom van Vollenhoven, who had just turned 19, was too good and played for the Police's first team alongside the veteran Hannes

Brewis – and later scored three tries for the Springboks in the test against the Lions at Newlands.

In the winter of 1955, I watched my second and third international rugby tests. I was one of the 95 000 spectators in a packed Ellis Park in Johannesburg who saw how Jack van der Schyff narrowly missed a final conversion and we lost 22–23 against the British Lions.

My first test had been in 1949 as a schoolboy, when the Boks won the fourth test against Fred Allen's All Blacks on the Crusader field in Port Elizabeth. Prior to this test, a group of us boys had been asked by enthusiasts in Uitenhage to queue through the night and keep their places until the ticket office opened in the morning in front of Brockett sports shop. Our sponsors had provided car seats for us, and also supplied blankets, flasks of coffee and sandwiches. We lounged on the seats and chatted, earning our reward.

But back to my career in the civil service. In January 1955, I was given a small office of sorts outside a storeroom at the Department of Forestry and had to report to a section head. He was not very informative.

Every day, I received piles of brown files about all kinds of subjects that were brought to me by the women from the mail service, known as Registration. You went through the files, directed them to the gentlemen in the various sections, and tried here and there to devise an answer for your section head. When you were at a loss, you simply took a pink sticker marked 'Pending', wrote a date on it that was a month into the future, and sent the file back to Registration, only for it to surface again in a month's time. A nice old laissez-faire world.

To combat my extreme boredom, I started teaching myself to type on a big old Remington typewriter I had stumbled upon in the storeroom – two-finger journalist style.

I noticed that the fellows in the general office got a copy of *Die Transvaler* in the mornings, and all eight of them would then each take a turn with the paper in the toilet. Talk about increasing your readership!

At teatime, we stood around. The guys flirted with the girls, and talked

CHILDHOOD AND FIRST YEARS IN JOURNALISM

politics and Blue Bulls rugby; here and there, a transferred Bolander in Forestry's employ would put in a good word for Western Province.

I made friends with Charles Brookes from the *Pretoria News*, met some of the other journalists there, and approached the editor about a trainee position. His advice was: first finish your degree. Ditto at the Pretoria office of *Die Transvaler*, where I met one of the best and most civilised newspaper people ever, Gus Cluver. Years later, I thought with a good dose of Schadenfreude that, if *Die Transvaler* had given me a job at that stage, things could have turned out quite differently for me and Perskor.

In April 1956, I was given leave and travelled home to Uitenhage. A family friend, the attorney Gideon Pieterse, paid us a visit. He was a correspondent for *Die Oosterlig* and wanted to go away on holiday, and asked me to stand in for him in his absence. I was keen, as I was twiddling my thumbs at home. I soon came across a few stories, one of which made the front page: a pretty woman was missing and everyone was worried.

I wrote the article and obtained a photo from the family. A day after the paper appeared, a chap accosted me: what was the problem? She was his wife, and was not missing – just cross with him. She had gone away for a few days.

Still, by the end of that stand-in period, the editor, Dirk de Villiers, phoned me and said I should come and see him. We had a good discussion, and he offered me a job as a reporter in Port Elizabeth from 1 May 1956. I submitted my resignation to Forestry in Pretoria by telegram. They did not approve of my conduct – one should at least thank one's employer and give a month's notice. I had absconded.

While writing this memoir, I came across a newspaper report that reflects something of my eagerness to become a journalist and come into my own.

The former US president Bill Clinton is a proficient orator. On 10 June 2016, he said in a tribute at the memorial service for the legendary boxer Muhammad Ali: 'I think he decided very young to write his own life story. I think he decided, before he could possibly have worked it all out, and before fate and time could work their will on him, that he would not be ever disempowered. He decided that not his race nor his place, nor the expectation of others, positive or negative or otherwise, would strip from him the power to write his own story.'

That paragraph really resonated with me. It took me back to the 17-year-old Ton, lonely but independent, who felt the very strong sense that he had to make something of his life, no matter what mountains might lie before him.

So, there I was, back in Uitenhage, a journalist, 19 years old, inexperienced but brimming with enthusiasm.

Dirk de Villiers initiated me into the mysteries of Nasionale Pers. His first message was a lasting one: a journalist should be curious, and have zeal and stamina. This was sound and valuable advice.

Initially, I stayed in Uitenhage. I got up at 4:30 in the morning, walked about three kilometres to the station, took the 6:05 train to North End Station, and clocked in at *Die Oosterlig* just before 7:00. Then I would work on sport (my preference), and court and crime stories, and later in the day cover meetings, such as those of the city council's committees, or the then divisional council, or church meetings – sometimes till late in the evening. Occasionally, I would catch the last train at 23:05, and get into bed at one in the morning. At 4:30 I was up again! Talk about stamina.

Later, I acquired a scooter to eliminate the walk to the station. Three scooters and two accidents later, I moved to PE. There, I boarded on the hill not far from the editorial offices and started making friends with other young, single colleagues. I came to know the magical camaraderie and brotherhood of newspaper people, and enjoyed it thoroughly. You worked hard, but played hard too.

I think Dirk de Villiers appointed me because something in me may have reminded him of his own career. A clergyman's son from Paarl, he had not gone to university either. Instead, he got a job at *Die Burger*. He became a capable, versatile journalist, in the best tradition of *Die Burger*, and progressed to the level of news editor. The editorship at *Die Oosterlig* was his first, and he systematically expanded and renewed the paper.

CHILDHOOD AND FIRST YEARS IN JOURNALISM

Dirk later became editor of *Huisgenoot* and general manager of Nasionale Tydskrifte before being transferred to Johannesburg in 1965 as general manager of the Sunday paper *Die Beeld*, alongside Schalk Pienaar as editor. There, Dirk's path and mine would cross again.

I reported in Port Elizabeth, opened an office in Uitenhage, and met my counterparts Clive Cowley and John D'Oliveira, who worked for rival papers the *Herald* and the *Evening Post* respectively. We became good yet competing colleagues; at times, we would exchange stories when no conflict of interest was involved. Later in my career, I would maintain this kind of collegiality with most press people. This was probably how a part of me was formed for the times that lay ahead.

Cowley later became head of his group's service in the old South West Africa, which then became a focal point of international politics. D'Oliveira rose to the position of parliamentary reporter for the old Argus group, became a friend and confidant of Prime Minister John Vorster, and wrote a biography about him. Sadly, this energetic and excellent journalist died at an early age of a heart attack.

My younger colleagues at *Die Oosterlig* included Franz Kemp, who became the famed newshound of *Huisgenoot*; Schalk Burger and Ben Louw, who both worked later at *Landbouweekblad*; and the verbose Cornelius (Boet) Uys, who would go on to become a spokesperson for Eskom. Another was Arthur Blake, a redhead from Stellenbosch. He owned a Messerschmidt with a convertible top, a three-wheeled, aeroplane-like scooter that everyone gaped at. When he was broke, he would collect empties (bottles for which a deposit had been paid) for money and groceries. He later became an authority on military history.

The young Dutch-born Jacques van der Elst went to Potchefstroom and ended up as a professor in Afrikaans-Dutch, and later became chief executive of the Suid-Afrikaanse Akademie vir Wetenskap en Kuns (South African Academy for Science and Art).

For relaxation, I played rugby for *Die Oosterlig*'s house team, along with my sports editor, Alex Kellerman. When Alex later became a senior journalist, Dr Danie Craven persuaded him to become the secretary of what was then the South African Rugby Board. Another member of our newspaper team was a young typesetter from the factory, Derek Minnie. He later played centre for Transvaal, and became chief executive of the big paper group Mondi and a member of the head committee of Transvaal Rugby. His son, Derick Minnie, is now a livewire flanker for the Golden Lions.

As a journalist, I became increasingly interested in national politics. At *Die Oosterlig*, I got my first taste of political reporting when I accompanied minister of the Interior Dr Eben Dönges on a visit to Jansenville, in MP Andries Vosloo's Somerset East constituency (no relation). Editor Dirk de Villiers had organised a lift for me in MP Vosloo's Dodge, an example of how Pers and Party co-operated in those days.

Before the meeting in Jansenville, the charming and cultivated Dönges, later the state president-elect, visited the tiny town hospital and shook hands with two or three patients. I photographed this, helping the paper to disseminate a benevolent image – or, to put it cynically, propaganda for the National Party. Much later, the term 'embedded journalism' was created for the journalism of papers that act as mouthpieces for political parties. But in the 1950s and 1960s, we neither thought nor realised that we were 'embedded'.

I had taken a sheaf of press telegram forms with me to Jansenville, on which I had to type my report using my portable typewriter. That evening, after the meeting, I had to take my report to the post office to be transmitted to the main post office in Port Elizabeth. From there, it was sent via teleprinter to *Die Oosterlig*'s editorial staff. I had to arrange with the postmaster in advance to come in at 9:30 to perform his task; he typed out my report with one finger on the old-fashioned Morse-code machine.

Think of today's high-speed, worldwide digital communication, then spare a sympathetic thought for journalists of the past who had to get the job done with the means available to them at the time!

A good story about earlier communication methods is that of the veteran South African journalist and writer Tony Delius, who in 1962 sent a background feature to *Time* in New York from Addis Ababa. He received a cordial thank-you letter, which pointed out that the article had cost the price of a new Cadillac: all the things that had to happen to investigate a news story at its source, prepare it for publication, and then get it onto the pages of a newspaper or magazine could be very expensive in the days before the digital world.

*

My beat at *Die Oosterlig* was police matters. In the evenings, I would drive with the flying squad in pursuit of fresh news. I also joined the Police rugby club to get even closer to the news. The secretary of the club happened to be the court orderly at PE's main magistrate's court. In the mornings, he allowed me to be the first to look at the 'book' of cases on the court roll, gaining me a lead over rivals from the *Herald* and the *Post*.

My beat expanded: sport, news, crime, general news and, later, politics.

Margaret Rheeder, a 33-year-old, was charged with having poisoned her husband Benjamin Rheeder with arsenic to eliminate him as an obstacle to her affair with a young stoker. It was a sensational murder case, and colleague Lorna van der Merwe and I were instructed to cover the trial.

The trial attracted attention countrywide; Rheeder was sentenced to death with no mitigating circumstances. She was hanged at Pretoria Central Prison. Lorna and I were asked to follow up on the trial with a series of articles about Margaret's origins in the southern Cape and to dig up the full story. We did this so successfully that *Die Oosterlig*'s sales jumped from an average of about 8 000 per day to 13 000, the highest in the paper's existence up to that point.

The camaraderie with Lorna, a bright journalist and a teacher of maths and Latin, led to a relationship, and we were married in 1960. Until her retirement, she was a first-class journalist and mentored a string of competent female journalists such as Reinet Louw Kemp, Elsa Kruger, Elretha Louw and the well-known Amanda Botha, who had been a protégée of Lorna's in the 1960s at *Die Landstem* and, later, at *Die Beeld*. Amanda was the first female member of the sports desk – a first for women in South African journalism.

The murder drama led to a job offer from the now-defunct weekly tabloid *Die Landstem* in Cape Town. Its editor was the energetic Piet Beukes, who had an MA in history from Oxford. He had been a member of Jan

Smuts's information staff during the Second World War.

During the war years, *Die Burger* had experienced opposition in the Western Cape in the form of a UP paper, *Die Suiderstem*. The paper lured several senior journalists away from *Die Burger*, including the writer and future politician Abraham Jonker, the father of the poet Ingrid Jonker. Among the editorial staff and contributors were the poet Uys Krige and the future politician Blaar Coetzee.

It became a fierce battle. But *Die Burger* held its ground and, when the UP lost the election in 1948, it was also the end of *Die Suiderstem*. Beukes and others found themselves jobless. Opposition leader Sir De Villiers Graaff and one of his friends, mining magnate Harry Oppenheimer, as well as the English-language group of morning dailies (South African Associated Newspapers) and the *Cape Times*, were persuaded by Beukes to invest in his creation: an Afrikaans weekly, published on Wednesdays in the Western Cape and distributed in the rest of the country on Thursdays and Fridays. *Die Landstem*, with its human-interest articles, light sprinkling of politics and juicy personal stories about sports stars, was a huge success.

Beukes enticed me with a monthly salary of £90, as opposed to the £45 I was earning at the time. And so I landed in a two-man subediting office with Jan Prins, who would later become chief executive of Nasionale Koerante. Jan was the chief expert in layout and page make-up. I did copy-editing, wrote general and sports articles, and enjoyed myself tremendously in the pleasant atmosphere of Cape Town and in modern offices, poles apart from the archaic *Oosterlig* setup in PE.

From October 1958 to July 1963, I got my first exposure to parliamentary reporting. In 1960, I accompanied Wilson Whineray's All Blacks on part of their tour, and in 1962 I toured with Arthur Smith's British Lions. And as I mention later, Lorna, who was working at *Die Landstem*'s magazine *Mense* at the time, and I were tasked with accompanying Miss South Africa 1962, Yvonne Ficker, to London for the Miss World competition. She came fourth. We also used the opportunity to visit countries in Western Europe, and I conducted a variety of interviews with politicians, industrialists and government officials in France, Germany and Italy. The boy from Uitenhage began to discover that there was a *big* world out there.

Back at the office, Piet Beukes sent me to Parliament. Because Tos Wentzel from the 'Sap' paper *Die Weekblad* and I both wrote for weeklies, the surly parliamentary secretary Mac McFarlane arranged that we had to share a visitor's card for the parliamentary lobby. We could not both be with MPs and senators in their leisure and smoking space at the same time. It was not a problem; we arranged our appointments with MPs and had opportunities for interviews and chats over a cup of tea or a drink.

Some MPs were friendly; others shunned you because you were not from a Nationalist paper. Some always had a joke on hand. The one who could tell the most salacious jokes I ever heard was Captain Jack Basson, MP for Sea Point. He was an ordinary farmer from the Sandveld and father of the great business leader Whitey Basson. With our political correctness, Jack would have had a hard time today had his jokes leaked out.

The Nasionale Pers reporters from *Die Burger* and *Die Volksblad*, as well as the journalists from *Die Transvaler* and *Die Vaderland*, were reserved and stiff towards me. Tos Wentzel and I were not 'one of them'. With journalists from the English-language papers the relationship was more comfortable, but the biggest jellyfish in the press gallery was the chairperson, Arthur Classen, leader of the team from the South African Press Association (SAPA).

Classen set such great store by his dignity and self-importance that he just about choked whenever he saw me or Wentzel. As chair of the Press Gallery Association, he advised McFarlane on seats in the press gallery and did not really want Wentzel or me there.

It was there that I met *Die Burger*'s witty political columnist Schalk Pienaar. I found him quite different from some of his stiff-necked colleagues. Schalk was pleasant and always keen for a chat. Before the House of Assembly adjourned at seven in the evening, he would put away a few generous tots of brandy and then type his brilliant columns – containing political insights that would eventually make him the country's foremost political commentator.

For me, life in the press gallery was a revelation. I felt that I was sitting above the political boxing ring, looking down on the scene where the course and history of the country were determined. I saw the relatively new prime minister Dr Hendrik Verwoerd in action with his relentless logic, a man who commanded respect from both friend and foe. Even the sole Progressive Party MP, Helen Suzman – who had fought fiercely for the democratic dispensation we got in 1994 – had respect for his intellect, although not for his opinions.

I have a story about Suzman. It is common knowledge that she had an affair with the leader of the Progs, Dr Jan Steytler. On Tuesdays, it was question time in Parliament; the member who asked the question usually had to be present for replies. Steytler had a question on the list. When the speaker put the question, neither Suzman nor Steytler was in the House. When the speaker inquired about Steytler's whereabouts, Minister Paul Sauer, who had been resting his forehead on his hands, called out instantly: 'To Helen gone!'

In the eyes of many people, Verwoerd's legacy is so abominable that, when the liberal commentator Allister Sparks said in 2015 in front of a DA audience that Verwoerd was 'smart' and his remark was published, he was excoriated for having dared to express even a shred of praise.

In the House of Assembly, I was able to experience how many scoffers there were in the dominant National Party. Among the far-right members there was scorn for Suzman and contempt for Sir De Villiers Graaff and his United Party. Sir Div was a civilised, honourable person, not without a sense of humour. When he accepted the position of leader of the UP – and hence leader of the opposition – a journalist asked what he most enjoyed doing for relaxation. He replied: 'Well, it depends. And if it depends, fishing is the most enjoyable.'

There were also thinking parliamentarians who looked further than the naked racism of the NP: people such as Japie Basson, Piet 'Weskus' Marais, Alex van Breda and Blaar Coetzee, and a later group of younger members, such as Barend du Plessis, Dawie le Roux, Sam de Beer (very *verlig* – 'enlightened', or liberal – after an earlier far-right period) and Wynand Malan.

But the soul of the NP caucus was deeply *verkramp* (conservative). Albert Hertzog and his select supporters, such as Jaap Marais and Willie Marais, Daan van der Merwe, Tom Langley, Cas Greyling, Andries Treurnicht,

Connie Mulder, Gert Bezuidenhout – the vast majority of MPs and senators – believed in hard apartheid and, later, in the splitting up of South Africa with its 'Bantustans'.

They had grown up with and steadfastly believed in 'white domination', as articulated in the credo of the former prime minister Hans Strijdom, who had said bluntly: 'We believe in white *baasskap*.' Then, Verwoerd opened the door with his announcement of the Bantustans – or, as Schalk Pienaar called it, 'separate freedoms'. In the black homelands, Pienaar and Piet Cillié, editor of *Die Burger* and later chair of Naspers[1], saw a possible escape route, away from the numerical superiority of black people in South Africa. It gave us a brief interregnum, lasting about a decade, in which we continued to live in a dream world.

I, too, once shared that dream, and would later, in an essay written at Harvard University, depict a utopian fantasy of a commonwealth of independent Southern African states co-existing in harmony: Transkei and Kwa-Zulu and Mozambique and Zimbabwe, etcetera, etcetera. I am still red-faced about that opus, which I keep in a bottom drawer. Hindsight is an exact science.

I reported from Parliament between 1959 and 1970. Later, my reporting was done on behalf of the Sunday paper *Dagbreek en Sondagnuus* and, from 1965 onwards, for *Die Beeld*. My parliamentary stint was a valuable training ground, where I built up contacts that would prove to be of great help later in my career as an editor and in my lobbying efforts as a businessman.

I used to subscribe to the view that a journalist could not be considered well-rounded unless he or she had notched up a few parliamentary sessions. Parliamentary reporting was a training ground for future editors, on both the Afrikaans and English sides of the media landscape.

After one visit to the new democratic Parliament in the post-1994 era, I have felt no urge to return. To my mind, it has degenerated into a political circus, with no solid debating or well-honed arguments being pitted against each other. What Malema and his gang have been doing to parliamentary proceedings of late is below par, illustrating our country's deterioration as far as public life is concerned.

In early 1963, the big boss of Dagbreekpers, Marius Jooste, invited me to meet him. He was a burly, self-assured man, a former marketer who had started a newspaper of his own with some others: the Sunday paper *Dagbreek*. The editor was Willem (Wollie) van Heerden, an independent thinker who occasionally sounded cautious notes in his columns about changes that inevitably had to come.

Mr Jooste, in a spruce double-breasted sports jacket, met me in the bar of a Sea Point hotel. He buttered me up and offered me a job as a reporter in Johannesburg.

I bargained with Jooste and secured positions for me and Lorna, editor of the magazine *Mense*, to move to the north of the country for R550 per month. My own salary was R300. Lorna was appointed at the magazine *Fleur*.

For me, the writing was on the wall in 1963 when *Die Landstem*'s circulation reached 150 000 and the paper added the jubilant line above its masthead: 'The biggest Afrikaans paper in the world.' I found that a bit thick. Its sales then started to stall, and I anticipated that the paper would take further knocks as a result of the expansion of *Dagbreek* and the *Sunday Times* to the Cape. Besides, I was getting bored with the predictable diet of articles. (By the way, *Huisgenoot* now refers to itself on its front cover as the biggest Afrikaans magazine in South Africa. Such boasting makes me uneasy.)

In late June 1963, Lorna, our two-year-old daughter Nissa and I arrived in a grey, freezing Johannesburg in our Volkswagen. We rented a spacious flat in Van der Merwe Street, Hillbrow, and soon adjusted to the fast pace of our new life as Johannesburgers.

That move to the country's North (the Free State and Transvaal, a region I discuss in Chapter 11), changed my life. I had big dreams, but did not know just how far they would take me.

CHAPTER 2

The metamorphosis of Naspers

Today, Naspers, which I came to preside over unexpectedly and somewhat to my surprise in May 1984, is a big player on the international media and technology scene. With operations in more than 130 countries, the group has been called the seventh largest in the world in its field. How did this huge leap from an Afrikaner-centred company to a global conglomerate come about?

It is a fascinating, exciting story. I was intimately involved in the company's metamorphosis, initially as managing director of Nasionale Pers from 1984, and then for 23 years as chair, at executive and then non-executive level, until April 2015. My years in management were preceded by turbulent years as a journalist from 1956 to 1983.

The outlook was fairly gloomy when I went to Cape Town in March 1983 to work for a year as assistant MD alongside my predecessor, Advocate 'Lang' David de Villiers[2]. Gloomy, because the print media had been competing for advertising with the new South African television service, monopolised by the SABC, since 1976. This novelty in South Africa – advertisements on television – had a devastating effect on the revenue of newspapers and magazines. Until that stage, the print media in South Africa had done well; the country entered the television era exceptionally late – in 1976, twenty years later than Australia, for example – so the print media had been spared this reduction of revenue for an exceptionally long time.

I had been a newspaper journalist all my life, and my switch from editor of *Beeld* in Johannesburg to MD of the entire Nasionale Pers organisation was an enormous surprise. The move was not only a promotion, but a drastic change, of course, as far as my own career was concerned.

The chair of Nasionale Pers[3] (as it was still known at the time), Piet Cillié, had asked me to succeed Lang David. I remember that day in my office in Johannesburg. 'Why pick on me?' I asked, dumbfounded.

I had never set my sights on a management position. Cillié said I had a track record of success as co-founder of three successful Afrikaans newspapers: the Sunday papers *Die Beeld* in 1965 and *Rapport* in 1970, and the daily *Beeld* in 1974.

On 13 August 1981, I wrote in my diary: 'Piet Cillié was in my office at 2.25 p.m. He knocked me for a six: I'm being considered as successor to Lang David and had to think it over. I was stunned.'

Cillié concluded with an anecdote that was probably intended to keep me humble. It was about the young clergyman who ascended the pulpit brimming with confidence to deliver his first sermon, only to descend afterwards with drooping shoulders. He was then told by the head elder that if he'd instead ascended in the way he descended, he wouldn't have descended as he did!

I was audacious enough to let myself be persuaded. My reasoning was: Nasionale Pers had been built around print media: books, newspapers, magazines, printing works and distribution. I was completely at home in the world of print media. My instinctive feel for ink-and-paper products, what the Germans call *Fingerspitzengefühl* (the feeling in your fingertips), emboldened me to accept the great challenge.

In my years as a journalist from 1956 until I became editor of *Beeld* in 1977, I had started thinking more widely. My general knowledge, insight, opinions and skills as a political commentator and editor had developed strongly.

Nasionale Pers was the ally of the National Party (NP), and our dailies were the party's official (*Die Burger* and *Volksblad*) and unofficial (*Beeld*) mouthpieces. In the days when I started working at Nasionale Pers, employees had to confirm in writing that they supported the 'Nationalist' ideals of the company. Our journalists were therefore the crusaders of the NP, throughout the party's tough opposition years in the first half of the twentieth century and, after 1948, as rulers of the country.

Nasionale Pers had been founded in 1915 to serve as a mouthpiece for Afrikaners, who were economically and politically weak in the wake of the Anglo-Boer War of 1899–1902, also known as the Second War of Independence, the English War and, more recently, the South African War. Political journalists who defended the policies of the National Party had been embedded in the culture of Nasionale Pers from the outset. They promoted the NP's political ideology in their reporting.

And so I found myself in Cape Town in 1983 in a totally new position and role. I immersed myself in the top-management mysteries of Nasionale Pers's board and management, and familiarised myself with the state of affairs of all the subsidiaries. I attended courses to hone my management skills and refresh my financial knowledge.

I had good colleagues among top management, people I knew well but who were considerably older than me: Hennie Conradie, the finance chief; Jurie Naudé, head of the magazine division Nasionale Tydskrifte; Jan Prins, head of our newspaper operations Nasionale Koerante; and Heinie Jaekel, head of the book-publishing division Nasionale Boekhandel.

Some of them were rather sceptical about me, but I enjoyed the support of colleagues such as Jan Prins (generally known as 'Prince Jan' among subordinates) and Jurie Naudé. In an earlier phase of our lives, we had been fellow journalists. And my staunchest supporter was Gideon Engelbrecht, our Northern chief executive, with whom I had fought in the trenches in the cut-throat Northern press world.

My predecessor Lang David had been blessed with many talents. A top advocate, De Villiers had led the South African legal team at the International Court of Justice in The Hague with success on the South West African conundrum. He was a fighter for the underdog, and a proponent of the dismantling of the NP's race-based policies. This stance led to serious clashes with the Cape leader of the NP, PW Botha, for one. Botha still sat on the board of Nasionale Pers at the time.

Lang David's term held another advantage. With his level-headed approach, he commanded the respect of English-speaking newspaper editors and CEOs.

Piet Cillié – former editor of *Die Burger*, chair of Nasionale Pers and a loyal NP supporter, but a far-sighted individual – had shielded Lang David, and he was able to conclude his career with the best net profit in the company's history in the financial year ending 31 March 1984: R21 million. It was immediately dubbed our boom year.

As designated leader, I had one obsession: how to take the Pers, as we referred to the company in our own ranks, forward. Our newspapers were doing well, *Beeld* was headed for solid profits after huge start-up costs, our magazines were thriving, and the schoolbook publishers were then still flourishing.

My obsession was partly politically driven: under my leadership, *Beeld* had conquered the North for our *verligte* standpoint. In political columns and commentary, I had prepared the way among our readers for a momentous political change: acceptance of our black compatriots as equal partners.

While the word '*verlig*' has now mostly fallen into disuse, after becoming a buzzword about fifty years ago in combination with its polar opposite – '*verkramp*' – and denoting a category of mainly Afrikaner pro-reform voters, it may be necessary to explain its meaning. The term was coined in the 1960s by Dr Willem (Wimpie) de Klerk, brother of future president FW de Klerk, in combination with the concept '*verkramp*'.

From the 1960s until the first half of the 1980s, '*verligtheid*' did not yet mean that the *verligte* individual necessarily believed in a one-person-one-vote dispensation. Rather, the term denoted a willingness to reflect critically on the status quo and to accept relatively radical change. A *verligte* was open to persuasion, and prepared to embrace reform.

The concept of *verligtheid* also took on a wider meaning, namely an inclination towards less coercion and censorship, towards greater cultural freedom and modernity, and towards the rationality that needed to temper the Afrikaner-nationalist impulse. It was associated with a less patriarchal mindset, with understanding for the struggle for greater women's rights, and also with greater tolerance for homosexual people. The 1980s were, among other things, characterised by Afrikaans literature's 'coming out of the closet'.

Readiness to accept change: that is perhaps the most concise definition one can give of *verligtheid* among the Afrikaner voters of the day.

To some semi-*verligtes*, holding talks with the African National Congress (ANC) was initially seen as going too far; even in the early 1990s, a *verligte* could have reservations about the full consequences of one person, one vote, or about testifying in front of the Truth and Reconciliation Commission (TRC). Someone such as Dr Beyers Naudé, who had associated himself with the ANC as far back as the 1970s, would not have been referred to as *verlig*: he had a more radical view.

Verligtheid as a mindset nevertheless helped make the one-person-one-vote dispensation possible by ensuring the victory of the Yes vote in the referendum of 1992. *Verligtheid* was, to some extent, comparable to glasnost, a mindset that resulted in the dissolution of the Soviet Union in 1991.

An important gamble, given the views of many of our readers and the political pressure to which the Pers was subjected, was a column in 1981 in which I wrote that, at some point, the NP would be forced to sit down at the negotiating table with the ANC. It was extremely daring for its time.[4]

In 1974, Beyers Naudé, while on a visit to the Netherlands, predicted that the ANC would come to power within ten years. This was a change that would only happen twenty years after 1974, but one which I, too, foretold in a column in 1981, on account of the forces that were building up below the surface.

PW Botha hauled me over the coals about the column, which evoked a strong reaction. But the time had come for South Africa and the Pers to start paving a new way towards the future for Afrikaners and all South Africans. I think the leaders in the NP had already realised by then that the status quo was indefensible. My column was given coverage in international newspapers, with one paper viewing it as a message that negotiations with the ANC had to be considered.

As managing director, I reasoned, I had to take the Pers forward politically so that the organisation could survive the time of political change that lay ahead. The company also had to remain financially strong in the changing environment, especially taking into account the loss of revenue as a result of television.

I used the first leadership conference of the Pers to spell out my aims to a fairly sceptical audience. Under Lang David's leadership, the company held an annual conference for top management. Invitations were highly sought-after; the summit offered the top leaders in the group the opportunity to get better acquainted and to exchange ideas, both formally and informally. Leaders were issued with topic assignments beforehand, and we also brought in eminent external speakers to counteract 'inbreeding' on our part. Female leaders – who were in the minority at the time – were included.

Thus, Lang David invited the political analyst Anna Starcke as guest speaker to shake up our stultified political thinking. Female contemporaries who were invited included Jane Raphaely, June Botha, Dene Smuts, Jane Kinghorn and Rieta Burgers. The conferences boosted the Pers's enthusiasm and conveyed an image of hopeful innovation and unanimity. The impression was created of a dynamic group, a leader in its field, thanks to Lang David's excellent and *verligte* leadership.

My theme at that conference was 'continuous renewal'. At the same time, I wrote in our in-house magazine to the full staff complement – who numbered 6 000 at the time – that it was now a question of adapt or die. In the print media, I wrote in this inaugural address, we had indeed arrived at a crossroads. 'As the prehistoric animals had to do, we have to adapt ourselves or, like the coelacanth, become fossils.'

When all was said and done, you were alone at the top – with all the challenges.

You have allies, you have fellow colleagues in top management, but the ball is in your court. *You* have to manage and lead, and the board will judge *you* by how you perform in that regard.

My phone rang late one afternoon in December 1984. The caller was Koos Bekker, an MBA student at Columbia University in New York, previously of Stellenbosch and Wits universities and subsequently at the Young & Rubicam advertising agency in Cape Town; his wife Karen Roos was, at one stage, on the staff of *Sarie*, the Pers's women's magazine. I had met him in Johannesburg when I addressed a group of young, *verligte* Afrikaners of Johannesburg known as Peil.

On this call, Koos told me he believed he had a solution to the print media's struggle against the SABC's TV monopoly. He gave me a brief outline of his proposal.

During an academic year at Harvard University as a Nieman Fellow in 1970–1971, I had become acquainted with the recently launched television service Home Box Office (HBO). It was the world's first pay-television channel and transmitted movies for a monthly subscription fee.

What Koos had in mind was an adapted version of HBO for South Africa. My interest was aroused at once. My head of newspapers, Jan Prins, happened to be on a mission in New York; I called him and said he should immediately invite Bekker for dinner or tea and suss him out.

Prins took Koos to the Russian Tea Room in the heart of New York. He called me back: I should pursue the matter. So began a 32-year association with Koos Bekker.

When Koos had told me his story during our first phone conversation, I grasped the merit of his concept at once, thanks to my familiarity with HBO. It struck me later that, had someone else occupied my chair in 1984, Koos's proposal would probably have fallen on barren ground due to a lack of the kind of knowledge I fortuitously happened to have. The luck of a pressman!

I instructed Koos to set out his proposal in a memo to the Pers's board. With the document in hand, I went off to the lions' den.

Well, when it comes to a new appointment in the position of managing director, there are two truths. One applies to the new leader, and the other to the board of directors who are due to be led. In his first year, the leader has to take big decisions and then submit his proposals, support them with facts and arguments, and get them accepted. A board does not turn down such a leader lightly: its members want a leader with a venturesome approach at the helm. The board members, for their part, have to afford the new leader the opportunity to show what he intends to do, and not frustrate him.

I asked the board to appoint Bekker as my personal assistant with a confidential mission, a budget of R50 000, and an office and a secretary on the premises of our Magazines group in Johannesburg.

Koos accepted my offer and set to work in 1984. He displayed a drive and capacity for work unlike anything I have ever experienced. The man was and is brilliant – someone who has always coupled his insights with hard work and dedication.[5]

The future of the project was entrusted to me. I had to generate the political will on the part of the government to grant us a licence.

I knew what to do. I started with PW Botha. As a political reporter in Parliament from 1959 to 1970, I had come to know our country's political leaders – including PW – well. I knew he was besotted with newspapers, despite his frequently launching scathing insults at the very papers that were sympathetic to him in his political speeches. I knew, too, that he had written articles for the Free State daily *Die Volksblad* in his youth. Botha was a Free Stater from Bethlehem, and he treasured *Die Volksblad*.

My strategy was to spell out clearly how SABC TV choked printed newspapers to death. TV has the advantage of not requiring paper and printing presses, yet it draws mass, national audiences. It is a state monopoly with which we are not allowed to compete; the advertising revenue it captures is largely derived from advertising lured away from newspapers. Unlike the SABC, newspapers do not have the benefit of compulsory licence fees and have to pay tax. In short: it was an extremely unequal fight.

What we were requesting was not a state subsidy, I explained, but merely the right to compete. As a result, daily papers could have a future: not only those that supported the government, but from across the political spectrum. Think of the tiny *Natal Witness* in Natal, the 'last outpost of the British empire', or the marginal *The Friend* in Bloemfontein, or the leftist *Daily Dispatch* in East London, and many others. In this way, one would keep the country's broad democratic conversation alive.

From conversations with ministers Piet Koornhof and Pik Botha, I started suspecting that this plea could fall on fertile ground, especially when it came to Pik: we had got to know each other over many years. Always game for a challenge, he secretly welcomed the initiative as a fresh influence on the media landscape that would keep the SABC on its toes.

One day, Pik told me that the television service was Nasionale Pers's baby, but that we should also include Perskor, the once mighty Northern press grouping. Moreover, he suggested, we should broaden the base even further and bring in the English press groups. If we did not, we would always be the target of vitriolic criticism from the English media and political opponents who would say the licence was a concession to connected newspapers to make money, not unlike the controversial fishing concessions granted to connected Nationalists of an earlier era. We took Pik's view to heart and expanded the consortium to include all dailies in the country.

But first, the various press groups had to be united. There were six of them, with strong mutual antagonisms: Perskor and Nasionale Pers were arch-rivals, and the Argus and Times Media groups were even involved in litigation against each other. I went to each proprietor in turn and persuaded them all to join. The diverse press leaders obliged me, although they, too, must have been sceptical about the venture's chances of success. Through presentations and pleas, we eventually brought all six groups together in one consortium, under the leadership of Nasionale Pers. (Our eventual stake of 26 per cent was only fractionally bigger than that of the three other top groups, at 23 per cent each.)

But that was not the end of it – we had to jump through another hoop. The government appointed a task group with a panel of independent external experts to investigate the introduction of pay television. The group was headed by Dr FJ Hewitt, deputy president of the Council for Scientific and Industrial Research (CSIR). There were 40 applications for licences.

In the event, our consortium – the Electronic Media Network, abbreviated to M-Net – was awarded the licence, subject to a string of conditions. Among other restrictions, we were prohibited from broadcasting news – that was the prerogative of the SABC and its boss, the government. The National Party's message as conveyed by South Africa's television services had to remain under government control.

The relationship with the SABC kicked off on a strained note. When M-Net was about to start, the new SABC head, Koedoe Eksteen, and I often negotiated about specific aspects. Then, out of the blue, he announced that the SABC planned to launch a commercial TV channel, TV4.

The M-Net team realised at once that such a channel would be a death blow to M-Net. Accordingly, I made Eksteen an offer: the SABC gets 20 per cent of M-Net, and we get 20 per cent of Channel 4. He would control his Channel 4 and we would control M-Net, but we would eliminate a battle for sports rights and programmes and there would be space for both. Koedoe took the offer to his chair and his former boss at Foreign Affairs, Dr Brand Fourie, who said no.

With hindsight, this was probably one of the worst decisions the old SABC ever made. Imagine how much money it would have raked in with 20 per cent of the M-Net giant ...

In 2015, I bumped into the film producer André Pieterse in Stellenbosch, who told me he had presented a proposal for a cable network to the chair of the SABC, Dr Piet Meyer, as far back as 1970. According to Pieterse, Meyer and the Information minister had responded extremely negatively to the idea.

The TV licence was granted only to daily papers, not to Sunday papers or magazines. Our standpoint was that daily papers were vitally important to the discourse in the country. They had a watchdog function, encouraged open conversation and endeavoured to open doors. They were the oxygen of public life; indeed, this is still the case. The success of M-Net meant a huge financial boost for all our partners and shareholders.

The first years were tough, however. When we had to appeal to our shareholders for funds for a second time, Perskor withdrew from the consortium. In terms of our agreement, its stake reverted to Nasionale Pers. Two years later, when we were making money, Perskor bosses Willem van Heerden (chair) and Koos Buitendag (MD) came cap in hand to ask whether they could buy back their stake. I said yes – but at a new price, because of the progress we had made. But Koos Bekker restrained me and recommended that we take them back without a penalty. It was a magnanimous gesture on Bekker's part, but for me it went against the grain in view of the bruising, years-long press war I had experienced firsthand in competition with Perskor in Gauteng.

The establishment of M-Net was the biggest and most radical initiative in the history of Nasionale Pers up to that point. In her unpublished manuscript titled *Naspers 100: Chronicle of a company, its people, its country and its world*, Professor Lizette Rabe writes that the founding of M-Net 'can be regarded as the actual quantum leap at the end of Nasionale Pers's seventh decade. With that, it launched itself from a print media company into the electronic age, and thereby amassed enough financial muscle to enable it to ride the wave with the advent of the digital age.'

This step changed Nasionale Pers irrevocably. The income from M-Net led to the further diversification of the company. It started in the early 1990s with the establishment of MTN as a cellphone business in South Africa. The cellphone industry was still in its infancy, but our clued-up engineers had grasped the value of the product. By that time, I had even made a cellphone call to Cape Town from a taxi in Stockholm, Sweden!

In the case of MTN, too, the task of obtaining approval fell to me. In 1990, I approached Posts and Telecommunications minister Dr Piet Welgemoed, previously a lecturer in transport economics at the Rand Afrikaans University, now the University of Johannesburg. I discussed our plans to develop this industry in South Africa. Welgemoed was young and open-minded, and sounded positive.

Even so, the first feedback was sluggish and unenthusiastic. We were ordered to present our business plan for digital cellphones to the Post Office (the predecessor of Telkom), since they operated a primitive C450 analogue system that allowed calls to be made from cars – through a large brick hidden in the boot. Our team went to make a formal presentation to the Post Office's board. Weeks later, we were informed by letter that they did not think this thing would work, and that our projection of 300 000 subscribers was totally overoptimistic.

But I remained undeterred. After many peregrinations and compromises, two cellular network licences were finally awarded in 1994 – one to a consortium in which the Post Office was a partner (they had changed their tune in the meantime). They were allowed off the mark first, so Vodacom soon built up a lead in the market. The second consortium included us. We had brought in a strong black-empowerment partner in the form of NAIL, led by Dr Nthato Motlana (who had been Madiba's doctor), as well as a foreign partner, Cable & Wireless, which could contribute technical expertise.

Naturally, big money was required to erect masts and buy computers – time and again, the partners had to dig deep into their pockets. But today, MTN is one of the business giants on the African continent, a huge and cash-flush company.

It was precisely this that created a huge dilemma for M-Net and our group. The digital era was at hand, and M-Net had expanded internationally with FilmNet in Western Europe. But we did not have sufficient capital for both industries. Bekker recommended that we stick to the television side, as cellphones were, in his view, a 'mono product'.

Of course, digitisation benefited the entire cellphone industry enormously, and the era of smartphones has made it one of the largest and fastest-growing industries in the world.

Bekker came in for much criticism about his decision, but had the last laugh later: thanks to digitisation, the DStv service could connect with cellphones, laptops and tablets – so, today, the cellphone companies are major rivals of the DStv offering in its various forms and industries worldwide.

All these changes altered Nasionale Pers fundamentally. I was at the helm as chief executive and, later, as executive chair. When the digital age arrived, I passed the baton to Bekker as the new CEO of Nasionale Pers in 1997, when I was 60 years old. I could have stayed on in my position for three more years, but I motivated my decision to step down as follows: I came from the age of print media and, while I knew the ropes when it came to television, the digital age was Greek to me. It is an age for young people, and Bekker was eminently equipped to take the helm.

In fact, in my own mind I had already picked Bekker as my successor years earlier; in my opinion, there was no one in the Nasionale Pers group, or in our entire media industry, who was better suited to the task of leading the company. The board of Naspers – the company's official name from 1998 – supported the recommendation unanimously. Thereafter, Bekker and I, as chief executive and non-executive chair respectively, would work together for 15 years to develop the Naspers group.

The name change from Nasionale Pers to Naspers was not without disagreement.

Bekker wanted a completely new name. I reckon he was sensitive about the political baggage of the old Nasionale Pers, its name and its origins. The directors discussed the matter and, for the first time in my 32 years on the board (and perhaps in the history of the Pers), we were about to make a decision that was not unanimous.

Director Mike de Vries, former rector of Stellenbosch University, requested that his dissenting vote be placed on record if we changed the name. De Vries was probably still in the shadow of his late father-in-law Dr Phil Weber, who, as ex-editor of *Die Burger* and group chair, had been one of the greats of Nasionale Pers.

The board decided unanimously and wisely on the abbreviated, recognised name 'Naspers'. Nasionale Pers listed on the Johannesburg Stock Exchange (JSE) in 1994 with this shortened name. Today, it is the global trade name for our group.

Bekker made massive leaps with Naspers, with digital technology that opened worlds. For many years, I was chair of Naspers as holding company, as well as of subsidiaries such as M-Net, MultiChoice, SuperSport, and offshoots outside South Africa.

We moved into the international league, and I was particularly proud of the exceptional expertise of our group's teams. With South African experts at the forefront, we simply stood out above international opponents, succeeded internationally and commanded respect. Koos was the talisman, and he deserves all the praise for his insights.

My role became increasingly that of a patron who watched over Naspers's interests locally, but also as a global player. Bekker could pull everything off, but with the blessing of Naspers.

The chair's role is not one of micromanagement. He has to be informed by his CEO and meet regularly with board committees to keep abreast of developments. He has to keep pace with changes in the industry; in the case of the upward-surging Naspers, this was a must. He has to watch over the interests of the group constructively and serve as a sounding board for top management. On the board, a chair has to lead with calm confidence. He should not be an egotist and try to dominate.

I thank the Lord that in all my years I could lean on remarkable boards of directors at Naspers. People of integrity and intellect such as Piet Cillié, David de Villiers, Jeff Malherbe, Elize Botha, Pieter de Lange, Fred Phaswana, Rachel Jafta, Yuan Ma, Don Ericson, Ben van der Ross, Lourens Jonker, Fran du Plessis, Neil van Heerden, Boetie van Zyl and the American Craig Enenstein made it a privilege to chair meetings. With individuals of that calibre at your side, you do not need Cadbury or King corporate governance prescriptions to lead a business successfully.

Was the expansion of Naspers, with the creation of M-Net as the first wedge, a wise decision?

Today, Naspers is a far cry from the one-dimensional, party-bound company it had been from its founding years until the late 1960s. In the 1980s and 1990s, it contributed to the democratic turnaround in South Africa in that its promotion of *verligte* thinking was instrumental in securing the victory of the Yes vote in the 1992 referendum. Without this outcome, the democratic election and the transfer of political power in 1994 would have been stymied temporarily and ultimately would have had to be brought about with far less mutual goodwill and possibly more violence.

After the general election of 1994, the role of the old governing National Party and the alliance between the Party and the Pers in South Africa came to an end. Freed from the supervision and pressure of the NP, Naspers could become independent and was able to liberate its newspapers from a party-political affiliation that had increasingly become a burden to the company.

When it came to the print media in Afrikaans, Naspers could continue to offer Afrikaans-speaking writers, journalists and readers a cultural space for expressing their talents, interests and views, as well as a forum for their participation in the political life of South Africa – something to which all language and cultural groups in the new, democratic South Africa are fully entitled.

It was also possible to promote diversity and offer huge opportunities to a new kind of reader and writer, journalist or editor who identified with the new order. In this way, Naspers and its Afrikaans publications were able to contribute constructively to the new democratic dispensation.

Apart from that, Naspers's business operations branched out in new directions that had no connection with party politics, but created value for South Africans. The company aligned itself with the latest approaches in its practices, and surprised both friend and foe with its renewal on all fronts.

In my last speech, at a farewell function that Naspers held for me in February 2016, I answered the questions about our own transformation as a business group as follows:

> If one looks at what we were before 1994 and before the era of digitisation, before the earth-shaking transformation of our society in 1994, then the answer is that we are fully on the right road.
>
> If we had not embarked on that road with the gravure-printing process and the building of our giant magazine-printing plant in uncertain times; the establishment of *Die Beeld* and *Beeld*; the founding of *YOU*; the acquisition of *City Press*, *Drum* and *True Love*; and if we had not, with M-Net, MTN and MultiChoice, taken the digital road into Africa, across the world, all the way into China, Russia, Brazil – 133 countries – if we had not taken that road, Naspers in its hundredth year would have been a faint shadow of its former strength.
>
> If Naspers had not taken the huge strides required by the surrounding society and global technology trends in good time, we would have been sitting in sackcloth and ashes today in an ever-shrinking little corner, fear-stricken and futureless. Renewal has always been my motivating force and, fortunately, I could drive the renewal with the calibre of colleagues of our group and its boards.

The near-utopian post-1994 situation has passed, and the demographic realities have created new rules and requirements. The digitalisation of information poses the biggest challenge the print media have ever faced.

I concluded my farewell speech as follows: 'My successors are inheriting a healthy multinational business group and I can only wish them the best insights in the times that lie ahead, albeit that this evokes the unpleasant prospect of the old negative Chinese adage: may you live in interesting times.

CHAPTER 3

A global giant

The so-called law of unintended consequences only strikes one in retrospect. This is certainly the case with the listing of Nasionale Pers in 1994 and the growth that followed this step. When making economic claims, one always needs to reckon with the uncertainty and unpredictability of the global economy. But in 2017, at the time of writing, Naspers was the largest company in South Africa and Africa by market value. It ranked among the top ten media and communications giants in the world. This is a mammoth achievement.

The story of Naspers's astounding growth fills me with pride. But humility is also advisable. One's humility has to lie in an appreciation for the vagaries of the global economy, which have bloodied the nose of many an economic giant.

Nasionale Pers was quite small compared to the giants in the South African business world when we listed in September 1994. The big companies were the so-called blue chips, such as Anglo American, De Beers, Rembrandt, Richemont, South African Breweries and many others. The saying among investors was, 'Never sell a blue chip.' Today, a considerable number of the blue chips are gathering dust.

In my years as MD and later as executive chair, one of my major objectives was to unlock value for Naspers shareholders. From the company's beginning in 1915, the share was hedged within a framework of protection against hostile takeovers. Nasionale Pers had been founded for the purpose of playing a political role in society.

When it came to finances, the policy was conservative. My predecessor as chair, Piet Cillié, used to talk about 'remainder' or 'surplus' in his reviews instead of 'profit'. Profit was, in his opinion, a swear word within an organisation with the high Afrikaner ideals of Nasionale Pers. Dividends were kept low in order to build up the company's reserves. This approach was referred to as a 'Joseph policy', a bulwark against adversity or lean years.

Nasionale Pers was the only public company in which the auditors issued a positive qualification every year. In other words, according to them, the assets were valued at too low a level. This policy took shape in the capable hands of leaders such as Recht Malan, Phil Weber and Hubert Coetzee – and, in my time, those of the financial director, Hennie Conradie. It was a policy that stood Nasionale Pers and its shareholders in good stead.

As good as this management plan was, the modernisation of the South African business world was making new demands on companies. I realised soon after my appointment as managing director in 1984 that Nasionale Pers would be unable to survive as an unlisted company in its entrenched-control form.

Mof Terreblanche, an investment expert and an ardent campaigner for Nasionale Pers's listing, gave me valuable advice on the road to listing – a road that proved to be quite long. Some of my fellow board members were of the view that listing would lead to the relinquishment of the company's independence, and that it would lose its 'Afrikaans culture'.

The eventual listing in 1994 took place against the backdrop of South Africa's transition to an inclusive democracy under the leadership of the ANC, with Nelson Mandela as state president. 'Afrikaans culture' as such, in so far as Nasionale Pers was involved in something like that, was itself in urgent need of reorientation.

The decision in favour of listing was taken on 3 June 1994. A three-man committee had done the required spadework: Murray Louw and Jannie Grobbelaar, both seasoned corporate experts, and Nasionale Pers's financial director, Eric Wiese. The fears on the part of shareholders and directors that Nasionale Pers could fall prey to hostile takeovers were allayed by means of an entrenched-control structure, the brainchild of Murray Louw.

In January 1994, I convened a special board brainstorming session to discuss the listing. I submitted a document titled 'To list or not to list' to the directors. Below are excerpts from the rationale I provided for the listing:

> The main reason for accepting the principle of listing is not, in the first place, financial. Obviously, the financial side carries great weight, but I have a problem with leading Nasionale Pers in the new circumstances if our structure remains unchanged. We have been overtaken by changed circumstances.
>
> At present, we are probably the biggest general publisher in the country if we take into account the reach of our newspapers, magazines and books. Our prominence is amplified by the degree to which our publications participate in the public conversation.
>
> Our newspapers insist – and it is our own company outlook – that our country needs openness, transparency, in public administration. We must do business in such a way that it does not seem as if we have something to hide.
>
> Whether we like it or not, our handling of shares and the restriction on voting rights and on tradability have created the impression that we are clinging desperately to control, to the extent that we are a '*volkstrust*'.
>
> This impression elicits negative reactions – it makes us a target. In our potentially unfriendly atmosphere from government quarters, we have to get the general public on our side. At the moment, we are a 'soft target', judging by the increasing poor publicity we are getting about the perceived favouring that resulted from improper relations with the government.
>
> Our own position is in contrast to our partnerships and investments, for example in M-Net, where we are the only unlisted stakeholder.
>
> We need a setup that is democratic, modern and in line with prevailing business practices. It is quite possible that in a future order we may be forced to lift voting rights restrictions, and then all the initiative to create a favourable control structure would be out of our hands.

The board and management may wrongly be seen as undemocratic and old-fashioned, people who feel safe and comfortable in protected conditions, and who are out of step with the new environment. It is far better to be proactive now than to be forced to change under less favourable circumstances.

It is expected that a new government will subject press groups in particular to close scrutiny. From a strategic and tactical perspective, it is better to change to a more representative control structure at this stage.

I spelt out the financial considerations for listing in the document and noted this argument, among others:

We must be seen in the new circumstances as a public company in the fullest sense of the word, in which the whole of South African society can participate. At present, this is not the case. If we continue to cling to the status quo, it can prejudice us financially. I cannot overemphasise this point.

To my mind, the whole share arrangement of private trading has led to a measure of mounting frustration, even irritation, on the part of shareholders.

The eventual listing on 12 September 1994 released the steam from the pressure cooker, to the great joy of shareholders. The closing price on day one was R21, three times higher than the last tender price in June 1994. The total value of shares traded on that day was R132,5 million. The value was equal to 44 per cent of the average daily turnover on the JSE. At the time, R132,5 million was the highest value ever obtained for a single share traded on a given day.

From a study of our list of shareholders, I estimated that our listing created more than 1 200 millionaires on day one – certainly the biggest empowerment ever of Afrikaans supporters.

Just by way of comparison: in August 2017 – 13 years after listing – the market capitalisation was R1,2 trillion – that is, R1 200 000 000 000.

A GLOBAL GIANT

On day one, we were the 14th-largest company on the JSE by market capitalisation. In 2017, at the time of writing, the company was hands down the largest listed South African company in South Africa and in Africa.

I was very proud of Nasionale Pers's boards and managements who facilitated the turnaround with flying colours.

The first step in this direction – the first company from our stable to go public – was M-Net in 1990. Koos Bekker was at the helm. He deserves all the credit for his ability to grasp superb new opportunities, launch them with powerful initiatives, and carry them through with hard work. With M-Net, he blazed a trail for Naspers by showing how to position a company in the so-called New South Africa of 1994. Soon, his vision would stretch far beyond the borders of our country.[6]

At M-Net's head office in Johannesburg, colour and gender discrimination were done away with from the outset. Parking spaces were occupied on a first-come-first-served basis, with no bays reserved for management. Koos instructed that he was Koos and not Mr Bekker, to the consternation of Johann Rupert when he phoned Mr Bekker one day and could not get hold of him. The reason? The switchboard knew only of Koos.

The listed company subsidiaries SuperSport and MWEB flowed from M-Net. The founding of MTN followed. And, later, the digital family was brought together as MultiChoice Africa and MultiChoice South Africa Holdings.

Naspers was the paterfamilias behind all these businesses. Before long, the quantum leap across South Africa's borders had happened – first with FilmNet in Western Europe, and later with the Greek television service. Thereafter was the big outreach to Africa. The cherry on top was the investment in Chinese technology giant Tencent, to which a chapter in this book is devoted.[7]

What was particularly satisfying was the investment in the empowerment schemes Phuthuma Nathi I and II. In these schemes, R50 shares were sold to black investors at R10, with a R40 loan redeemed from dividends. The scheme has paid out millions to shareholders. In this way, Naspers could start to redress inequalities and let historically disadvantaged people share in its financial success. Media24, the print media business, launched its own Welkom Yizani empowerment scheme. Owing to the effect the advent of digital technology has had on the print media industry, with a shift away from print publications, Welkom Yizani's path has not been as rosy as that of Phuthuma Nathi.

In 2016, Naspers as an awakened giant received an incidental compliment from Dr Daniel Matjila, CEO of the Public Investment Corporation (PIC) that manages government pension funds. The PIC had lent R2 billion at a ridiculously low interest rate to the Sekunjalo consortium's Independent Media Group (the old Argus Group). Sekunjalo's executive chair is Dr Iqbal Survé, an avowed ANC propagandist. He is a verbose individual with breathtakingly ambitious plans for a media empire.

During a briefing to a parliamentary committee in August 2016, Dr Matjila was questioned about the rationale behind the big loan to an unprofitable group. He said that the Independent group was previously owned by Irish shareholders (Dr Tony O'Reilly's group of companies), and much of its profit had flowed out of the country. When the group found itself in trouble, he explained, the PIC saw the opportunity to bring Independent Media back into South African hands. The PIC believed that, with South African ownership, the Independent group would attract government contracts and advertising, but this never materialised.

According to Matjila, what was happening to the Independent group at the time had to be compared with what had happened to Naspers in the early 2000s when the latter, too, had struggled financially.

'Naspers is the biggest company on the JSE. It used to be known as a company that burnt cash. It is only fair to give blacks a chance to create a Naspers.'

Shortly afterwards, in September 2016, Dr Survé, who glorifies himself in his own papers practically every second day, launched a slanderous attack on Naspers. One of the factual errors in his allegations was that Dr Hendrik Verwoerd had been the founder of Naspers. In 1915, when Nasionale Pers was founded, Dr Verwoerd was a 14-year-old boy! Moreover, in his years as chair of Perskor, Dr Verwoerd had been involved with an organisation that

A GLOBAL GIANT

fought tooth and nail to thwart Nasionale Pers's entry into the Northern media market.

As a rule, Naspers's management did not respond to attacks of this nature.

It was kind of Dr Matjila to hold up Naspers as an example worth following. However, his view that Naspers had struggled financially in the early 2000s was incorrect. Except for a brief period in 2001 when the so-called dotcom bubble burst, Naspers never showed a loss from 1950 to 2017.

Naspers always made its investments from its own reserves and has never turned to the state or state corporations for funds. This forms part of a legacy of independence. Naspers has launched substantial empowerment actions on this basis, to the benefit of the whole of society and not reserved for a particular race, as Dr Matjila's investments sometimes appear to be.

The unintended consequences strike one, or a company, in retrospect: the listing of Nasionale Pers in 1994 was indeed a case of a small pebble that was cast far, with positive ripple effects.

I write, next, of our best investment – in fact, one of the best investments ever.

CHAPTER 4

Tencent, the colossus in the stable

The big, winged stallion in the Naspers stable is the Chinese company Tencent.

This instant-messaging company's logo was initially two little penguins. But today, the company is a colossus in all respects. The fortunes of Tencent exert such an influence over Naspers that, if it catches a cold, the Naspers share price shows symptoms of pneumonia.

Through two top executives' firsthand accounts, I can share the full story of Naspers's Chinese investment more widely.

It is Tencent's success that has propelled Naspers as a media group to its position as the seventh largest of its kind in the world. The story is one of tenacity in the face of challenges in foreign parts. Getting to the top in Chinese society and culture, unfathomable to us, requires quite exceptional talents.

Koos Bekker deserves the credit, because the investment in Tencent is an extension of the strategy he has followed from the outset: unlocking and exploiting the commercial potential of nascent television, telecommunications and information technology at an early stage and with enormous drive.

He had help, however. The indispensability of good collaborators with their own initiatives and zeal is illustrated by the Tencent story. The groundwork was laid by two members of his management team. Naspers, for its part, has stood behind Bekker's gamble through thick and thin.

One of the two colleagues who did the spadework was Charles Searle, the CEO responsible for the group's listed Internet assets, including Tencent and the Russian Internet company Mail.ru. He is also a director of Tencent and Mail.ru. The second person was Hans Hawinkels, the erstwhile chief executive officer of MIH Asia. At present, Hans is an entrepreneur in Johannesburg who aims to market a well-known South African cider brand in China on behalf of another business group. Charles's story appears below, in his own words. I have kept his account as it was conveyed to me – I cannot improve on it:

> In 1996, Naspers sold its European pay-TV business – jointly owned with Richemont – to Canal Plus of France for US$2,2 billion. With money to invest, the big question was where and what sector to invest in.
>
> The group knew pay TV well, but new investment opportunities were rare and overpriced. Several print-media acquisitions were chased in Brazil, Argentina, China and India. A few print investments were actually made, and most of those lost the group money, severely so in the case of Abril in Brazil.
>
> Another sectoral possibility was the Internet, which had recently launched in the US, especially San Francisco. In terms of geography, Koos was keen on China, pointing out that in recorded history China was more often the leading economy in the world than any Western country, and predicting that the historical pattern would recur.
>
> Koos started visiting China and was joined by senior members like Cobus Stofberg and later Jim Volkwyn, head of pay TV. Eric Li provided valuable cultural introductions.
>
> Hong Kong was the logical gateway to China and the group chose it as its base in Asia. The office opened soon after the Hong Kong handover in 1997, and headed up by former head of pay-TV operations in Africa, Hans Hawinkels, the group's deputy chief investment officer, Mark Sorour and business development manager Ian Barnard.
>
> As the then chief investment officer of the Internet division, I joined

them shortly thereafter. The focus for the Hong Kong office was to look for opportunities both in pay TV and also for those in the rapidly developing Internet sphere.

At that time big international companies displayed little interest in China from an Internet perspective. With no experience of China and little in the Internet, Naspers went in almost blind, the team feeling their way – with the support of some rather expensive consultants.

After failing to identify a satisfactory entry vehicle to enter China, Naspers decided to go it alone. In 1998, using technology and systems imported from South Africa, and a mixture of expatriate and local managers, a Chinese language portal and Internet connectivity service provider called Maibowang was launched in Beijing with much fanfare.

The Maibowang venture blossomed briefly on the global Internet bubble that would eventually lead to the dotcom crash of 2000, but ultimately it failed as it was outperformed by home-grown Chinese competitors. Our expat team knew little about the local market and cost-conscious Chinese consumers shunned it in favour of cheaper alternatives. Naspers had sunk US$46 million into Maibowang by the time it was closed down – the whole investment was lost.

Regrettably it wasn't the group's only mistake in China. During the same period, there was a string of doomed investments: one of the first privately held Internet data-hosting centres in China, a Shanghai-based financial portal known as Eefoo and an Internet sports portal trading under the name of Sportscn – all of which failed. It was a huge cost to the group in both financial and human terms.

However, critical lessons were learnt from these failures. The most important was that globally successful business models don't always work in China. Secondly, that local Chinese managers were often of superb quality, surpassing Western managers in work rate and sometimes in strategic capability. Thirdly, that instead of setting strategy and then entering a country, it may be wiser to find the best local entrepreneurs and follow them, respect them, and listen to them. These lessons would become valuable not only for the company's future investments in China, but in other emerging markets around the world.

TENCENT, THE COLOSSUS IN THE STABLE

The group started probing websites that focused on community-related services, ones in which users created their own content and built relationships. This was a nascent area and companies such as MySpace, Facebook and Friendstar were not yet born. The dotcom crash of 2000 shook many Internet businesses and IDG Technology Venture Investments, one of the earliest investors in the China Internet, was among those hit by the crash. IDG invited the group to review a portfolio of some 50 companies, among which was Tencent.

I was responsible for managing corporate relations with Chinese partners, regularly reviewing portfolios for potential opportunities to co-invest, consolidate and acquire companies. I was joined in the assessment by Neville Meijers, Hans Hawinkels and the fluent Mandarin speaker David Wallerstein.

Unlike most Internet companies, Tencent's website didn't give an e-mail address or telephone number – instead it gave an OICQ[8] number as a contact. According to Netease's web ranking system – the Alexa[9] of China at the time – Tencent was one of the highest-ranked websites and leader of the Chinese social-networking sites.

Founded in November 1998 by a group of college friends, Tencent was based in Shenzhen, across the border from Hong Kong. Ma Huateng – better known as Pony Ma – as well as Tony Zhang and Charles Chen were core founders. After graduating in computer science at Shenzhen University in 1993, Tony Zhang did an MSc in computer applications at South China University of Technology and Pony Ma joined China Motion Telecom Development Limited as a software developer.

At first, they focused on pager text messaging, but in February 1999 they launched an instant messaging service called OICQ, one of the first in China. In late 1999, Tencent received funding from venture capitalists IDG Technology Venture Investments and PCCW Ventures.

Tencent's profile was unlike most big Chinese Internet companies at the time – it wasn't based in Beijing or Shanghai and its founders hadn't attended the prestigious Tsinghua or Beida Universities like many successful Chinese Internet entrepreneurs.

Initial contacts between our team and Tencent were rather tentative. The Tencent team did not have wide experience of international deals and our team had to swallow the hard fact that Tencent earned no revenues and was likely to lose cash. Gradually, a relationship of mutual trust and respect began to develop.

There was something very special about the Tencent management team. Cohesive and confident, the founders were passionate about engineering and their product, as well as where they were going strategically. Pony Ma in particular had exceptionally clear strategic vision for so young a CEO.[10]

However, Naspers wasn't the only company interested. Tom.com, then one of the big Chinese Internet players, was keen and talked lofty valuations, but when the tech bubble burst, was no longer a suitor. Likewise, Richard Li, who had just taken over at PCCW, was also interested but ultimately burned by the Internet crash. The balance gradually tilted in favour of Naspers, but there were many obstacles to overcome and it was a year before the investment was completed.

The decision to invest in Tencent was not unanimous. Some members of the Naspers management had reservations about investing in a fledgling, high-risk company with no revenues, even though it had a growing user base. Internet history is littered with the corpses of companies that failed to turn popularity into cash. Others were still shellshocked by Naspers's dismal investment track record in China and reluctant to spend the company's last resources on another wild-goose chase. Indeed, the string of failures in China and elsewhere in Southeast Asia pushed Naspers into a loss and a share price below R12.

Naspers managers debated the pros and cons vigorously and then sought board approval. It was a credit to our board that they approved committing the last of the group's available cash resources to this high-risk investment.

It was also a bold decision on the part of Pony Ma and his partners to place their trust in a little-known South African/European company.

After long talks and tense investment-committee meetings, the deal went through in 2001 and Naspers invested US$32 million for a 48 per cent stake in Tencent. In fact, the investment in Tencent was the last significant Internet investment Naspers made for the three tough and turbulent years that followed.

Immediately after the deal was completed in 2001, Naspers invested a little extra money to shore up Tencent's finances. Later that year, Tencent teamed up with giant state-owned mobile operators China Mobile and China Unicorn to forward Internet-originated messaging to mobile phones, for which they were able, eventually, to earn some Chinese revenue.

From the get-go, the partnership was committed to sharing ideas and complete mutual trust. As a multinational company, Naspers was able to share ideas based on its understanding of some markets elsewhere around the world, but of course all decisions were always made by Pony Ma and his exceptional founder team who best understood the Chinese market.

By 2004, Tencent had reached revenues of some US$130 million. Tencent decided to [register an] IPO[11] and Martin Lau headed the Goldman Sachs team. Tencent's offering raised US$184 million. Impressed by Lau's handling of the IPO, Tencent invited him to join their management team as the chief strategy and investment officer, and in 2006 he was promoted to president. He proved as far-sighted and astute as the founders.

One of Tencent's core strengths from very early on was its exceptional executive team. This was augmented with their external hires; in the early days, each founding member oversaw details of different aspects of the business. Tony Zhang, who served as the chief technology officer, dealt with technology issues; Charles Chen, chief administrative officer, dealt with legal affairs and government issues. Daniel Xu was the chief information officer.

Tencent has long nurtured strategic relationships with telecommunications operators and terminal-device manufacturers in China. It is also committed to investing in developing its innovation capabilities – more than 50 per cent of Tencent employees are technical engineering staff. In 2007, Tencent invested more than US$16 million in setting up the Tencent Research Institute, China's first Internet research centre, with the aim of promoting innovation in core Internet technologies. It has campuses in Beijing, Shanghai and Shenzhen. Later, it pioneered the Internet Plus initiative in China.

Tencent has struck a balance between providing free services to attract users and offering payment options for users keen on more. In addition to its instant messaging platform QQ, it has a web portal QQ.com, WeChat, QQ Games, Qzone, 3g.QQ.com, SoSo, PaiPai and Tenpay – which meet user needs for communication, information, entertainment and e-commerce.

In April 2014, the 15-year-old QQ platform hit a milestone – 200 million people using the service simultaneously. That same year, Tencent reported 808 million monthly active users on QQ.

After Tencent, investing in and trusting founding entrepreneurs became Naspers's key business model. The focus was now on searching for promising Internet businesses and conducting thorough due diligence, but the deciding factor was always the founders. If they were smart, passionate and committed, Naspers invested and respected them to manage the business.

In 2007, Naspers acquired a 30 per cent stake in one of the largest Internet companies in Russia, Mail.ru. And then came a string of investments in e-commerce ventures. Allegro in Eastern Europe and OLX in Brazil were exciting additions. Some flopped, like Multiply in Indonesia and Buscape in Brazil.

In 2013, Koos Bekker wanted to improve the operational savvy of top management and brought in Bob van Dijk, a senior eBay executive, to head up the e-commerce segment. Just as this sector was taking off, tragedy struck when the overall head of our Internet operations, Antonie Roux, was diagnosed with pancreatic cancer and died a few months later. As the head of Internet, Roux was the board's first choice to replace Koos Bekker when he stepped down as CEO the following year. Instead, Bob van Dijk was fast-tracked from global e-commerce to CEO of Naspers.

Naspers isn't the same company it was 20 years ago. It has matured and adapted to the new economic climate and, through a series of successful pivots, has found its current e-commerce niche. Mergers and acquisitions are still a critical part of the business and the group continues to invest at a rate of half a billion to one billion US dollars a year, as it has done for the past decade. But alongside that, the e-commerce operations have been significantly bolstered by deep operational experience.

Tencent has grown to become one of the most influential Internet companies in the world. Now ranking as the top online gaming company globally, it is also an advertisement for the skill of Chinese managers. Both Koos Bekker and I serve on the Tencent Board.

The market is much more competitive than it was 20 years ago, with a lot more money chasing fewer assets. Smart decision-making and building scale have become critical. Founders remain the critical factor in deciding whether to invest in a business, but the benchmark for delivery is now set even higher. The M&A[12] team, headed by Mark Sorour, scours our industry for deals with potential.

That concludes Charles Searle's account of how the paths of Naspers and Tencent crossed. Next, Hans Hawinkels, who was CEO of MIH Asia at the time, describes the execution of his assignment from his own perspective, after he had prepared the ground for the deal:

I was appointed CEO of MIH Asia to be based in Hong Kong from January 1998 after successfully launching DStv across Africa. Koos Bekker had returned to South Africa from Europe after the Naspers European interests had been sold to Canal Plus and asked me to go to Asia to find both pay-TV and Internet opportunities in Asia for the Naspers group.

I successfully concluded a merger between UTV and IBC in Thailand to form a successful UBC pay-TV business – other opportunities were hard to find.

We were looking for Internet opportunities across Asia – mainly focused on the Internet service provider model as well as portals. It was still very early in the development of Internet businesses globally, so there was no certainty as to the success and sustainability of these businesses.

Naspers was usually at the forefront of developments in media and Internet businesses, as was demonstrated by its early introduction and successful launch of the digital satellite pay-TV business in Africa.

However, the group had a control philosophy from its business which limited the opportunity set we could look at, as there were a number of Internet businesses where the group could have acquired a minority interest, but these were turned down, for example, Netease, which today is a successful Nasdaq-listed Internet company.

We made a number of interrelated investments across China, Thailand and Indonesia. We partnered with a company called IDG Ventures in an Internet hosting business in China called 21 Vianet – IDG were minority partners in the deal.

It was IDG who called me in early 2001 to say that it had a 25 per cent interest in a company called Tencent based in Shenzhen. The other 25 per cent shareholder was PCCW, a Hong Kong-listed company that had just done a deal to buy Hong Kong Telkom from the British.

IDG said that the Chinese founders – four of them – were very unhappy with the situation as PCCW were not good shareholders, and were 'drip feeding' them money for development and not giving the founders any strategic advice.

IDG said that if I could convince the founders that MIH would be good shareholders, the founders would support me in a deal and IDG would sell their shares to MIH. But I would then have to convince PCCW to sell as well.

Tencent was a desktop instant-messaging communication platform called QQ – so not the typical business model we were looking at – and had 22 million users, but no revenue.

It should also be noted that the dotcom crash came in April 2001, so everyone was concerned about the future of Internet-related companies.

After a number of meetings where I convinced them of how MIH could assist them both financially and strategically – particularly the revenue model – the founders were in agreement to support MIH in its efforts to acquire the two VC companies' (IDG and PCCW) combined 50 per cent shareholding. They also liked the fact that we were a media company.

There were intensive discussions within Naspers whether to proceed or not – we were not sure of the business model, but liked the founders and the potential of an instant-messaging platform. There was one other global example of this called ICQ, owned by AOL in the USA, but it also had no revenue.

Eventually, Koos gave me the go-ahead to proceed with negotiations – a brave decision given the negative post-dotcom-crash environment.

I had extensive negotiations with PCCW – they were very reluctant to sell. But they simply did not know what to do with their Tencent shareholding and had no business plan for it.

After three months of discussions and much persuasion, in September 2001 PCCW eventually agreed to sell their 25 per cent shareholding to MIH at a company valuation of $66 million, and then IDG followed.

I was involved for the next six months with the Tencent management team working on a business plan to be presented to the Naspers board.

Unfortunately, my contract with Naspers was not renewed by Koos and I left the group in December 2002 and returned to South Africa. As you can imagine, I was deeply upset by this and was not able to share in the benefits of this acquisition.

As this account shows, Hans fell victim to Koos's guillotine. The affable, friendly Koos could be implacable once he had made up his mind about an individual or an issue. As this was a management matter, far away from Naspers and light years away from the giant that Tencent would become, the board did not ask many questions.

Koos then put Antonie Roux in charge as our action man on the board of Tencent. Koos himself took up a directorship, which he has retained to this day, including during the two years he was on a sabbatical.

Roux was a dynamic addition. He had started out quite modestly at the old Nasionale Pers with a diploma in electronic engineering, where he and Jac van der Merwe formed a formidable team that put Nasionale Pers on the electronic highway. The gifted Jac was later sent to Europe to help develop the decoder used by our group. Roux joined Jac, Koos Bekker and Cobus Stofberg in the Netherlands to grow our pay-TV subsidiary, FilmNet.

Jac van der Merwe died tragically in 1994 together with his instructor in an aircraft accident in the Swiss Alps, while he still had his student pilot's licence.

Antonie Roux did stellar work in Tencent on behalf of Naspers. More than anyone else from the Naspers side, he infused us with enthusiasm about Tencent's growth possibilities. Quarter after quarter, he would regale the board with images of rising growth graphs and mind-boggling predictions of future growth. The predictions were all realised.

And then Roux was diagnosed with pancreatic cancer. His death in 2014 was a grievous loss to Naspers. Bekker had been due to succeed me as chair in 2014, and we were in agreement that Roux would be his successor as CEO of Naspers. Roux's death meant that we had to postpone the plans for a year until the choice fell on Bob van Dijk – a seasoned e-commerce specialist from Europe.

Pony Ma is Tencent's other hero. He and four friends had built up the company; Searle's and Hawinkels's accounts explain how they acquired Naspers as a partner.

Ma (a name as ubiquitous in China as Van der Merwe or Smith in South Africa) is a self-effacing person who lives very modestly. Though he has been called China's wealthiest man on occasion, up to now he has purchased an apartment for his wife, his daughter and himself in Shenzhen and, later, one for his parents, who hail from the countryside. He drives a modest car. His biggest philanthropic initiative to date has been a donation of billions to the Chinese state, in the form of a fund that supports education and medical care in the country.

In my time, Naspers awarded Pony Ma our group's highest accolade for performance, the Phil Weber Award. Pony declined the prize because he did not want to attract attention in China with this foreign tribute. He sets great store by a good relationship with the Chinese authorities. Under his leadership, Tencent ploughs large contributions into the Chinese economy.

A hardworking and inspiring leader, Pony Ma has grown Tencent systematically from an instant-messaging service to a conglomerate offering more than 10 000 services. He is involved in a leadership battle with Alibaba, headed by the hugely enterprising Jack Ma, whose group is Tencent's main rival.

Calling Tencent a whale in Naspers's pond may perhaps illustrate how dominant this component is. In the 2002–2003 financial year, Naspers paid $32 million for 48 per cent of Tencent. By October 2016, the stake stood at 34 per cent after listing, and it was worth $90 billion!

Tencent's market share in China is enormous in global terms. In March 2017, the instant-messaging service had more than 900 million customers, and its social-media and messaging app WeChat over 1 billion active users.

Tencent is by far the jewel in Naspers's crown, and the sharpest arrow in its quiver, to employ yet another metaphor. As already stated above: if Tencent coughs, the Naspers share contracts pneumonia. In 2017, at the time of writing, the contribution of the old Naspers's South African subsidiary, Media24, made up only about six per cent of the whole. Naspers has diversified into e-commerce and online classifieds services, and is now probably the biggest in the world outside the United States. In Naspers's combined assets, Tencent is the overwhelming acquisition.

In his contribution to a collection of essays published in 2015 at the time of Naspers's centenary, the experienced economist and stock analyst Dr Chris van Wyk gives an outsider's view of Naspers and Tencent titled '*Waagmoedig gebore – 'n sakeperspektief* (Audacious from birth – a business perspective).[13]

Van Wyk writes that Naspers's stake in Tencent is generally valued by professional analysts at levels representing roughly 100 per cent of the group's total valuation. 'It is argued that investors in Naspers get the rest of the group 'for free', implying in turn that the share price is currently trading at a discount, which some analysts reckon is unjustified.'

According to Van Wyk, the contribution of Tencent to the group's valuation holds a risk for investors. 'Should the current and future performance of Tencent be subdued, it would certainly reflect negatively on Naspers's valuation.'

Van Wyk does say that the majority of professional analysts believe too little cognisance is taken of the further growth potential of the core investments outside of Tencent. 'They hold the view that the future earnings growth of core interests should be given greater weight in the current valuation of Naspers shares.'

During my years as Naspers leader, after the investment in Tencent I was bombarded with more questions about this stake than about any other aspect of the group's activities. I would simply reply that China, with its 1,5 billion people, was currently in a development phase. There was still an enormous amount of blue sky left, and if Tencent maintained its course with good management, I saw no reason why it would not flourish.

The investment in Tencent, and then later in Mail.ru in Russia, with its subsidiary, Vivo, has meant that Naspers owes an enormous part of its wealth to investments in the two leading former communist countries. Today, the Chinese economy is indeed capitalist-oriented, and the Russian Federation is democratic in name. But the questions one may pose about these two countries are well known.

I used to say that my predecessors such as Phil Weber and Recht Malan were probably turning in their graves because South Africa under the National Party had fiercely opposed communism. But, I would add, Piet Cillié, the master of dialectics and the great path-breaking thinker of Nasionale Pers, supported the new initiatives quite philosophically.

To the question of whether it bothered us to do business in a dictatorship such as China, my reply used to be that the whole world exports to and imports from China, and that this trade takes place on a commercial basis. We do not judge our participation in the Chinese economy by the degree of press or media freedom that exists or is lacking in the country. We have no real understanding of Chinese government policy that is geared towards the stability, prosperity and advancement of an unimaginably vast population. And we certainly have no say in it. Limiting trade with and within China to that which measures up to South African principles would relegate us to the sidelines in an internationally accepted economic game.

I was able to witness the magic carpet of Naspers China on several occasions and to experience firsthand the mystery of the Great Wall under a full moon – *and* to stand amazed at the ways of the human being and society.

CHAPTER 5

Koos Bekker, the talisman

Out of a telephone call 32 years ago, a relationship was born that would turn the old Nasionale Pers Limited on its head.

The relationship between Koos Bekker and me started at the end of 1984. The two of us braved many storms together. We weathered them; so did Naspers, as the company has been known since 1998. There were magical highlights and many memorable experiences. M-Net, our first venture together, was like the bottom rung of a ladder on which we could climb ever higher.

There were also difficult days in our relationship, which is par for the course. But we overcame the sticking points. Today, we still do not necessarily see eye to eye on all issues. There is also some unfinished business. How else could it be in the complex world within which Naspers still stands squarely, and in which it has to blaze new trails?

Koos – as he insists on being called, or as almost everyone calls him – is a global figure in the communications industry. He is also an enigma: not much is known about him, and he keeps a strict watch over his private life. Some of his activities have nonetheless brought him and his family much publicity.

Still, as the colleague who has worked with him for the longest, I can indeed claim that I know him well.

From the outset, when he took up the reins of the start-up M-Net in

1984, he announced that he was Koos. No Mr Bekker. No preferential parking. No hierarchical structure. Open-plan work spaces.

When Koos had to fly down to Cape Town one day and the Pers's driver, Pieter Prins, collected him from the airport, Koos told him: 'Call me Koos.' Whereupon Pieter retorted: 'Mr Bekker, the day you call Mr Vosloo Ton, I'll call you Koos.' A fitting reply, because Koos has never called me by my first name. I am Mr Vosloo to him, just as in my own days as MD I never called our chair, Professor Piet Cillié, 'Piet'. The age gap was simply too big, and we had grown up in an era in which one respected seniority.

This 'Koos' appellation also gave rise to the saying 'KSS' in the workplace. It stands for 'Koos says so'.

Our relationship was always relaxed but courteous. We rarely socialised. On only one occasion during our 32 years, in the early days of M-Net, did we go out for a meal on our own and polish off a bottle of red wine. We did not frequent each other's homes.

Don't get me wrong: Koos was invariably polite and considerate, and over the years he was unstinting in his generosity and attention to personal weal and woe, such as birthdays and times of trouble. He is the perfect gentleman.

His generosity stretches far. A consignment of mielies from his farm in the district of Heidelberg, Gauteng, used to be sent annually to the staff of the group across South Africa. Nowadays, the gifts are plums from the farm Babylonstoren in the Boland.

In Johannesburg, the staff were treated to an annual ox braai, with the meat coming from his farm. Apropos of the mielies, a satirist from the *Financial Mail* once wrote that Naspers was in such dire straits financially that the staff were getting mielies instead of raises!

Koos's left hand knows what his right hand is doing. But his good deeds are never publicised. He has made the publication of significant books with a historical element possible. Through personal sponsorship of refresher projects for lecturers and bursaries to students, he contributes to the advancement of training and education.

From the start, our working relationship was exactly how it had to be, in my opinion. As managing director of M-Net's founder, I entrusted the reins of the new company to him. I did not look over his shoulder. But when matters needed to be discussed, we talked openly and candidly.

Koos would give me feedback when problems arose. And the M-Net launch was dogged by problems – for one, the struggle to sell the concept to politicians, a job for which I was responsible.

As minister in charge of the SABC, Piet Koornhof was not exactly helpful in establishing M-Net, which would compete with the SABC. Fortunately, Pik Botha, his successor, was keener on the idea of innovation and competition, and showed greater open-mindedness.

We also had to prepare thoroughly for the presentations to the task group headed by Dr FJ Hewitt of the CSIR, which had to hear applications for the licence. We cleared this hurdle successfully.

And then we were faced with the mammoth challenge: marketing pay television to a public to whom this concept was completely foreign. On top of that, we had to go in search of new technology in the United States. I remember having to fly as far as San Diego in California to persuade companies to share their decoder technology with us.

Furthermore, South Africa was burdened with sanctions. The US government was highly suspicious: it had come to light that the South African government had successfully enriched uranium at Valindaba, with an accompanying programme to develop nuclear explosives and weapons.

To make matters worse, the decoder technology was classified by the US military. We had to obtain permission for its use from the military via the State Department. We were granted this permission; the gods had smiled on us.

On 24 January 1985, I received a phone call from Pik Botha, Foreign Affairs minister and also in charge of the SABC. He asked whether the two of us could speak frankly. When I said yes, he hesitated before asking: 'Why has Nasionale Pers appointed a private detective to spy on Sol Kerzner and me?' Botha had received 'irrefutable evidence' from a security agent that the said detective had been tasked with compiling a file about him and Sol; if Naspers failed to get the TV contract, the information in the file would be used to 'destroy' Pik.

I was gobsmacked. My immediate inquiries established that what had reached Pik's ears was just talk. He and Sol Kerzner had a good relationship, and Kerzner's 'palm-greasing' in the then 'neighbouring states' of Transkei and Bophuthatswana was no secret.

The matter ended there, but I aged considerably in the space of an hour.

The relationship between Koos Bekker and me was tested over the years. When the M-family expanded internationally, we founded a few dozen separate companies that I chaired for many years.

The relationship is well captured in the book *Gorilla in the Room: Koos Bekker and the Rise and Rise of Naspers*[14] written by Anton Harber, journalism professor at the University of the Witwatersrand, in 2012. He writes: 'Bekker had made all these moves with Ton Vosloo right behind him …'

Professor Harber is so kind as to describe the part I played as follows: 'But a big part of the credit belongs with Vosloo, the corporate paterfamilias who spotted Bekker at the age of 31 and has backed him ever since, even when things looked dire.'

On the other hand, Professor Harber emphasises the drive Koos displayed: 'So there is a team and a father figure, but Bekker is the driving force.'

This representation of the situation is spot-on. As chair of the Naspers board, my job was to keep a vigilant eye on the management teams and measure them against the implementation of the annual budget, in the interest of the shareholders. But a budget is not cast in stone. The board receives monthly, quarterly and half-yearly reports so that the temperature of the firm and its components can be gauged continuously. From this position, I was able to observe and support Bekker's progress.

Bekker is an enigma, as I have noted above. Harber cites one of his colleagues who summed up this intensely private person as follows: 'Koos Bekker is an introvert in an extrovert's job.'

According to Bekker, managers should shun the limelight, in their own interest and in the interest of the concern they serve. On page 11 of

Gorilla in the Room, Harber quotes what Bekker once said: 'When you run media, you soon discover that managers who love playing in the limelight often get dazzled and bump into the furniture. The stars in our groups – the journalists, the TV personalities, computer whizzes – they take centre stage and they bow to the audience. Our managers stay away from the flashlights.' Koos's introversion is therefore also linked to his professionalism.

Bekker's refined aloofness does not mean indifference – the opposite, in fact. With his full energy – he is extremely thorough and hardworking – he is involved in and focused on his enterprises. His painstaking preparation for an agreement or a crucial business discussion saved our bacon on many an occasion. He would coach his top managers rigorously and have them do simulation exercises. He would then present the package to me as chair, or to the relevant board committees. Once all the hitches had been pointed out and the finishing touches put to the strategy, Koos would go off into the lion's den. We won many battles in tough negotiations purely because of our team's meticulous preparation.

Bekker is a slave driver in that he expects others to follow the same standards he sets for himself. If there is work to be done, business hours do not apply. When we started with FilmNet in the Netherlands, our first international venture in 1991, Koos would often summon staff for a Saturday or Sunday conference. The Dutch employees complained bitterly that he messed up their weekends.

In business, Koos did not hesitate to risk big money in the pursuit of opportunities. This approach has cost Naspers's shareholders billions of rands over the years, but earned them billions more. He is renowned for his ability to see around the next corner and then act swiftly and decisively. His visionary entrepreneurial approach is best exemplified by what happened in 1995, with the switchover from the analogue television system to the digital one.

Koos phoned me and said that he wanted to switch MultiChoice to digital, a relatively new but exciting technology that only the DirectTV group in the United States had launched at that point. MultiChoice happened to be in the process of updating analogue, and this news caught the technical team off guard.

A while later, I received a call from the chair of the SABC, Professor Christo Viljoen. We were making the biggest mistake of our lives, he said. The technology was not mature, and we would run into great difficulties. I acknowledged that he was an electrotechnical engineer who knew more than I did about these matters, but told him I had faith in Koos's judgement; Koos knew what he was doing.

With hindsight, the move was a giant leap ahead. The present-day SABC is still analogue-driven. In terms of an agreement with MultiChoice, the public broadcaster has three channels for digital transmissions. Meanwhile, the offshoots of M-Net are able to broadcast on hundreds of channels throughout Africa and beyond.

This leap was typical of Koos. He has an instinctive feel for promising innovations. If he is convinced, he will convince his team, and also the controlling boards, regardless of cost. Some expensive mistakes were made, but measured against Naspers's success, the company had the right leader.

Among the expensive mistakes was the setback in 2001, when the so-called dotcom bubble burst and investors in Internet technology took heavy hits worldwide. Naspers's profits fell from R3,3 billion in 2000 to a loss of R1,9 billion; at one point, the share price plummeted from R100 to R12.

Management fought back with robust cost-cutting and the markets recovered. One can learn valuable lessons from setbacks.

The tipping point in putting Nasionale Pers onto a new trajectory was the introduction of pay television in South Africa. After the founding of M-Net in 1984, digital television followed over time. In between, it was the turn of the cellphone industry, followed by seizing new opportunities offered by the Internet, e-commerce and, of course, the investment in Tencent (see Chapter 4).

These steps took Naspers away from its original industry, the print media. As a print-media company, Naspers/Nasionale Pers, in its best publications played a huge and important role in South Africa. With its paper-and-ink products, the group was at the forefront as a provider of news, information and knowledge. Its newspapers and magazines offered a public forum for opinions and debate. It was an educator in the wider sense of the word. Some publications focused on special fields of interest or healthy entertainment.

The group offered open opportunities to writing talent in South Africa and produced superb products, such as numerous books whose value is beyond price. At the same time, it survived financially and did well for more than a hundred years. These services are still continuing.

But, in the last decades of the twentieth century and thereafter, the so-called graphosphere, the sphere of printed matter, has gradually been outvoted by the so-called videosphere, the sphere of the video screen. Naspers had to adapt and follow the signposts towards the future. And it had to do so in time. When I look back, it was my opportune discovery and appointment of Koos Bekker that pleases me the most.

Digital technology and the Internet dealt traditional print-media companies a death blow, especially financially. Koos Bekker was the person who, with a paradigm shift, made it possible for Naspers to escape a similar fate. His far-sightedness, powers of persuasion and can-do determination have made him Naspers's talisman. I grasped his potential at an early stage, won him for Naspers, and trusted, supported and complemented him; that was my role.

Measured by company performance, the transition was an enormous success. Venerable blue-chip shares have bitten the dust, yet Naspers has risen to become the most valuable company in Africa.

Why did Naspers – on Koos Bekker's advice, but that of others, too – venture particularly into the more economically uncharted parts of the world such as China, Russia, Poland, Indonesia, Thailand, the Philippines, Brazil, Colombia and Argentina?

When we moved out of Western Europe, we successfully launched a pay-TV service in Greece, but sold it in time at a considerable profit when the economic storm clouds started gathering over the Greeks. In our deliberations, we concluded that Western Europe and the United States were already too fully occupied and too expensive for investments, especially for us in South Africa, where strict exchange-control regulations still applied to exporting capital.

Naspers then started investing widely, through its subsidiaries, in technology that worked for it and had not yet been exploited strongly in those regions. Much of the success can be attributed to Naspers's chief investment officer Mark Sorour, who was (and still is) responsible for mergers and acquisitions. This former banker has exceptional insight when it comes to potential investments. He receives hundreds of offers every year; it takes keen powers of discernment and experience to separate the wheat from the chaff. Mark has this capacity, and he practically wears himself out as he flies around the globe several times a year!

As a result of new investments, Naspers now operates in more than 130 countries and directly or indirectly employs almost 67 000 people. The company is nothing like the Nasionale Pers of old with its Afrikaans orientation. In 2014, the lingua franca of the board of directors was changed to English on my recommendation – in that year, we had Afrikaans and English-speaking directors, as well as American, Brazilian, Chinese, Singaporean and Filipino directors, in our ranks.

Bekker is staunchly Afrikaans by birth, and does much behind the scenes to promote Afrikaans. But he believes that, in the business world, one should put business interests first. In the business world, there is no room for considerations or sentiments that may hamper one's success – hence his objections to a new name for the company that would in any way be reminiscent of the old Pers with its particular political associations, as I have mentioned before.

Here is a good example of how, after the name change, Bekker protected the new image of Naspers he wanted to build: in 2000, when he had been at the helm of Naspers for a relatively short time, he noticed that *Die Burger* was commemorating its 85th anniversary with an exhibition of front pages from the past in the foyer of the Naspers Centre in Cape Town. It included several exultant newspaper posters that celebrated National Party election victories. Bekker immediately instructed the exhibition to be removed.

When M-Net was founded, there was initially a strong emphasis on equal treatment of Afrikaans and English. The eventual bias towards

English drew much criticism of the chief shareholder, Naspers, from its traditional support base.

Digitisation brought along a neat solution: with the splitting of channels, an Afrikaans channel, kykNET, could be established. Today, kykNET is so successful that it operates three Afrikaans channels and makes excellent profits. Meanwhile, the Afrikaans channel VIA has been added on channel 147.

Koos Bekker remains an interesting person: he is a student of Mandarin, and sponsors a chair in Mandarin at Stellenbosch University; the group's biggest investment is in communist China. He is not ashamed of this, unlike what he might feel about Naspers's Afrikaans-nationalist past.

As far as Afrikaans itself is concerned, he immediately said yes when I approached him to support the re-establishment of the annual Aardklop arts festival in Potchefstroom with a generous contribution from Naspers. We wanted to revive the Northern Afrikaans arts festival after an ill-considered decision by the former board to close it down.

The most vehement disagreement in my relationship with Koos was about the publication of an official history of Naspers in celebration of the company's centenary in 2015. The board had approved my recommendation that Professor Lizette Rabe, head of the journalism department at Stellenbosch University, be commissioned to undertake the project. She worked on the manuscript for four years, on contract with Naspers. I assisted her as a sounding board, given that, as a former journalist, I had experienced more than forty years of Naspers's history firsthand. Various people invested time and energy in the manuscript; in my view, the result was an overall picture of the company's century.

When the project was almost complete, information about the digital era and the Chinese investment was still lacking. Rabe was unable to gain access to Pony Ma and his team from Tencent in China. Bekker asked two members of his top management team to compile contributions about these aspects. He was on a year-long sabbatical at the time.

However, at one stage, Koos sent three envoys to me in an attempt to persuade me to drop the project. They were his great confidant and fellow Naspers director Cobus Stofberg, financial director Steve Pacak, and company secretary Gillian Kisbey-Green.

I dug in my heels. With all due respect, none of the three envoys had detailed knowledge of Naspers's past. They were better acquainted with the final phase of its century, which had been ushered in by the start of the M-family.

When Bekker returned to work in May 2015, in the capacity of my successor as non-executive chair, he told me he was not going to have the book published. (It had been due to appear in an Afrikaans and an English version.) His reason was Naspers's thousands of black employees. If they were to read about the company's past, it would draw the attention of the ANC government to the company, which could be prejudicial to its regulated businesses, such as DStv and the digital expansions.

I told him his standpoint was wrong, because our history was public knowledge. So, too, was the reform we had brought about in the ranks of our own community from 1984 onwards. This reform had culminated in the Afrikaans-speaking community's willing and hopeful integration into the new, democratic South Africa. In my opinion, Koos's fears were excessive.

But Koos would have none of a book that was going to put the spotlight on Naspers's past. He held the trump card, as Naspers was the copyright holder. Ironically, I had had this copyright written into the contract myself, because Naspers had paid for the research.

In my farewell speech in February 2016, in front of an open audience, I appealed to Koos to reconsider his decision. I asked him after the speech whether I had embarrassed him with my appeal. He just said no and smiled.

It was never a personal issue for Koos, of that I am sure – merely an issue of viewpoint, policy and management. I disagree with him in the same respectful, professional manner, and would like to venture a prediction that this essential piece of South African history will appear in print after all.

The wise Piet Cillié once said during a lecture at Unisa on 26 April 1990: 'It is therefore surely necessary that a press organ or company's own history and performance from year to year should also be investigated and recorded searchingly and honestly. In short: we, press people, should not be so preoccupied with others' history that we neglect our own. Nasionale Pers's history as an institution or business is an integral part of the total history of the South African society.'

There was a much worse, really brutal example of internal media censorship of which I am aware. In 1988, Perskor Publishers planned to publish a novel about the media by Dirk Richard, retired director of *Dagbreek* and *Die Vaderland*, and a director of Perskor. The book was a thinly disguised attack on the life and work of the late Marius Jooste, former chair of Perskor, and his relationship with newspaper editors.

When the book, titled *Asof dit gister was* (As if it were yesterday), had already been printed, the executive chair of Perskor and a former lackey of Jooste's, Koos Buitendag, got wind of it. He summoned Richard and threatened to strip him of his directorship. The book was pulped.

There is another matter that I reflect on in my retirement: the entrenchment of control of Naspers in 2006 when Koos Bekker, Cobus Stofberg and Sanlam got into a position to ward off the raid by Jannie Mouton and Chris Otto to acquire control of the company.

Naspers's control structure is complex. The company is protected against hostile takeovers, a shareholding structure that the Johannesburg Stock Exchange recognised when the company listed in 1994. The Mouton bid drew attention to a vulnerability, according to Bekker, and this gap was plugged by unusual means. Bekker and Stofberg acted together and, at one stage, held talks with other senior executives to obtain financial support for an agreement with the largest outside shareholder at the time, Sanlam.

Sanlam then sold 13 per cent of Naspers's high-voting A shares to a new company, Wheatfields 221. The deal was only between Sanlam MD Dr Johan van Zyl, Bekker and Stofberg. No other staff members or directors were approached to invest in the transaction.

Bekker and Stofberg paid R135 million for 50 per cent of Wheatfields. It is not known what their respective contributions were. Sanlam held the other 50 per cent, and per agreement would not vote against Naspers's vote. Sanlam mentioned the transaction in its annual statements. Thus a block vote was established that lay outside the control structure, but which would serve as an obstacle to a hostile takeover.

The board of Naspers was notified of the transaction with the explanation that a raid had been fended off. Wheatfields was the white knight. Dr Van Zyl has since vacated his position, and Sanlam's 50 per cent of Wheatfields is now a matter for Sanlam management.

The point is that the initiative raised questions in my mind about the future of Wheatfields. It can be accepted that Bekker and Stofberg will deal with this valuable instrument in the best interests of the company. I am fully satisfied that the matter will be dealt with in such a way that it cements the independence of Naspers.

When all is said and done, one cannot help returning to the high praise that is due to Koos Bekker. With exceptional intelligence, dedication and drive, he has made Naspers into a shining gem of a company.

Outside the office, Koos has a strong love for and interest in land. He owns a maize and cattle farm in the district of Heidelberg, Gauteng. He has developed the tourist farm Babylonstoren near Franschhoek beautifully. In recent years, he and his wife Karen have been developing an estate in the county of Somerset in England. This estate has long-standing ties with the descendants of Emily Hobhouse's family – a piece of history that interests Koos intensely. The Bekkers are pouring millions of rands into the project.

Thanks to his three per cent direct interest in Naspers, per a contract that I concluded with him on behalf of the board, Koos has sufficient means to live out his passion projects. He deserves to enjoy them to the full.

Now, I must take you back to earlier days.

CHAPTER 6

The press and politics: Vanguard thinking and paving the way

Nasionale Pers was founded in 1915 to help demoralised and impoverished Afrikaners get back on their feet in the wake of the South African War. Within the newly created Union of South Africa, it was possible to give Afrikaners as a group a new sense of hope, unity and urgency through initiatives such as the establishment of the National Party and Nasionale Pers.

The success Nasionale Pers achieved in this regard can hardly be overestimated. But it would be a mistake to confuse a new sense of solidarity among white Afrikaans speakers or co-operation between Nasionale Pers and the National Party with complete unanimity within this group of people. Likewise, it would be wrong to think that the Pers was subject to pressure from the Party without exerting strong pressure in reverse, especially after the NP became the governing party.

In fact, at no time, whether before or after 1915, have Afrikaners ever been closely united in ideological or other respects without resistance from dissidents or progressive thinkers in their own ranks. The news, views and polemics published by the newspapers and magazines of Nasionale Pers since 1915 attest to this.

At the time of South Africa's unification, emerging Afrikaans literature was characterised by Afrikaner-nationalist writers such as Jan FE Celliers. But the best writers were figures such as C Louis Leipoldt and Eugène N

Marais, with modern ideas that were at variance with the notion of a self-isolating community united by Christian-national values. Nasionale Pers published the works of both Leipoldt and Marais, but not, of course, some of their first editions, which were published prior to the Pers's becoming a book publisher.

Within a few years after 1948 – even before this time, actually – an onslaught on the political culture that was associated with the National Party came from within the ranks of Afrikaans literary writers. In the work of writers such as Uys Krige, Peter Blum, Etienne Leroux and Jan Rabie, and later Breyten Breytenbach, André P Brink, Adam Small and Ingrid Jonker – and eventually Antjie Krog – Afrikaans literature revolted against the sociopolitical situation under the National Party. By the 1980s, this was the predominant mindset among Afrikaans fiction writers and poets.

Academics such as the philosopher Johan Degenaar, clerics such as Beyers Naudé and politicians such as Frederik van Zyl Slabbert continued to stimulate resistance within the Afrikaner community. Some, including proponents of 'loyal' dissidence such as NP van Wyk Louw, had already embarked on this in the 1950s.

Nasionale Pers published the work of the majority of these dissidents – not necessarily to promote their views, but to afford them a turn to speak. In their letters pages and opinion columns, the newspapers of the Pers always offered dissenting voices the opportunity to be heard.

This balance between supporting the policies of the NP and facilitating and publishing criticism typifies the relationship between the Pers and the Party in those days.

Through the years and decades after 1948, the Pers remained loyal to the National Party, and the group's journalists had to help defend the NP. But in the meantime, its journalists also had to deal with the political news on a daily basis. Many of them formed their own critical opinions in this regard.

As far back as the early 1950s, some journalists started seeing their role as that of people who could criticise constructively from inside an influential institution. The great leaders of pioneering thinking within Nasionale Pers were the 'terrible twins' from Stellenbosch, Piet Cillié and Schalk Pienaar. The thoughts of the celebrated poet NP van Wyk Louw also appeared in the Pers's publications. His stance of *'lojale verset'* (loyal resistance), as he called it, sometimes caused great annoyance within the National Party.

When Prime Minister HF Verwoerd announced the possibility of sovereign black states in 1959, the homeland policy was welcomed by the Pers as a way of trying to bring about a situation of justice and fairness in South Africa. But later, on 17 February 1961, *Die Burger* also expressed its reservations: 'The stone-cold truth is that at this moment the policy is still confronted with massive incredulity, and that this attitude is not limited to opponents of the government. In our own Nationalist ranks the question is asked whether the policy is still possible, and if it is indeed possible, whether we are serious about implementing it.'

Among senior journalists, there was at times barely concealed irritation about the harsh measures to enforce racial segregation and the foolish decisions the NP government often took in its inflexibility, to the detriment and shame of South Africa.

In short: as far back as the 1950s the Pers started exerting strong critical pressure on the National Party in its role as governing party. This groundwork continued in the 1960s and the years that followed.

The end of the matter was the total rejection of apartheid by the National Party itself, the policy's demise, and the advent of the democratic era in 1994. A fully inclusive election was held 82 years after the founding of the African National Congress in 1912, and 80 years after the founding of the National Party in 1914.

Nasionale Pers's journey on the road to the new South Africa of 1994 proceeded in fits and starts, with many a pothole along the way. In its own ranks, political fear and political hope sometimes tugged at opposite ends of a decision. By 1987, for example, our papers were not yet ready to accept the Dakar mission of *verligte* Afrikaners led by Van Zyl Slabbert, and slated the initiative. With hindsight, this stance was a mistake and an embarrassment.

Dr Van Zyl Slabbert, former leader of the Progressive Party in the old House of Assembly, had resigned from Parliament: the country was burning as a result of escalating resistance to apartheid, while the government under PW Botha continued to fight the introduction of truly effective reforms. Large parts of South Africa were virtually ungovernable, with rioting, arson and brutal clampdowns by the police and army the order of the day. Against this backdrop, Slabbert took a group of mainly Afrikaans-speaking academics, businesspeople and journalists to Dakar in Senegal for a conference with a delegation from the ANC in exile. The event was organised by the poet and writer Breyten Breytenbach.

Afrikaans newspapers spewed vitriol at the Dakar travellers – this, when leaders within Nasionale Pers had already foreseen the ultimate consequences of apartheid almost forty years earlier.

The opening salvo of opposition to the policies of the NP government was fired by the editor of *Die Burger*, Piet Cillié, when he wrote in 1950: 'Putting the coloureds on a separate voters' roll and pegging their representation permanently at three members, and that with a majority like ours, is an ugly thing and no sophistry will prettify it.' In 1953, the chair of Nasionale Pers, Dr Phil Weber – a very conservative Nationalist – dared to say: 'We shall have to face the fact one day that our policy of apartheid is an absurdity.'[15]

What was really the view of leading figures within Nasionale Pers who were discomfited by, and reacted critically to, what they regarded as policy errors on the part of the NP government?

In the early 1950s, people like Piet Cillié and Schalk Pienaar were loyal Afrikaner Nationalists who supported the Party's policy and defended it against criticism of whatever kind. But once Afrikaner power had been consolidated, Cillié and Pienaar, like NP van Wyk Louw, began to cast a critical eye on the quality of Afrikaner life and what they saw as the flaws or errors that would ultimately put the Afrikaner's survival at risk.

For example, they maintained that the emphasis placed on white '*baasskap*' (domination or overlordship) by Hans Strijdom, who became prime minister in 1954, flew in the face of the Afrikaner's own struggle for freedom from British domination and would therefore nullify this

Afrikaner struggle in the long run. How could you deny another group realisation of the same principle that had inspired you and not expect this to lead to your own downfall?

The way coloured people were treated in 1950 disgusted someone like Piet Cillié. The views of people such as Piet Cillié and Schalk Pienaar were in keeping with Van Wyk Louw's credo, 'survival in justice'. In his works *Liberale Nasionalisme* and *Lojale Verset*, Louw posed questions such as: 'If I am not for myself, who will be?' And: 'But if I am only for myself, what am I?' Louw warned that a nation, after having done everything in its power to survive, could find itself faced with the final temptation: 'to believe that mere survival is preferable to survival in justice'.

Meanwhile, questions about the apartheid system also started cropping up in religious circles. The large Afrikaans churches, representing different denominations within South Africa's Dutch Reformed tradition, were, as it were, custodians of the 'Christian' half of the Christian-national principle.

In 1952, a book appeared that questioned the scriptural grounds for apartheid: theologian Professor Ben Marais' *Die Kleur-krisis en die Weste* (the English version was titled *Colour: Unsolved Problem of the West*). The book caused a furore, and Professor Marais was denounced by the General Synod of the Dutch Reformed Church (DRC). His detractors were led by Dr Koot Vorster, John Vorster's theologian brother, who justified apartheid on scriptural grounds.

After Ben Marais, there was cautious questioning of the NP's racial policy on the part of Professor Bennie Keet. But he received little support. His book *Suid-Afrika – Waarheen? 'n Bydrae tot die bespreking van ons rasseprobleem* (South Africa – Quo vadis? A contribution to the discussion about our racial problem) appeared in 1956.

When the former Transvaal province is typecast as the home of narrow-minded, ossified apartheid thinking in the 1960s, one should not forget that the Potchefstroom University for Christian Higher Education was among the first institutions in Afrikaner ranks that strongly questioned South Africa's racial policy.

The Doppers of Potchefstroom, members of the Reformed Church who had broken away from the Dutch Reformed Church in the nineteenth century, measured the inflexible racism of our national policy against principles of Christian charity. Their church magazine *Woord en Daad* (Word and Deed) was used to this end. This select band, if I may call them that, can be seen as some of the first real nonconformists to oppose apartheid orthodoxy. It was from this environment that Willem de Klerk came.

The quarrels about apartheid within the Afrikaans churches made for stimulating reporting and debate in the newspapers. The mentality of a figure such as Dr Koot Vorster could by no means be reconciled with the thinking of Nasionale Pers's leading lights, such as Cillié and Pienaar. The way in which the apartheid doctrine was cloaked in Calvinist garb in Dr Vorster's pronouncements and actions often made him the butt of jokes in *verligte* circles.

Leaders such as Piet Cillié and Schalk Pienaar realised that Afrikaners would have to adapt themselves to a changing world in which the old colonial orders were crumbling. The Afrikaans churches had to figure out for themselves how they could salvage their Christian mission with a defence of apartheid.

Questioning apartheid started gaining strong momentum in the 1960s, including as far as the involvement of the churches was concerned. Landmark events were the Cottesloe conference organised by the World Council of Churches (WCC) with delegates from their South African member churches in December 1960, the visiting British prime minister Harold Macmillan's 'wind of change' speech, the Sharpeville tragedy, and the assassination of Dr Hendrik Verwoerd.

The Cottesloe conference's closing declaration amounted to a condemnation of the apartheid order by the WCC. Someone who would later become a model of loyal resistance among the Afrikaners, Dr Beyers Naudé, writes in his autobiography, *My Land van Hoop* (My Country of Hope): 'I don't think any of us realised how soon this dynamite would explode in the faces of some of the DRC's delegates.'

The Cottesloe declaration contained 17 resolutions, but four of them in particular drove the Afrikaans churches into a corner. These pertained to people from all race groups worshipping together, mixed marriages, land ownership, and the political status of coloured people.

On 1 January 1961, Dr Verwoerd launched an attack on the Cottesloe delegates by declaring: 'In reality, the churches have not yet spoken. The voice of the Church must still be heard, to wit, at their synods where the members as well as the clergymen will be represented.'

The fat was in the fire. According to Beyers Naudé, the Transvaal Afrikaans dailies, *Die Transvaler* and *Die Vaderland*, were scathing in their condemnation of the Cottesloe delegates. 'Fortunately,' he writes, '*Die Burger* in Cape Town voiced a different view.' Naudé continues:

> On 19 December 1960 this paper wrote very sympathetically about the Cottesloe resolutions in a lengthy editorial, stating among others that the Church had the right and the duty '… to test political policies against moral laws … to admonish and correct the rulers of this world and to do so fearlessly because the Church, if it is purely attuned to the Reality behind the reality, represents a Higher Authority than governments, political parties or the will of the people'.

In that period, Piet Cillié clashed head-on with Verwoerd about the place of coloured people in our political system. He advocated direct representation of coloured people in Parliament, while Verwoerd condemned this as a step towards complete integration, 'even biological integration'. Verwoerd eventually won the battle against Cillié, in the sense that the latter had to moderate his resistance.

The vanguard thinking of *Die Burger* was bolstered in 1965 by the establishment of the Johannesburg-based Sunday paper *Die Beeld* under the editorship of Schalk Pienaar, with colleagues such as the *verligte* journalists Johannes Grosskopf and Rykie van Reenen at his side.

Pienaar's leadership of *Die Beeld* was described by his friend, the poet DJ Opperman, as the 'biggest, the most daring, the most forceful, the most provocative', 'just short of a total ban by court, state, church, academe'.

Die Beeld, as a Sunday paper, was a new kind of venture for Nasionale Pers. The success this paper soon achieved, in terms of both circulation and political influence, resulted on the one hand from the resolute fearlessness and journalistic talent of Pienaar and his editorial team. On the other hand, the success was due to the wide spectrum of readers *Die Beeld* managed to reach and attract. There was something that appealed to the university rector, but also something for the wage labourer to read for an overview of the week's events; something for the Cape reader, and something for the reader in Pretoria and Johannesburg – all written in reader-friendly language and presented with eye-catching typography.

The front page frequently featured sensational breaking news: the Sunday paper did its own investigations into events of the past week and issues that would arouse readers' interest. Inside, readers could expect intellectually stimulating articles, for instance, a riveting book review by André P Brink. The front-page news, thought-provoking articles and political reports constituted an exciting, sometimes daring, brand of journalism that tested boundaries. *Die Beeld* was a paper that created new readers. A paper for all tastes, distributed across large parts of the country. A winning recipe.

It waded into forbidden territory and slaughtered sacred cows. As *Die Beeld*'s political reporter, for example, I exposed the role of provincialist pressure groups in the decision-making of the National Party and its government. Dr Verwoerd, chair of the Northern Afrikaans press group, regarded the advent of *Die Beeld* as a declaration of war by the South against the North.

Nothing could daunt Pienaar. As he put it: 'The oath I swore was that if I should ever occupy a position of authority at a newspaper, I would inform the people about the things they ought to know about, and inform them in such a way that they know what I am talking about.'

This vanguard thinking within our papers was continued after the assassination of Dr Verwoerd in 1966, when John Vorster took over as prime minister. Vorster, Cillié and Pienaar had been contemporaries in their student days at Stellenbosch, and for a while Nasionale Pers's papers endorsed Vorster's so-called outward-moving (détente) policy that was aimed at finding partners among leaders of African countries.

Vorster's attempts to shake hands with willing African leaders and his changes to the country's sports policy soon incurred the wrath of *verkrampte* members of the NP caucus. *Die Beeld* and Nasionale Pers's dailies gleefully exploited this situation. From the perspective of the *verligtes*, a breakaway that would rid the National Party of its *verkrampte* wing was a hopeful development.

The right-wing rebellion eventually led to the establishment of the Herstigte Nasionale Party (HNP, or Reconstituted National Party) in 1969, a definitive split from the National Party. The HNP's founder, Albert Hertzog, was the son of JBM Hertzog, who had been a founder of the National Party in 1914.

But this internal political realignment in South Africa did not cause external criticism to abate. In fact, during Vorster's and Botha's time, the ANC's onslaught from outside led to gruesome attacks on civilians and a low-intensity civil war on our borders.

The turbulence in Afrikaner politics was reflected in the Afrikaans press industry. It gave competition between newspapers a political slant, fuelling discord among party members. A 'forced marriage' was even arranged between Nasionale Pers and Perskor. In an effort to settle the press war between the two rival groups, NP cabinet ministers who served on the boards of the two groups helped to bring about a 50/50 joint ownership of a new Sunday paper.

In November 1970, *Die Beeld* merged with Perskor's *Dagbreek en Sondagnuus*, with which *Die Landstem* was incorporated, to form *Rapport*, with equal shareholding. *Rapport*'s first editor, Willem Wepener – known by the nickname Ysterman (Iron Man) among his journalists – continued the *verligte* thinking and was the first editor of an Afrikaans newspaper to advocate the release of Nelson Mandela.

But this did not spell the end of Nasionale Pers's dreams of a Northern daily. In 1974, the Sunday paper *Die Beeld* returned to life as the daily *Beeld*; in 1977, I found myself in its editor's chair.

In our commentary, my editorial team and I opposed with all our might what was referred to as the escapist thinking of the government. This gained *Beeld* the reputation of a trendsetting daily whose reformist agenda paved the way for radical political change.

THE PRESS AND POLITICS

In his autobiography, *Kroniek van 'n Koerantman* (*Chronicle of a Pressman*), my assistant editor and later head of the newspaper section of Nasionale Pers, Hennie van Deventer, described our course as follows: 'By constantly providing reasoned arguments and motivation, [Nasionale Pers's papers] strengthened the government's hand to bring about essential changes. At the same time, the broad reading public was induced to become more accepting of inescapable realities.'

At the start of 1981, the inevitability of radical change impelled me to write the political column in *Beeld* to which I referred in Chapter 1. The column attracted attention internationally. In the political 'silly season', on 9 January 1981, I wrote: 'The day will surely come when a South African government will sit down with the ANC at the negotiating table.' (A translated version of the full text of the column appears at the end of this chapter.)

It struck me at the time that a number of government leaders such as Pik Botha, Barend du Plessis, Dawie de Villiers, Kobie Coetsee and others did not follow PW Botha's example, and refrained from slating the column. This restraint was perhaps connected to the fact that the government was at that stage negotiating behind the scenes in Geneva with Swapo about the future of South West Africa (Namibia).

The ANC, like Swapo, could be seen as a black nationalist organisation, with sentiments that were not so different from those of Afrikaners who had fought for their freedom in South Africa. One could ask oneself whether the talks in Geneva were not perhaps a harbinger of future developments.

The New York Times, *The Guardian* and *The Financial Times*, as well as German and Dutch publications, carried reports on my column. *The Guardian* wrote: 'The Johannesburg-based Afrikaans daily which has close links with the Botha administration and which has campaigned strongly in favour of the "reformist" policies of the prime minister, Mr PW Botha, has come out openly in favour of government talks with the banned ANC.'

The Dutch daily *Trouw* published a prominent report from its Johannesburg correspondent Hennie Serfontein with the following comment: 'The article by Vosloo is the most astonishing "evidence" ever given in high government circles, because it concedes openly that the government's strategy has failed.'

There were also reports from the Netherlands that put a rather different slant on my column. Anti-apartheid organisations such as Azapo were concerned that my plea could indicate that there was something wrong with the ANC. Why would the government of South Africa want to negotiate with them all of a sudden?

In my political opinions and general outlook, I was positively influenced by politicians and influential individuals such as Piet 'Weskus' Marais, Theo Gerdener, Japie Basson, Pik Botha, Neil van Heerden, Anton Rupert, Pieter de Lange, Elize Botha, Flip Smit and Willie Esterhuyse. And I was negatively influenced by Verwoerd, Vorster and Botha, not to mention the *verkramptes* of my time, such as Albert Hertzog, Jaap Marais, Andries Treurnicht, Gert Beetge and many more – also my old schoolmate, Barry Botha. He later became editor of the extremely pugnacious far-right mouthpiece *Veg*.

My journalism mentors whom I rate most highly are Pienaar, Cillié and Rykie van Reenen, and my first editor, Dirk de Villiers. He was my editor at *Die Oosterlig* (now *Die Burger-Oos*) in Port Elizabeth. From May 1956 to October 1958, Dirk de Villiers initiated me into the Nasionale Pers environment and taught me the virtues of a newspaper journalist: curiosity, zeal and stamina.

A footnote in passing: one of my fiercest journalistic disparagers was Beaumont Schoeman, the former *Vaderland*'s political correspondent when I was at *Dagbreek* and *Die Beeld*. He later became editor of *Hoofstad*, with Andries Treurnicht as editor of Jaap Marais' right-wing political mouthpiece, *Die Afrikaner*. *Die Afrikaner* folded, which left Schoeman in a precarious financial position. He was in the prime of his life, with a family to support. Schoeman was a good language editor and a thorough journalist, and I helped him to become chief subeditor of our financial magazine *Finansies & Tegniek*. He got back on his feet, but sadly died unexpectedly of a heart attack after only a few years in our employ.

The road to a more expansive world was also opened to me by Piet Beukes, an old Free State *Bloedsap* and devotee of Jan Smuts. Beukes was the founder-editor of the controversial weekly *Die Landstem*. For five years, he and his colleagues afforded me opportunities that extended my journalistic skills immeasurably.

My thinking about our national affairs was influenced decisively by the year at Harvard University that I was able to enjoy in the northern-hemisphere academic year from September 1970 to 1971. This sabbatical exposed me to the cutting-edge thinking of world-renowned academics such as Karl Deutsch, an expert on the history of nationalism, and to the ideas of Raymond Vernon, Sam Huntington and Herman Kahn of the Hudson Institute. During my Harvard year, I sent frequent short opinion articles to *Rapport*.

In February 1971, Arthur Ashe, who would go on to become the first black tennis player to win the Wimbledon men's singles title in 1975, was in the news. He had been asked to play at the South African Open tournament, but the South African government had denied him a visa, evidently because he was black. I deemed this action hurtful and damaging to South Africa, and promptly wrote so.

The day after my article was published in *Rapport*, our ambassador in Washington, HL Taswell, phoned and reprimanded me for having the cheek to denounce the South African decision. I told Ambassador Taswell bluntly what a stupid decision it was.

After my return to South Africa, *Rapport*'s editor Willem Wepener showed me a note he had received from Nasionale Pers chair Phil Weber, requesting him to warn me against my own impetuousness. Wepener had never forwarded the note to me.

I continued the work of paving the way for a new order in my role, later, as editor, with articles directed at our own staff and at the public as well as in discussions within the company. Doing so also prepared me for my subsequent role as managing director and chair of Naspers. This innovative thinking led to the outright victory of Nasionale Pers's papers over

Perskor's ambivalent dailies in 1983, when the latter disappeared from the morning market.

The *verligte* onslaught of Nasionale Pers's papers from 1965 onwards contributed to a turnaround in the NP, with the *verkrampte* elements stymied, PW Botha being elected as prime minister in 1978 and, later, FW de Klerk, who took his place. We contributed to the process that led to negotiations with the ANC and, ultimately, to the inclusive democratic election of 1994.

Column published in Beeld on 9 January 1981 (translation)

Like Swapo, the ANC lies ahead

I have much more to say to you, more than you can now bear (John 16:12).

Amid the smokescreens and diplomatic equivocations, the real hard news about the South West Africa conference in Geneva is the fact that South Africa has sat down at the negotiating table with a so-called liberation organisation, Swapo.

And in second place, by a short head, is the hard news (made public by *Beeld* and later confirmed) that South Africa's direct negotiations with the Marxist regime of Angola made the talks possible.

So, I suppose one has to say it bluntly: the day will surely come when a South African government will sit down with the ANC at the negotiating table.

We should not live in the dream world that the status quo of a white government speaking for and on behalf of the entire country will obtain for all time in the Republic. If that is the case, may Ian Smith's infamous 'thousand-year' UDI rule jerk us back forcibly to reality.

Of course, there are numerous preconditions one could set, foremost of which is that the ANC would have to undergo a purge with respect to its behavioural pattern before an SA government would talk to it.

Maybe the Progs under Dr Van Zyl Slabbert would like to confer with the ANC in its current guise. The Progs and their camp-follower media are, of course, only too keen on holding a national convention.

From this side of the fence, it can be said that the ANC is the mother of organised black politics in South Africa. It could be called the National Party of the black nationalists, in a manner of speaking. Hence it cannot be ignored.

The ANC has come under communist influence, and today no white person has the assurance that the ANC is not a communist body to the marrow as far as its leadership is concerned. In other words, it has no other goal in mind than to take over South Africa and rule the country according to a communist model.

It would seek to raze our system to the ground – not apartheid, but the capitalist-Western system that makes us part and parcel of the Western world, a sphere of influence with which we trade and which benefits and strengthens both parties.

Everyone knows very well that if the dismantling, the demolition, of our system is the condition for the ANC's participation in SA politics, we would be heading for war – the current skirmishes would turn into a hot war.

The ANC and its sympathisers – millions of black people in the Republic can probably be counted among them – have to accept the following as non-negotiable: the Republic of South Africa is a sovereign state.

In the long run, limited peace will only come if the ANC accepts that the mixed and numerically unequal makeup of our population requires a political order that deviates from the 'winner-takes-all' principle.

A split-up state lies in store for us. Transkei, Bophuthatswana, Venda and Ciskei cannot simply be erased, and the model of a confederation/federation must be accepted.

The ANC would have to renounce its Marxist ambitions and take its seat at the negotiating table along with the political groupings being established under the bountiful and protective hand of the Nationalist policy.

It would be one of many such interest groups and not the sole anointed one of the UN, which is the status Swapo now has.

From a white perspective: this is our country, but it is also the country of black people, because the realist understands that a split-up state would probably be unable to absorb more than ten, twelve million of our black population politically. The balance would have to be negotiated with, and the balance would be the urban blacks, among whom the ANC's influence is arguably the strongest.

I started off with a text, because for all of us there still lie many things ahead 'that we cannot now bear'. Whites would simply *have* to trust our realistic rulers.

But in the meantime, we can combat the ANC in its current guise with full conviction by keeping the following saying of the Chinese philosopher Han Yu (768–821 AD) in mind:

'If the enemy's ideas are not stopped, we will not be able to disseminate our own ideas without impediment; if the enemy's ideas are not removed, we will be unable to popularise our own ideas.'

Our highest preference is to make the Defence Force cliché of winning the hearts and minds of black people for our cause practical policy on a gigantic scale. We must prove visibly that our system is better than the system the ANC can offer. That is a tall order.

If we are not up to it, we will be doomed to sit down at the national convention on Prog terms, under the most unfavourable conditions possible, with the ANC in the driver's seat. Or to emigrate.

CHAPTER 7

Invasion of the North

The political power struggle inside South Africa in the second half of the twentieth century made for an exciting and challenging journalistic life.

When I joined the Sunday paper *Dagbreek* as a political reporter in July 1963, Dr Hendrik Verwoerd was our prime minister. He was also chair of the board of the press group Dagbreekpers, on which he served along with a bunch of Cabinet ministers. Dagbreekpers was a forerunner of Perskor. The opponent in the South, Nasionale Pers Limited, also had ministers on its board.

The National Party sought to influence and control the Afrikaans papers, although Nasionale Pers in particular also exerted influence in the opposite direction. In the end, after 1994, the Pers could follow its own path, with the Party having finally thrown in the towel.

In 1963, Verwoerd was firmly in control of the country. After the failed attempt on his life by David Pratt in April 1960, he had recovered miraculously from the injuries caused by two bullets to his face. Not only could he resume his career, but Afrikaners idolised him.

In his first speech after the assassination attempt, on 31 May 1960 in Bloemfontein, Verwoerd, who was not an active churchgoer, attributed his recovery to God.

Nationalist Afrikaners worshipped Verwoerd; in the general election of

1966, he also received considerable support from English speakers. He was seen as a man of unyielding firmness of principle, a leader with a granite-like character. In an article published on 26 August 1966 that was highly critical of apartheid, the US news magazine *Time* nonetheless referred to Verwoerd as 'one of the ablest white leaders Africa has ever produced'. In 1964, Dr CW de Kiewiet – the world-famous historian from Cornell University in the United States, who had grown up in South Africa and risen to the position of president of Cornell University and the University of Rochester – even likened Verwoerd to the French statesman Charles de Gaulle.

Hermann Giliomee cites De Kiewiet in his autobiography *Historian* (2016). According to De Kiewiet, Verwoerd was confronting the country's grave problems with 'boldness, shrewdness and even imagination'. It was by no means absurd, De Kiewiet wrote, to suggest a comparison between Verwoerd and De Gaulle, 'the stern, headstrong but deeply imaginative leader of France'.[16]

As the sole Afrikaans Sunday paper, *Dagbreek* expected me as political reporter to cover the prime minister's activities. During the parliamentary recess, which started in June, politicians usually lived in their constituencies and performed constituency work among the voters. The political '*stryddae*' (rallies) in the Highveld winters were plentiful, and usually took place on Saturday afternoons. One soon learnt to eat the traditional fare of wors and mieliepap with fried-tomato-and-onion relish.

Verwoerd kept the media at a distance. He was not one for small talk. Everything was arranged through his private secretary, Fred Barnard. An interview would be granted if the premier thought it would have the desired effect.

One such interview in 1957, with the astute Rykie van Reenen, had inadvertently resulted in the big story that Verwoerd had actually been born in the Netherlands, not South Africa. This revelation was an enormous embarrassment to Verwoerd. Maybe that was why he restricted interviews.

Rykie's interview was published in *Die Burger*'s 'Byvoegsel' supplement. Verwoerd's condition was that he would have the chance to read the text before it was published. The only information he wanted the paper to cut was the reference to his birth on the Jacob van Lennepkade in Amsterdam in 1901. But this fact was not removed.

Verwoerd's attempt to obscure his true origins calls to mind similar public ignorance about the real origins of the iron-fisted Justice minister, Jimmy Kruger, of a later era. Kruger suppressed uprisings in the period from 1984 to 1987 harshly. Papers such as *The World* that stood up for the interests of black people were banned. Their editors were locked up at Jimmy Kruger's behest.

But Kruger was not this strongman's real surname. He had been born James Thomas, the son of Welsh parents. They had come to South Africa, where James's father had got a job in a coal mine. When his parents died in a car accident shortly after their arrival, James was adopted by an Afrikaner family named Kruger. Hence James Thomas became the 'boerseun' Jimmy Kruger. This secret was exposed by *The Star*, to the minister's embarrassment.

Though Verwoerd was invariably courteous, everything revolved around him. His Cabinet ministers were in mortal fear of him. One day, he summoned the minister of Public Works, Willie Maree. Expecting an important assignment, Maree was instead ordered to ensure that his department keep the shrubs and flowers on the traffic island in De Waal Drive neatly maintained. Verwoerd drove along that road every day from Groote Schuur to Parliament, and the untidiness offended him.

Verwoerd and his wife Betsie lived a private life with their large family. They were not interested in social intercourse of the convivial or glamorous kind. They were in the service of the Party and the Afrikaner *volk* – an image of irreproachable civility and politeness befitted this role.

On *stryddae*, Verwoerd would stand up after the formalities and, with enviable logic and eloquence, speak fluently for up to two hours, without notes. He was cheered to the rafters; people thought he could walk on water. I was the only journalist who was present when, on a Saturday afternoon in July 1965, Verwoerd dropped a bombshell with a policy statement on sport. His sports policy, which I explain in Chapter 16, eventually led to our complete isolation in the field of sport.

Verwoerd, though a man of granite, nevertheless gave indications here and there that he could adapt his standpoint. In 1967, I discovered in the memoirs of the former Australian premier Sir Robert Menzies, for example, that Verwoerd was not absolutely opposed to direct representation of coloured people in the House of Assembly. Verwoerd wrote to Menzies in 1960 that coloured MPs representing coloured constituencies in Parliament was 'one of the possible alternatives' envisaged for the future.

This story appeared in *Die Beeld* on 22 October 1967, and was interpreted as a crack in the granite firmament of our racial policy. In our Afrikaans publications, the word 'kleurlinge' (Coloureds) was replaced over the years by the term 'bruin mense' (brown people), as the distinction between white people, brown people and black people sounded more neutral than other terms, which have a pejorative connotation.

With Verwoerd as chair of the board of *Dagbreek*, Marius Jooste, managing director of Dagbreekpers and later Perskor, was soon able to get huge sums flowing into its coffers. Instructions were given that the government printer had to award certain contracts to Jooste's empire. The Transvaal Education Department under Dr AJ Koen spent close to a hundred per cent of its schoolbook budget at Perskor. On his retirement, Dr Koen was promptly rewarded with a seat on Perskor's board.

The high-minded Verwoerd was also not disinclined to accept veneration and gifts. Jooste and his fellow Afrikaners in the North granted him a life interest in a house on the banks of the Vaal River, a place of rest where he could relax and go fishing. The name of the farm was Stokkiesdraai (Playing truant). In addition, he received a powerboat named *Boekanier*, a name referring to the Buccaneer fighter planes that South Africa managed to get hold of in years when it was difficult for the country to do so. The donors took back the place of rest not long after Verwoerd's assassination.

Jooste brought about a merger between *Dagbreek* and the former Vaderland press company, a company in which Minister Albert Hertzog had a large stake, to form Perskor. There was suspicion in the air that Nasionale Pers intended to launch a Sunday paper – and, who knows, maybe even a daily, too – in the North.

Northern Afrikaners dominated more than Afrikaner politics: their prevailing one-way thinking had filtered through to Afrikaner institutions such as the Afrikaner Broederbond, the FAK (Federation of Afrikaans Cultural Societies), the ATKV (Afrikaans Language and Culture Association), the SABC, the Suid-Afrikaanse Akademie vir Wetenskap en Kuns, theology faculties, junior political movements and student bodies.

Nasionale Pers kicked off its entry into the Northern newspaper market by founding the Sunday paper *Die Beeld* in November 1965. I contacted my first mentor, Dirk de Villiers – the new general manager of *Die Beeld* – and was summarily appointed political reporter.

Perskor ordered me to clear my desk on the double and get out – but not before I had attended an executive committee meeting of the Transvaal NP in Braamfontein as *Dagbreek*'s representative, two days before my departure. At this meeting, the general secretary of the NP, Jack Steyl, delivered an emotional declaration of war against Nasionale Pers and the Cape liberalists. *Die Beeld* would be up against a 'real Transvaal revolt', he vowed.

I was able to convey the fury of the Transvaal NP to Dirk de Villiers and Schalk Pienaar.

Then, Verwoerd's assassination on 6 September 1966 hit the country like a tsunami. Verwoerd and the NP had just won a general election with an overwhelming majority. Everyone was on tenterhooks about which direction Verwoerd would take in the face of international pressure. Tsafendas's knife stunned the country to a standstill.

On that day, I was working at *Die Beeld*'s head office in Johannesburg on a magazine article about the election for the weekend's edition. Parliament had just resumed, after a recess. My part in the mourning period was to assist our team at the state funeral for Verwoerd at the Union Buildings in Pretoria on Saturday 13 September.

Die Beeld managed to get our rolls of film and the article – which was still only in Rykie van Reenen's head at that point – to Johannesburg post-haste by having her race back past the heavy traffic on a Hell's Angels motorcycle. It was a clever bit of innovation for those days, a plan conceived by news editor Tobie Boshoff.

The best anecdote about a journalist who almost missed out on a major story also has to do with the attack on the prime minister. Former *Cape Times* editor Tony Heard writes in his memoirs *The Cape of Storms* that the paper's political correspondent and columnist, Gerald Shaw, was working in his press gallery office during the parliamentary lunch break on that day. Shaw had ordered a hamburger and tea, as usual. The parliamentary messenger whose task it was to deliver the meal, Dimitri Tsafendas, was taking his time. The parliamentary bells were about to ring for the start of the afternoon session when Tsafendas finally brought the hamburger. The change he gave to Shaw was ten times more than it should have been; his thoughts were likely elsewhere.

Shaw returned to the House of Assembly just in time to see the hamburger deliverer stab Verwoerd to death on his prime minister's bench. When Shaw called his news editor Tom Jessop to convey the news, Jessop initially refused to believe him, thinking it was a prank. Shaw was furious.

And so Balthazar Johannes Vorster, better known as John Vorster, became our new prime minister in 1966. Normally dour, but with a sense of humour when it came to golf jokes – he was besotted with the game – Vorster was a razor-sharp debater. He had the knack of landing devastating blows against the opposition while speaking off the cuff.

Under his hand as minister of Justice, Police and Prisons, the South African Police was converted into a highly competent anti-crime network. During Vorster's tenure, the police also operated underground, in large part to counteract the mounting activism of the ANC and the PAC. All political rebels from the ranks of black, coloured and Indian communities were branded terrorists.

Vorster always received me well and was open to a discussion, but he would wield the lash if he thought you deserved it. In his opinion, I was too liberal.[17] His big press buddy was the conservative Alf Ries, political reporter from the Nasionale Koerante group. Yet Vorster had his biography written by the political reporter John D'Oliveira from *The Star*, generally known to be liberal.

In Vorster's time, I was already the political reporter for Nasionale Pers's Sunday paper *Die Beeld*. My articles were aimed at publication on Sundays; in the course of the week, I would sniff around for articles others might have missed, or hunt for a scoop of my own.

Fortunately, I had a clear way: *Die Beeld* under Schalk Pienaar had ushered in the *verligte* era of Afrikaans journalism, and we piled in with gusto to loosen the oppressive grip of the *verkramptes* on our national order.

Vorster came down heavily on me about an article I wrote in March 1970 in *Die Beeld* regarding a speech by the minister of Mining, Planning and Health, Dr Carel de Wet – an article that contributed to De Wet's omission from the Cabinet. On 20 March, Dr De Wet, in a political speech in front of members of the NP's youth wing, the Jeugbond, responded to criticism from the HNP about an R8 million loan to Malawi, a country with which South Africa had good relations. In his speech, he referred to the building of an airfield in Malawi. On the audio tape, which I still have in my possession, he goes on to say: 'But suffice to say that in the invidious and dangerous situation in which we find ourselves, it would be very valuable to South Africa if an airport and an airfield that can also handle military aircraft, among others, were to be built in Malawi.' (Lengthy applause.)

The headline of the leader on page 1 read: 'SA base in the North?' Dr De Wet strenuously denied that he had talked about a military presence, even though his taped words were clearly audible. Defence minister PW Botha was highly irritated with De Wet for having publicly pronounced on *his* portfolio.

My article, and De Wet's announcements that industrial expansion would be limited to South Africa's economic hub, the Pretoria-Witwatersrand-Vaal Triangle region, led to his dismissal.

Then, I got an interview on 24 July 1970 with a visibly upset John Vorster. Was I happy, now, with what we had achieved with Carel de Wet? he asked at the outset. 'You sit in the press gallery, don't you, and you can hear how the United Party uses *Die Beeld* to attack De Wet and the National Party. It puts me in a difficult position,' Vorster said.

Next, he enquired what we were planning to do on the coming weekend with regard to the De Wet episode. I replied that we would publish a factual article, and that the editor would probably refer to the matter in his column.

He then said that he would just like to know, then, whether I was happy about the fact that the United Party quoted us so frequently. He had lumped *Die Beeld* and *Dagbreek* together, since both wanted to write the NP out of power.

One survives tiffs like these. Fast-forward to a scene eight years later, on 31 January 1978. Once again, I was talking to Vorster – this time, as the editor of *Beeld*. He praised the paper, and said we had campaigned well in the election of 1977.

We spoke about the government's shutting down the black newspaper *The World*, under the editorship of Percy Qoboza.

'*World* will stay closed,' said Vorster. 'Percy will be kept in jail for another few weeks. He lied to me three times. The man is a crook.'

He also said he intended to act against the *Rand Daily Mail*. In light of the international reaction to the closing of *The World*, he would not hesitate; if sanctions were imposed on us, closing the *Rand Daily Mail* would be the first item on his agenda. At worst, one can but lose one's head, Vorster said.

In 1983, as managing director designate of Nasionale Pers, I began to acquire titles from Jim Bailey's press group – *City Press*, *Drum* and *True Love*. Qoboza, like me a former Nieman Fellow at Harvard, was the editor of *City Press* at that stage.

In the meantime, John Vorster been forced to resign as state president on account of the Information Scandal that exposed his knowledge of the illegal use of state funds to launch an NP-supporting English paper, *The Citizen*. His attempt to silence opposition papers and, at the same time, co-operate with an operation to use taxpayers' money to establish an English paper that favoured the government ended his political career ingloriously.

My notebooks from 1978 give a glimpse of how Vorster viewed the international scene and South Africa's situation at the time. Sanctions lie in store for us, regardless of how we bend ourselves, Vorster anticipated. US president Jimmy Carter has committed himself to African countries to insist on one person, one vote. If we are to be saved by a veto, it would be that of the British. If you ask me with whom I'd prefer to be stranded on a desert island, it would be the British, Vorster said. He distrusted the French. America was superficial. Germans are either around your neck or around your ankles, according to Vorster.

From his appointment as prime minister in 1966, Vorster also served as chair of Perskor. He was not a rigid, uncompromising ideologue like Verwoerd. But he endeavoured to safeguard the security of South Africa with might and main. It soon became apparent that he was uncomfortable in his position. The *verligte-verkrampte* conflict bothered him greatly.

As a lawyer, Vorster was someone who could think on his feet. In his soul he was *verkramp*, like his elder brother, the former DRC leader and moderator of that church's General Synod, Dr Koot Vorster. They believed in 'white baasskap', as Hans Strijdom, prime minister from 1954 to 1958, had. Strijdom had not beaten around the bush, however; in his day, the world had not confronted South Africa as strongly as it would in Vorster's time.

Strijdom declared in a speech in 1955 that apartheid could be called 'paramountcy, baasskap or what you will', but it was indisputably 'domination'. Strijdom was brutally frank: 'I am being as blunt as I can. I am making no excuses. Either the white man dominates, or the black takes over … The only way the European can maintain supremacy is by domination … The government of the country is in the hands of the white man and for that reason the white man is baas in South Africa.'

It took Vorster a while to realise that, when he started moving away from the *verkrampte* members of the NP's parliamentary caucus, they began to undermine him.

To assess the lay of the land, he had to take cognisance of *Die Beeld*'s political reporting and commentary, a paper founded a year before he took office in September 1966. *Die Beeld*, under Schalk Pienaar's editorship, was fearless in its assault on the *verkramptes*.

In his gruff way, Vorster had started to incline towards a *verligte* direction. Like any party leader, he believed he was immune to crumbling support. He counted on the loyalty of younger MPs such as Daan van der Merwe, Thomas Langley, Gaffie Maree and others. Meanwhile, Dr Albert Hertzog was already gathering a following among MPs who opposed the relaxation of hard apartheid. Some MPs with *verkrampte* tendencies later saw the light and stayed with the NP. But a far-right splinter group was coalescing.

To an extent, *Die Beeld* stood alone in its battle against the *verkramptes*.

Die Burger, under Piet Cillié, was more reticent – Verwoerd had already persuaded it, with considerable pressure, to abandon its efforts to open a way into Parliament for the coloured people. *Die Volksblad*, Nasionale Pers's daily in the Free State, was also cautious: the Free State Nats were predominantly conservative.

In the Transvaal, however, Perskor's *Die Vaderland* and *Die Transvaler*, and later also *Hoofstad* and *Oggendblad* in Pretoria, committed their undisguised support to the Hertzog-Treurnicht faction. This led to the most acrimonious political provincialism that South Africa experienced in the second half of the twentieth century.

When Nasionale Pers, as a courtesy, informed Dr Verwoerd – as prime minister and as chair of the Northern press group – of *Die Beeld*'s launch in 1965, the reaction of Marius Jooste, executive chair of Perskor, was: 'You can publish a newspaper anywhere as long as it is on the other side of the Vaal River.'

Such political imperialism was unheard of. Nasionale Pers was seeking to expand from the less bustling Cape and Free State provinces to the more prosperous Transvaal, including the wealthy Pretoria-Witwatersrand-Vereeniging region. This was the country's economic heartland, after all.

The Northern Afrikaans press groups and the Transvaal NP viewed the move as a liberal assault.

There was a long history of suspicion between the two press groups. This had not been the case at first: Nasionale Pers had helped to establish *Die Transvaler* – in 1936, it had provided financial assistance and secured backing for the founding of this paper as a Nationalist daily in the North.

The chair of Nasionale Pers, Willie Hofmeyr, also became chair of *Die Transvaler*. The operation was aimed at counteracting *Die Vaderland* of the 'Fusionist' prime minister Dr JBM Hertzog. ('Fusion' referred to the coalition between Hertzog's NP and Jan Smuts's SAP, which resulted in the creation of the United Party. The members of Hertzog's party who broke away under Dr DF Malan to form the Purified NP used 'Fusionists' as a derogatory term for Hertzog's supporters.)

Verwoerd, a 35-year-old sociology and psychology professor at

Stellenbosch University, was appointed as the first editor. *Die Burger* invited him to join the editorial team for a few months to familiarise himself with newspaper work. Several senior journalists from *Die Burger* were also encouraged to join *Die Transvaler*.

But Verwoerd's views, policies and conduct as editor of *Die Transvaler* soon led to problems. For instance, he proposed a quota system for Jewish people on behalf of the Transvaal NP. *Die Burger* in Keerom Street was not amused. From a business perspective, too, the proposal was ill-considered. The consequences for the new daily were disastrous, as all Jewish companies summarily withdrew their advertisements.

In 1941, Verwoerd sued *The Star* for defamation, because the paper had called him a Nazi sympathiser. On 31 October 1941, *The Star* had written in an editorial titled 'Speaking up for Hitler': 'We had this week a rather better example than usual of the process of falsification which it [*Die Transvaler*] applies to current news in its support of Nazi propaganda.

'Its dishonesty is so easy to expose and it identifies *Die Transvaler* so closely with Nazi propaganda that it must assist in opening the eyes of those who read the paper in question as to the extent to which it is the tool of malignant forces from which this country has everything to fear ...'

In his judgment, Justice PA Millin dismissed Verwoerd's action with costs and said: 'Dr Verwoerd did support Nazi propaganda and made his paper a tool of the Nazis in South Africa.'

The cost of the libel action and the loss of advertising brought *Die Transvaler* close to bankruptcy, and its board decided to approach Nasionale Pers with a request for amalgamation.

WA Hofmeyr, founder and chair of Nasionale Pers and founder-chair of *Die Transvaler*, was not impressed, and proposed that *Die Transvaler*'s shares have a lower value than those of Nasionale Pers.

Nasionale Pers's proposal was not acceptable to the Transvaal NP leader Hans Strijdom, and the matter was not pursued further. *Die Transvaler* did manage to get back on its feet, but was never really profitable.

After Nasionale Pers launched the Sunday paper *Die Beeld* in 1965, the two parties agreed that the Capetonians would purchase a new printing press and *Die Transvaler* would erect a building in which both papers could be printed. This brought relief for *Die Transvaler*.

But the co-operation with Nasionale Pers came to an end when Marius Jooste bought out Voortrekkerpers, the owner of *Die Transvaler*, and merged it with his group, Vaderland Beleggings, to form Perskor. At the time, the accomplished *Sunday Times* editor Joel Mervis wrote in his weekly satirical column, The Passing Show, that Jooste was the 'hoofdrukker' (chief printer) and Verwoerd the 'onderdrukker' (oppressor).

The advent of *Die Beeld* with its *verligte* outlook in 1965, in a context in which the Northern press supported the conservative, obdurate element in the NP, sparked the mother of all provincialist battles. The rivalry and ructions continued from November 1965 up to the demise of Perskor in the 1980s. The following anecdote illustrates the extent to which Nasionale Pers and Perskor under Marius Jooste distrusted each other until the early 1980s.

Lang David de Villiers and some of his top executives were walking into Perskor's building in Auckland Park in Johannesburg to negotiate about points of convergence for a possible agreement. De Villiers said: 'Gentlemen, why am I thinking now of the American general Clark who had a word of warning for his officers in 1945 as they walked in to negotiate with the defeated Italian high command about their surrender? "The first one of you who calls our gallant new allies those fucking Ities," General Clark said, "will be court-martialled."'

John Vorster put pressure on the feuding parties to end the press war. Ben Schoeman, at that time the Transvaal leader of the NP and chair of Perskor, was at Jooste's side. Nasionale Pers was represented by its chair Phil Weber and the relatively new managing director, Lang David de Villiers.

Among other attempts to keep afloat, Jooste had taken the unorthodox step of buying out *Die Landstem* as a weekly and incorporating it into *Dagbreek*. This inflated circulation artificially. Nasionale Pers eventually agreed to a 50/50 venture between the two parties: equal ownership of a new Sunday paper, *Rapport*, which would replace *Die Beeld*.

Die Beeld's editorial team was dismayed and furious. In their opinion, they were winning the press war for Nasionale Pers. In terms of the agreement that would apply to the new paper, however, Nasionale Pers would exercise editorial control and appoint the first editor of *Rapport*, so the *verligte* course of *Die Beeld* could be continued. Perskor would appoint the first manager. It was a fresh new paper that was launched in 1970 under the editorship of Willem Wepener. *Rapport*'s sales exceeded 500 000 at some point – an unprecedented figure for an Afrikaans paper.

I was the first news editor designate of *Rapport* after my years as *Die Beeld*'s political reporter. I was only able to assume my duties in July 1971, being on a year's study leave as a Nieman Fellow at Harvard until June.

The year outside South Africa had given me a new perspective on our racial situation, the role of apartheid in society, the demands for integration on the part of the predominantly English-speaking opposition, and the political demands of the oppressed black majority. *Rapport*'s news editor designate therefore took up his role under the influence of his exposure to his Harvard year.

With the 50/50 agreement, Nasionale Pers retreated to an extent from the struggle against the Transvaal papers with their rigid apartheid thinking. But the ideal of an Afrikaans daily in the more affluent North was still latent. In 1974, the company announced its intention to establish the daily *Beeld*. This paper was launched on 16 September 1974.

Expectations of *Beeld* were high, but Perskor had been girding its loins for a new fight. Jooste founded two Afrikaans dailies in Pretoria, *Oggendblad* and *Hoofstad*. In Johannesburg, Perskor had *Die Transvaler* and *Die Vaderland* in its stable. Hence, it was four dailies against one; *Beeld* faced an uphill battle.

Along with several former journalists of the Sunday paper *Die Beeld*, I was eager to take up the cudgels against the four rivals. Willem Wepener was very unhappy about losing stalwarts among his staff at *Rapport* to the new daily.

I was appointed as one of the assistant editors of *Beeld*. Schalk Pienaar was appointed as editor-in-chief by Nasionale Pers, despite his ill health. Johannes Grosskopf became the senior assistant editor. When Pienaar stepped down after only three months, Grosskopf replaced him as editor.

Pienaar was suffering from serious heart problems and cancer, but his physician reckoned he would be able to hold out for a while. He was a vitally important leader of the team. Besides, Pienaar was the political commentator we needed to launch *Beeld* successfully.

CHAPTER 8

A tectonic shift

Following the general election of 1994 and the adoption of a new constitution in 1996, South Africa formally entered a democratic order that was acceptable to voters of all colours and races. Nearly 350 years of white domination had come to an end.

The NP government had voluntarily relinquished the power it could only, ultimately, maintain through unjustly strict measures. Political say was transferred to the representatives of the majority of the population in a spirit of reconciliation and liberation.

There was no disruption of public order of note during the 1994 election, partly because of the reconciliatory attitude of Nelson Mandela and his colleagues and partly as a result of the constructive co-operation of the old government's representatives. This political miracle was acclaimed worldwide.

That the Nobel Peace Prize was awarded jointly to Nelson Mandela and FW de Klerk in 1993 attested to an event that was almost as surprising and significant as the collapse of the Soviet Union in 1991. In fact, the two breakthroughs, in quick succession, were interrelated. The lifting of the 'Red Peril' removed the military and ideological pressure on South Africa that had emanated from the Eastern Bloc. This, in turn, helped make the lifting of the struggle against the 'Black Peril' in South Africa feasible.

The unforgettable moment of reconciliation in South Africa had been preceded by protracted military conflict on the country's borders, the ANC's acts of terror, and the activism of the ANC, PAC, Azapo and other anti-apartheid organisations inside and outside South Africa.

As already discussed in earlier chapters, nearly fifty years of National Party rule involved another struggle that intensified gradually from the 1960s onwards: a political struggle waged within the discourses of the white community. This battle was fought not only within institutions such as universities and media that opposed the National Party government. And it was not only the English-speaking white community that criticised and opposed the government's policies. On Afrikaans university campuses, and within the media established by Nasionale Pers, there were voices of protest and efforts to change the politics of the country.

A great deal of agonising accompanied the intra-Afrikaner debates and Afrikaners' conflict about how to come to terms with their black compatriots and the world community. The reason for this was that, during British colonial rule and particularly since the time of the South African War, the Afrikaners had found or felt themselves to be engaged in a battle for survival. The survival of their language, culture and religious values, as well as their actual survival as an ethnic group in an African country, was at stake when they reflected on a political order for South Africa. Moreover, they had to let go, finally, of a long-cherished nationalist ideal, which had eventually been realised by the National Party.

By the end of the 1980s, the NP government was not even close to the end of its possibilities of administering and policing South Africa effectively and defending it militarily. But the country had reached a point where the majority of white voters preferred a morally just, inclusive order that could satisfy the population as a whole, despite the risks such transformation might hold for them. Accordingly, in a referendum in 1992, the government was entrusted with a mandate to reach a negotiated settlement with the ANC.

This decision by an ethnic group willingly to surrender power and accept the numerical superiority of the ethnic groups to whom they had denied political power in the past is unique in world history. The influence that Nasionale Pers exerted on its readers to think along *verligte* lines and vote Yes in this referendum contributed greatly to the establishment of a democratic South Africa.

As a political reporter, newspaper editor and, finally, managing director and chair of Naspers, I witnessed the agonising and soul-searching, but also the ultimate ascendancy of the *verligte* school of thought I sought to promote as a stakeholder. In the country's stormy years, the Nasionale Pers (now Naspers) and its papers played an instrumental role in encouraging reform and ultimately making a fully democratic South Africa possible.

The relatively independent role of our group of companies went hand in hand with an increasingly critical engagement with people and schools of thought at the forefront of the times.

In 1948, the National Party came to power with an extremely narrow election victory. Dr DF Malan became prime minister at the age of 75. Dr Malan had been the first editor of *Die Burger* in 1915. In those days, newspapers were appropriate mouthpieces for political parties. Thus, a close bond developed between *Die Burger*, a product of Nasionale Pers, and the National Party.

The word 'apartheid' was used in a speech by Jan Smuts as far back as 1919. During DF Malan's tenure, it became a vogue word. But this word would soon acquire the strong stigma of racial segregation that was aimed at ensuring white racial purity and supremacy. DF Malan contributed to this negative image by campaigning for the abolition of the coloured franchise, and also for the removal from the common voters' roll of the limited number of coloured males in the Cape Province who had voting rights.

With its negative connotations and emotional value that reflected badly on South Africa, the word 'apartheid' was borrowed by most of the major languages without translation. In the changing world of the second half of the twentieth century, apartheid became South Africa's Achilles heel.

Among his followers, Dr Malan was beloved and respected. He was an erudite clergyman with a love for the Afrikaner cause and the Afrikaans language. His academic qualifications included a BA in music and science, an MA in theology, and a doctorate in divinity obtained at the University of Utrecht in the Netherlands.

When Dr Malan stepped down as prime minister in 1954, the office would be occupied by political strongmen such as Hans Strijdom, Hendrik Verwoerd and John Vorster. These were the sterile years of Afrikaner nationalism that were associated with brazen racial domination. This rigid mentality, associated with the powerful Transvaal faction of the National Party, affected the close bond between Nasionale Pers and the National Party. One should actually say that Nasionale Pers's loyalty no longer extended in equal measure to all factions within the Party.

Piet Cillié, *Die Burger*'s editor-in-chief, wrote with reference to the Sharpeville tragedy in 1960 that the apartheid policy had made South Africa 'the polecat of the world'. His words evoked the requisite indignation in the Transvaal. A year earlier, journalist and politician Japie Basson, a renowned *verligte* maverick who was averse to apartheid, had been expelled from the National Party. He subsequently joined the opposition.

We find a clue that Nasionale Pers had already distanced itself from dogmatic apartheid at an early stage in the attacks launched by SED Brown's far-right, blatantly anti-Semitic paper the *SA Observer*. Prominent Afrikaners such as Dr Anton Rupert, Advocate Lang David de Villiers and Piet Cillié were slandered as liberalists who were in cahoots with communism. Brown had the financial and moral backing of a large and influential group of Pretorians, people such as Dr Albert Hertzog, minister of Post and Telecommunications in Verwoerd's and, later, Vorster's Cabinet.

In 1965 Japie Basson, a quick-witted political sharpshooter, revealed in the House of Assembly that a former British spy was undermining the *verligte* direction of some people within Nationalist ranks. Two camps were clearly taking shape within the National Party: the *verligtes* and the *verkramptes*, as they would become known. Nasionale Pers was in the *verligte* camp. Hence Brown's attacks elicited counterattacks from Nasionale Pers's papers.

Within the context of 1965, Japie Basson sat on the opposition benches and I was political reporter of *Die Beeld*, Nasionale Pers's Afrikaans Sunday paper. I wrote an article about developments on the day of Japie Basson's thunderbolt that appeared in *Die Beeld* on the following Sunday, after Piet Cillié had published a 'Dawie' opinion column in *Die Burger* on the Saturday in which he pilloried SED Brown with withering scorn. Schalk

A TECTONIC SHIFT

Pienaar, editor-in-chief of *Die Beeld*, gave the reaction against the far-right an extra boost in his own column that Sunday. That was the state of affairs in those times.

The *verkramptes* drew their energy from the conservative leadership of Dr Hendrik Verwoerd. Following the shocking breach of national security that led to Verwoerd's assassination, John Vorster, a hardline communist-hunter, was elected Verwoerd's successor. The National Party rallied round Vorster on account of his record as a tough minister of Justice and Police who had waged the struggle against the ANC, the PAC, the Communist Party and other related organisations by harsh means.

Vorster's targets included activist student organisations such as Nusas (the National Union of South African Students), with the result that the security police also started operating on university campuses. Sometimes, the security police would fund the election campaign of a Students' Representative Council (SRC) member to find out what was happening in the SRC.

Vorster was not an implacable ideologue like Verwoerd, but his draconian measures conflated South Africa's status as 'polecat of the world' with that of a police state. Among the merciless measures he introduced to combat communism was the 90-day, and later 180-day, detention of suspects without trial. Liberalism, which was regarded as free thinking that could lead to seriously aberrant thinking, or something to that effect, was also targeted.

The incarceration of suspects led to many abuses and deaths, with the deaths of Steve Biko and Ahmed Timol two of the best-known examples. Between 1963 and 1990, a total of 73 people who had never been charged died in detention.

I got a personal taste of the government's intensified vigilance when I was charged under the Prisons Act in 1978. This Act, along with other pieces of legislation such as the Internal Security Act, the Terrorism Act, the Suppression of Communism Act, the Official Secrets Act and the Defence Act, characterised Vorster's tenure.

I was charged because *Beeld* had published a photo of a prisoner without permission. An article on the Afrikaner martyr Jopie Fourie, who was executed for his part in the 1914–1915 Rebellion against the government of the Union of South Africa, along with a photo of him from 1912, had appeared in the *Beeld*'s supplement *Die Byvoegsel*. I was charged for the use of this historical photo and slapped with a fine of R1 000 in the Johannesburg magistrate's court. My fingerprints were taken in the cells, but I could at least call our manager, Eric Wiese, to bring R1 000 in cash. If the fine had exceeded R1 000, I would have had a permanent court record.

This episode smacked of a gesture directed against Nasionale Pers's paper in the North.

While BJ Vorster was tightening the screws on state security, he maintained good relations with his former Stellenbosch student friends, Cillié and Pienaar. He was open to persuasion when it came to the idea that South Africa could not continue uncompromisingly with its apartheid policy. This *verligte* side of Vorster, if one could call it that, promoted resistance and a party-political breakaway on the part of conservative NP members.

Vorster's plan with his so-called outward movement or détente policy was to forge ties with African leaders. President Hastings Banda of Malawi, for example, was invited to South Africa for a state visit. Vorster also visited the Ivory Coast, and relations were established with states in the Middle East – even with Iran before the revolution there toppled the shah.

Johan Bruwer, an arts journalist for *Beeld* and later the arts editor of *Rapport*, was able to provide intriguing background information about Vorster's plans for reaching out to the frontline states in Africa. His father, Professor Johannes Bruwer, could have played an important role in bringing about an improvement in South Africa's relations with its neighbours, had he not been a passenger on the ill-fated *Rietbok*. This Vickers Viscount crashed into the sea near East London in 1967. Johan tells the story as follows:

> On 13 March 1967, about seven months after the death of HF Verwoerd, my father, Professor Johannes Bruwer, died in the *Rietbok*

A TECTONIC SHIFT

disaster. He was vice-rector and head of the anthropology department at the University of Port Elizabeth, and was the acting chair of the Broederbond at the time. A former commissioner-general of then South West Africa, he had resigned from that position in 1964 after a year because of irreconcilable differences with Verwoerd, who was on the wrong path and at the same time turned a deaf ear to advice.

Early in 1967 my father received a visit in Port Elizabeth from Dr Hilgard Muller, the then minister of Foreign Affairs. In the week after his death, my mother recounted that Muller and John Vorster had approached my father with a view to appointing him as roving ambassador to the frontline states. My father would have been based in Lusaka, the headquarters of Kenneth Kaunda, president of Zambia and also chair of the frontline states.

Kaunda was a personal friend and an ex-student of my father, who had been based in the former Northern Rhodesia (which became Zambia in 1964) for decades, from the 1930s up to 1952. Among other things, my father had founded a teachers' training college in Katete – he literally designed it himself and built it with the help of the students. On account of his contribution to the expansion of education in the then British colony, he was, according to my brother, offered an OBE (Order of the British Empire). My father apparently declined it because he did not consider himself to be part of the British Empire or the Commonwealth.

The proposed position of roving ambassador apparently met with Kaunda's approval. My father was evidently the appropriate person to bring about better understanding and connections between South Africa and its neighbouring countries.

On 13 March 1967 he was on his way to Pretoria where the appointment would have been finalised and announced at Cabinet level. The *Rietbok* disaster on that day ended both his life and the project.

My mother received messages of condolence from several black leaders with whom my father had formed ties over the years. She was, inter alia, invited by President Kaunda of Zambia and President Hastings Banda of Malawi to visit them as a personal guest. She accepted Kaunda's invitation and spent a week at his residence in Lusaka.

The *verkramptes* in the National Party noted this 'fraternisation' with black people with horror, and it expedited their party-political breakaway.

Vorster also tinkered with the government's policy on sport. The doors of international sport were slammed shut in 1965 after Dr Verwoerd had said at an NP youth congress at Loskop Dam in the old Eastern Transvaal that Maori players would not form part of an All Blacks rugby team that was due to tour South Africa. As a reporter for the *Dagbreek en Sondagnuus*, and the only journalist on the scene, I wrote an article that flashed around the world and plunged South Africa into greater isolation (I elaborate on this in Chapter 16).

After 1966, Vorster sought to break through this isolation, and the government voted money to make 'full-blooded tours' to South Africa possible.

In his way, Vorster did his little bit for the struggle of the *verligtes*, despite the cosmetic nature of his reforms, aimed at improving the image of South Africa outside its borders. For instance, Vorster did not see his way clear to granting the coloured community political rights, as the *verligtes* had encouraged him to do. Nasionale Pers's papers nonetheless lauded him for his adjustments, and in 1970 he would score a massive victory at the polls.

The *verkramptes*, on the other hand, lobbied against Vorster under banners such as those of Gert Beetge's Blanke Bouwerkersvakbond (white construction workers' union). The paper *Veg* attacked the National Party from Pretoria. The big spider in the resistance web was Dr Albert Hertzog, a member of Vorster's Cabinet who was later kicked out and who started his own party.

Under these circumstances, Nasionale Pers's papers could launch into the far-rightists with gusto. Schalk Pienaar took the lead with *Die Beeld*; *Die Burger* under Cillié was a tad more restrained; and *Die Volksblad* under Bart Zaayman was still rather fearful of the consequences of black land ownership and black participation in government.

The plea for a more open society in Nasionale Pers publications caused

A TECTONIC SHIFT

English papers such as the *Rand Daily Mail* under Laurence Gandar and, later, Allister Sparks, and the *Sunday Times* under Joel Mervis, to hope for a split in the National Party and increased support for the parliamentary opposition, the United Party (UP).

But something else happened. The more the far-rightists were marginalised by the mainstream in the NP, the more the UP fractured. The Progressive Party gradually supplanted it. The leading English-language papers did not give Nasionale Pers credit for its role in the reform of our political landscape. The hopes of a paper such as the *Rand Daily Mail* were, as far as the white electorate was concerned, pinned on the Progressive Party.

The Afrikaans press soon experienced a strong division between the papers of the Perskor group (and its predecessors) and those of Nasionale Pers (I discussed this in more detail in Chapter 6).

The citizens of countries that were not as well acquainted with South Africa as, say, Great Britain was, were sometimes under the impression that, in the apartheid era, the country's population consisted of a united stronghold of like-minded white oppressors and a majority of passive, oppressed black people. Many people in the Netherlands, for instance, harboured this view.

This image was not totally devoid of truth. But one of the facts overlooked in this scenario is that, in terms of the situation of its white voters, South Africa did constitute a parliamentary democracy. There was a high degree of press freedom and university autonomy, as well as elections, divisions between parties, divisions within parties, and victories and defeats at the polls. There were also personality clashes, scandals, political careers built and destroyed – all typical of a democracy.

Many coloured and black people strove for political freedom and power with all the means at their disposal: protests, violence, and also creative and intellectual writing, such as the work of Sol Plaatje or Adam Small and the dozens of black writers who followed after them.

In the four decades prior to 1994, the white House of Assembly, the prime minister and his Cabinet, and the newspapers that followed the course of events and commented on them, progressed by way of numerous tumultuous arguments, perturbations and convulsions to the eventual attainment of full democracy. The debates and strategic manoeuvres often revolved around the very problem that the black majority was not represented in the House of Assembly and the Cabinet.

The role of John Vorster, a man of law and order but also of secret operations in the interest of South Africa's security, played to its conclusion after the eruption of the Information Scandal in 1978. Dr Connie Mulder, minister of Information, and Dr Eschel Rhoodie, secretary of the Department of Information, had concocted a plan to use state funds for a propaganda war. Vorster had agreed that R64 million from the defence budget could be used to purchase international news agencies, to acquire the *Washington Star* newspaper and to establish *The Citizen*, an English paper that would defend the government's policies, in Pretoria.

This conspiracy is reminiscent of later ANC government's support of Gupta-backed media. Of importance here is that the Information Scandal effectively terminated John Vorster's political career. A battle for the control of the party and the government broke out shortly afterwards between PW Botha and Dr Connie Mulder.

Dr Mulder could count on the support of more MPs from the Transvaal in the caucus, and he was connected to all the so-called friendly organisations: the FAK; the Suid-Afrikaanse Akademie vir Wetenskap en Kuns; the SABC under Dr Piet Meyer; the Broederbond. Nasionale Pers's preferred candidate was the more reform-minded PW Botha, minister of Defence and leader of the Cape National Party.

Beeld in Johannesburg waged a ferocious campaign to expose Mulder's far-right links that made him the wrong man for the job of prime minister at that critical juncture. Botha won the leadership battle. It is my contention that *Beeld* had paved the way for him.

A helpful factor was that the far-right Conservative Party under Dr Treurnicht had lured away many of the National Party's right-wing supporters. Thanks to the guidance that *Beeld* and *Rapport* gave to their readers, and the splitting of the conservative vote, Botha was able to eliminate both Connie Mulder and Andries Treurnicht.

Beeld had gone flat-out to render assistance. We exposed the machinations of the Northern far-rightists with great fervour. In a final political contribution on 11 February 1983, written under my satirical-columnist pseudonym Lood, I recalled the collapse of the 'empire that was built around a few men'. I wrote that the 'mampoer triangle' had had one leg after the other kicked out from underneath it. The triangle had consisted of the SABC under Dr Piet Meyer, the Information coterie that had formed around Dr Connie Mulder's ambitions, and Perskor under Marius Jooste. My conclusion: their downfall owed less to the power of the press than to the ineptitude of those concerned.

PW Botha soon showed his more *verligte* colours, for example, by using the expression 'adapt or die' in a speech in Upington in 1979.

His attempts at reform produced the so-called Tricameral Parliament of the 1984–1994 period. Under the new system, Botha had the title of executive state president. Coloured and Indian people exercised a measure of authority in the Tricameral Parliament, but black South Africans were excluded from participation. By its nature, the Tricameral Parliament was unacceptable to the ANC and its fellow combatants. Botha's reforms were read as concessions that showed the regime was weakening.

Consequently, the ANC's onslaught from both outside and inside the country (with the help of the United Democratic Front) intensified. It was a time of violence, massacres, bomb attacks and protests. The country started burning, and the South African Police were unable to put out all the fires. The defence force was deployed inside the country's borders to maintain order.

Though Botha leant towards reform, his imperious and arrogant leadership style alienated his best friends, including Nasionale Pers's papers. After suffering a stroke on 18 January 1989, he stubbornly tried to cling to power. On 2 February 1989, FW de Klerk took over the NP leadership in an acting capacity.

An interview with PW Botha that *Die Burger* published on Saturday

4 March 1989 caused the national Cabinet under the leadership of FW de Klerk to unite against him.

In this matter, the Nasionale Pers as partner of the National Party played an unusual but important role in trying to push a wounded leader out of the camp in the country's interest. Our actions helped eventually to put FW de Klerk in the leadership role that would earn him the Nobel Prize.

Following his stroke, PW believed that by 2 March 1989 he had recovered sufficiently to fly down to Cape Town from his holiday home, Die Anker in Wilderness near George, to attend to matters again as president. He was set to hold discussions with members of his Cabinet in Cape Town.

I advised FW de Klerk and his colleagues to talk to PW as a group, and not to become divided among themselves. Owing to the independent conduct of some ministers, this advice could not be followed.

PW issued a statement after the discussions in Cape Town, announcing that he was fit, and intended, to continue in his office as state president. He had scheduled an interview for the following day, 3 March, with Nasionale Pers's political editor Alf Ries in Wilderness. This was evidently a move to consolidate his position.

Just before noon on Friday 3 March, the chair of Nasionale Pers, Piet Cillié, came to see me. He told me that PW's statement after the previous day's discussions had caused great discord in the Cabinet and NP caucus. According to Botha's statement, he was able to continue his job and could count on the support of his entire Cabinet. But medical evidence suggested that he would be incapable of performing his task to the full.

Cillié said it was imperative to clarify the situation urgently. Someone had to bell the cat. We talked the options through, and I undertook to speak to Wiets Beukes, editor of *Die Burger*, about an apposite column. *Die Burger* would play the key role. I also approached Bob van Walsem, editor of *Rapport*, and alerted him to Alf Ries's article that was due to appear in *Die Burger* on the Saturday.

Wiets was hesitant – in his view, party leadership matters did not fall within the remit of newspapers. I told him that there came a day, occasionally, when our group could play a decisive role, and that this was such a day. Wiets needed to stress in his 'Dawie' column how vital it was to

A TECTONIC SHIFT

get clarity soon, that the interests of South Africa and the National Party came first, and that our country could suffer serious harm if matters were allowed to drift in PW's direction.

Beukes agreed with me on all these points, but shied away from hitting out harshly at PW: politicians were weathervanes, and the wind could change after such a column. I also informed Wep (Willem Wepener, editor of *Beeld*). Then, I tried to get hold of FW de Klerk and left a message with his private secretary about the absolute urgency of FW tackling the matter firmly. FW later expressed his appreciation for our actions.

On Saturday 4 March, *Die Burger* and *Beeld* as well as *Volksblad* carried the planned articles. Read together, the lead story by Alf Ries on his conversation with PW, a shorter article by the political staff, and the 'Dawie' column were political dynamite. The lead story showed PW in his characteristic mode – combative and disdainful of his Cabinet colleagues. The shorter article by the political staff spelled out that he had become an embarrassment to the NP and the government.

I then phoned Alf Ries, Cillié and Dik David (DP de Villiers, former chair of Sasol and a senior director of Nasionale Pers). De Villiers cautioned us not to underestimate the *volk*'s compassion for PW. People such as Magnus (Malan) and Barend (du Plessis) would backtrack. De Villiers said he was on our side, but we had to tread carefully.

Cillié, as I told my then wife Lorna, had sounded like a little boy who had set a pile of dry grass alight and was now standing back and watching the fallout. It turned out that Cillié had drafted the article (by the political staff) and offered it to Wiets.

A week is a long time in politics. Even in the space of a weekend, a lot can happen. PW Botha, executive state president, had disparaged his Cabinet in a published interview. He had defied his doctors' findings and declared himself fit for office. He was standing by his rights and intended to resume his demanding duties. A crisis was clearly imminent. Nasionale Pers endeavoured to facilitate PW's retirement and was therefore deeply involved in the matter. Intensive tactical deliberations and telephone calls filled the days that followed.

On the morning of Saturday 4 March, I phoned *Rapport*'s editor Bob van Walsem to brief him on the latest developments. I had received phone calls from Dawie de Villiers, the minister of Minerals and Energy, and Kobie Coetsee, the minister of Justice.

Dawie said FW de Klerk had to act. He discussed with me the options he was going to present to FW. He would see FW (and also Alf Ries and others) at 12:00 at a braai at the Stellenbosch NP's sports day.

Dawie pointed out the craftiness of PW's working visit to Cape Town, followed by the statement of good health he had issued himself and the subsequent attack on his Cabinet in the interview he had arranged with Alf Ries. Dawie anticipated a clash between himself and Chris Heunis, minister of Constitutional Development and Planning, about an invitation that would be issued to PW Botha in the coming week to open the Cape NP's congress. Dawie felt that FW de Klerk should be invited to open the NP congresses of all four provinces.

Kobie called me from his Free State farm. He was upset about the interview with PW he had read in the *Volksblad*. But he had not yet seen the 'Dawie' column and the other articles. I undertook to have them faxed to him. He said he would cut the visit to his farm short and fly back to Cape Town on Saturday afternoon.

Kobie wanted to keep in contact with me, and we discussed the three options he wanted to mention to FW. The first was action by the National Party. The second was for a delegation of carefully selected people to engage with PW Botha. The following names were mentioned: Piet Cillié, Dr Piet Neethling, a long-standing friend of PW's, Pieter de Lange, chair of the Broederbond, and Dik David de Villiers, head of Sasol and a director of Nasionale Pers. They were all people for whom PW would presumably have respect, and who were not under his control.

Kobie's last option was that people should speak to PW's advisers, who were acting out of self-preservation. I could guess who they were. Kobie did not want to mention names over the telephone, but I suspected he was thinking of Dr Jannie Roux, secretary of the Cabinet; PW's private secretary, Ters Ehlers; and his press spokesman, Jack Viviers. Among other things, Kobie was upset about a reference to

A TECTONIC SHIFT

corruption in PW's conversation with Alf Ries, and thought PW had a special axe to grind.

Jack Viviers phoned me at 13:10 that afternoon. He asked what I had thought of Alf Ries's interview with PW. Jack and I had been colleagues for many years, inter alia at *Rapport*, but he was now attached to PW's office. Against our grain and after persistent requests from PW, he had been seconded to the position of the state president's press spokesman.

I told Jack that the interview with PW had muddied the waters, and that things were looking bad. I suggested he come to see me in his own best interest.

Jack arrived at 17:00 that afternoon. He had failed to grasp the political significance of PW's interview; I pointed it out to him. But FW and the younger men could not govern the country, he said. He asked whether I was aware that the Transvaal had resolved to break the Cape NP and the influence of Nasionale Pers.

That was rubbish, I said. FW was a man of integrity, and the country's problems took precedence over the provincial ambitions of the Transvaal NP. I advised Jack to unhitch himself from PW in his own interest. He could be caught in the crossfire and get hurt. He remained loyal to us (Nasionale Pers), Jack said, but also to PW. He could not leave PW in the lurch now.

After a lengthy discussion, Jack indicated that, while PW could not win the battle, he should not be left embittered by insensitive treatment after 55 years in public life. PW should be welcomed back cordially, be allowed to be the elder statesman, and be afforded the opportunity to allow someone else a chance. Then PW could call an election, announce when he would retire, and exit gracefully.

After Jack had left, Alf Ries phoned to report on the Stellenbosch braai. He said Heunis's speech had been unpleasant, seen by people there as a swipe at FW. Ries was unhappy about it. Only one person at the braai thought *Die Burger* had gone too far with its articles. It was Keppies Niemann, for many years a Cape party official and later an MP – a PW Botha acolyte.

I informed Ries that FW had called me. The press statement FW wanted to make was in line with a draft statement I had read out to him earlier over the phone. My draft read as follows:

> First of all, there is great understanding of the fact that the state president should get ample opportunity to recover after his stroke. One has high appreciation for his excellent service to the NP and the country. Botha has now chosen this time to grant a press interview that publicly touched on several issues that affect the very essence of the NP leadership and our form of government.
>
> He [De Klerk] has taken note of President Botha's views and intends to address these matters incisively and expeditiously within a party context, where they belong.
>
> As national leader of the NP, he appeals to Nationalists to unite and to put the greater and highest interests of the party and the country first at all times. Our strength lies in unity and selfless service.

FW greatly appreciated our ardent support and friendship.

PW Botha resigned as state president on 14 August 1989, just over five months later, after a protracted and bitter battle. Wrathful, he took his hat and left, amid mounting political instability, economic problems and diplomatic isolation.

How aggrieved he felt on the day of his resignation, and the distrustful and harsh way in which he treated the members of his Cabinet, is visible in the exchange of words between the ranting PW Botha and FW de Klerk, the man who would succeed him. A confidential source provided me with a record of the altercation, from which some translated excerpts appear below:

> **Min FW de Klerk:** I'm afraid, President, I'm by no means trying to be prescriptive, but there is a serious risk that the conclusion will be drawn that you indeed suspect us of having changed our standpoints in this matter, and that this may elicit an enormous debate. (De Klerk was

referring to the insinuation that the Cabinet without Botha had 'gone soft about the ANC'.)

Secondly, President, our suggestion with regard to Wilderness - I know you don't like it - relates to a concern we have about your state of health.

Pres PW Botha: Yes, that is now a cowardly way of going about it. In other words, you are now taking the cue given by Mr Eli Louw this morning, that I can't think for myself. That's what you actually want to say. Why don't you say it?

Min De Klerk: President, that's not what I am insinuating.

Pres Botha: Look, you people want to go too far now. I'm healthy. I'm healthy. Are each one of you able to present a medical certificate stating that you are in good health? Let's hear, how many of you are sitting here with pills in your pockets? Then you drag my state of health into it. What an outrageous thing. Oh, this will be a new way, this will become a new propaganda. He's not compos mentis.

Min De Klerk: No, that's not what we're saying.

Pres Botha: Oh yes, that's what you're saying. Where have you seen that my health will supposedly conk out? I'm leaving tonight. From tomorrow, I'm going to relax. You don't have to worry about my state of health, leave it in God's hands.

Min De Klerk: We shall, and we shall hope—

Pres Botha: And you'd better keep your relationship with Him right.

Min De Klerk: We'll do so, President. So it seems, President, as if—

Pres Botha: It's an outrageous thing that you're raising here. You are more tactless than I thought you were.

Min De Klerk: You were frank, President, and you have asked us to be frank.

Pres Botha: But I didn't cast aspersions on your person, did I. Why are you casting aspersions on my state of health? Is that the story with which you with your henchmen want to go into the world?

Min De Klerk: I don't have henchmen, President—

Pres Botha: Oh yes, very much so.

[Later]

Pres Botha: I've made you an offer that I'll leave tonight. You want me to leave tomorrow already, and I have to appoint an acting man. You have been thinking these things through since Saturday, haven't you?

Min De Klerk: It relates to your health, President.

Pres Botha: Oh, so in other words, I have to lie to rescue all of you. No, I'm sorry, colleague, I'm not prepared to draft the kind of stuff you managed to get adopted at the Federal Congress through hypocrisy.

Min De Klerk: It was not meant like that, President. It was meant sincerely. But, President, you have rejected our idea and put your own idea in its place, and we accept it, President.

Pres Botha: No, but you now have to tell me what I have to say, don't you, why I am appointing an acting man?

Min De Klerk: If you resign, appointing an acting man doesn't apply, President. Then the constitution regulates it differently.

FW de Klerk's proposals for reforming South Africa's political order were unacceptable to PW; on 6 May 1990, PW resigned from the National Party as well. Until his death on 31 October 2006, he stood steadfastly by his old convictions – for example, turning down the ANC government's offer of a state funeral.

On 3 July 1989, the Cape NP leader Dawie de Villiers told me about a discussion that the NP's provincial leaders had held with PW Botha at Wilderness on 16 June. Three of the four leaders were present: FW de Klerk, Kobie Coetsee and Dawie himself. The Natal NP leader, Stoffel Botha, was overseas at the time.

When PW was notified that the provincial leaders wished to talk to him, he asked that some of his supporters be invited as well. He wanted Pik Botha, minister of Foreign Affairs, Magnus Malan, minister of Defence, and Barend du Plessis, minister of Finance, to be present. Pik and Magnus sent their apologies because of work pressures; hence, only Barend was in attendance as a supporter.

Dawie said PW was well prepared, with a file filled with evidence. He

A TECTONIC SHIFT

hauled the visitors over the coals and accused the federal council of the NP of disloyalty. But the primary object of his outrage was Nasionale Pers, and particularly *Die Burger*. 'That editor', as he referred to the good Wiets Beukes, without ever mentioning his name, had undermined him in his illness.

According to Dawie de Villiers, PW harboured a much greater grudge against FW, but unloaded his bitterness by elevating Nasionale Pers to the position of scapegoat.

Thus, the era of National Party rule came to an end after 46 years. The new era dawned with hope, but also with old heroes who had taken their fall hard.

The great directional shift in South Africa was made possible inter alia by the groundwork done by Nasionale Pers's papers, certainly as far as the acceptance of the new South Africa by Afrikaans-speaking people was concerned. The *verligte* struggle waged by *Die Beeld* from 1965, then *Beeld* from 1974 along with the Sunday paper *Rapport*, facilitated massive reforms in our history. The sister papers *Die Burger* and *Die Volksblad* also helped make the reforms possible.

PW Botha may not have been completely off the mark on 16 June 1989 when he held Nasionale Pers responsible for the entire shift.

CHAPTER 9

Connecting with our black compatriots

An unprecedented youth uprising in Soweto in June 1976 sent shock waves through South Africa. As a result of efforts either to minimise the impact of the revolt, or to maximise it for propaganda purposes, there were divergent estimates of the number of people who were killed or injured. The highest figures were about 700 killed and 1 000 injured; the generally accepted estimate is that about 180 people, including schoolchildren, were shot dead by the police.

The immediate cause of the youth revolt was the Afrikaans Medium Decree of 1974, in terms of which black learners were forced to be taught certain school subjects in Afrikaans from 1975. The medium of instruction in different subjects would be split between English and Afrikaans on a 50/50 basis. One of the arguments used to justify this policy was that black learners would later be working for English- or Afrikaans-speaking employers.

The language issue was a spark that ignited a bigger fire. It set the frustration and rage of the black youth in South Africa in particular ablaze. The ANC movement and its supporting organisations could count on new animus in the struggle against white domination and privilege, and also on international shock and outrage that would drive the NP government deeper into a corner. The idea that Afrikaans was 'the language of the oppressor' spread across the world.

CONNECTING WITH OUR BLACK COMPATRIOTS

Today, Youth Day on 16 June commemorates the Soweto youth uprising of 1976 that had offshoots throughout the decade that followed, with the result that South Africa started to become virtually ungovernable in places.

At *Beeld* and *Rapport*, the editorial teams took a strong stand against the imposition of Afrikaans on the schools in Soweto. The responsible deputy minister was the right-wing Dr Andries Treurnicht, at that stage still a member of the National Party.

Rapport commented forcefully: 'Stop it! We don't want blood on our language.' This remark illustrates the forthright criticism of NP government measures that Nasionale Pers papers allowed themselves by this time.

The divide and suspicion between the race groups grew significantly in the wake of the Soweto revolt in 1976. In 1977, I decided as editor of *Beeld* to make contact with the editor of *The World*, Percy Qoboza. He had been nominated for a Nieman Fellowship at Harvard in 1975, as I had been in 1970.

Nieman Fellowships are awarded to mid-career journalists to reflect on their careers and hone their skills. At a distance from their normal working environment and within the stimulating academic environment that Harvard offers, they are able to take stock and look ahead with new insights and fresh ideas.

Our Nieman Fellowships provided an ideal basis for contact, mutual understanding, shared experiences and co-operation. We were two colleagues from different ethnic backgrounds in South Africa, each limited to an extent to his own cultural sphere because of the separate communities into which the NP government had divided the country – ample reason to build a bridge between us.

We decided to exchange views. Some of Percy Qoboza's columns appeared in *Beeld*, and some of mine in *The World*. The same applied to editorials. Our hope was that the readers of *Beeld* and *The World* would gain an understanding of one another's worlds, concerns and hopes. It was vital that the people of the country did not live past one another – that they got to know one another's humanity. The co-operation between our papers was a step forward in South Africa's press industry.

Not everyone was happy about this development. The head of the Bureau for State Security, General Lang Hendrik van den Bergh, slated *Beeld* as 'the world's biggest Afrikaans communist paper'. Today, it sounds ludicrous that the security service saw Reds under every bed, with a communist viewed as some kind of demon and even Nasionale Pers's newspaper *Beeld* being suspected of communist evil. In mitigation, however, one has to take into account that the communist Soviet Union and Cuba were providing substantial support to the border wars against South Africa at the time.

On 19 October 1977, not very long after we had embarked on our cooperation, *The World*'s offices were closed down and the paper banned. Qoboza was detained without trial for five months in terms of security measures, the handiwork of the minister of Justice, Jimmy Kruger, with John Vorster in the background.[18]

Exchanging articles with *The World* was in keeping with a changing situation – one in which various Nasionale Pers publications no longer followed loyally in the National Party's footsteps, and levelled frank criticism when it was deemed necessary. Voices other than our own – including that of a black intellectual such as Qoboza – were welcomed.

Nasionale Pers's role as a supporting organisation of the National Party, right or wrong, was abandoned to a large extent. The fact that *Beeld* regularly carried articles by Percy Qoboza, after which he was detained without trial for five months by the NP government, indicates how the relationship between us and the governing authority had changed. Our initiatives contributed in all kinds of ways to the freedom that black people finally won in 1994.

Nasionale Pers did not suddenly adopt this *verligte* role when the winds of change started blowing more strongly from 1976 onwards. There had been a long lead-up to this critical and innovating role. On founding the Sunday paper *Die Beeld* in 1965, Schalk Pienaar wrote: 'It is unacceptable to act as if the Afrikaners were the only inhabitants of South Africa.' In 1967, Piet Cillié, editor of *Die Burger*, wrote, perhaps with the philosopher

CONNECTING WITH OUR BLACK COMPATRIOTS

Socrates at the back of his mind: 'The press is a kind of midwife for new thinking that is waiting to be born.'

Schalk Pienaar also wrote: 'Afrikaners should remember their own oppression, not be disdainful and hostile towards others, and free themselves of the fear that co-operation and friendship with other races would lead to their destruction.'

With pronouncements like these, personalities such as Cillié and Pienaar made themselves unpopular among some in their own circle. Pienaar was, on occasion, vilified from within Afrikaner ranks as 'a traitor, an enemy of the Afrikaner, a communist fellow traveller, a pornographer and an atheistic iconoclast'.[19]

Neither the National Party, nor Nasionale Pers, nor the broader Afrikaans-speaking community was ever a bulwark of rigid and immutable unanimity. Nasionale Pers has been grappling with change for a century. This explains why its readers, too, found it possible to embrace radical reform by 1994.

Owing to the independent steps and views that papers in the Nasionale Pers stable in particular allowed themselves, tensions between the Afrikaans press and the party ran so high at one point that Prime Minister John Vorster met with the leaders of Nasionale Pers and Dagbreekpers (later Perskor) in March 1969 and presented them with a 'Code of Conduct for Nationalist newspapers'.

Dagbreekpers chair Ben Schoeman and MD Marius Jooste readily accepted the proposed code of conduct on behalf of their papers. But not Nasionale Pers. In Schalk Pienaar's words: 'With that, the code was done for, and the bosses of Nasionale Pers defended the independence of other editors against their own bosses.'

Pienaar's desire for an open conversation about the country's challenges, it has been said, 'ran like a golden thread through the editions of *Die Beeld*'. Replacing open conversation with a code of conduct was unthinkable.

Nasionale Pers chair Phil Weber wrote in his diary at the time: 'We have resisted state control all these years, and it would create a serious crisis if we now suddenly had to advocate it. Our journalists are not paid advocates or hirelings.'

In 1969, Nasionale Pers got a new chief executive – Advocate Lang David de Villiers, an outspoken *verligte*. In his court days, he had often defended the interests of the so-called underdog. De Villiers reasoned that, as CEO of a press company, he could achieve more to bring about adaptation and reform, and an end to South Africa's clash with the rest of the world, than he could as an advocate or, perhaps later, as a judge. Prior to his appointment at Nasionale Pers, he had already served occasionally as an acting judge.

Unlike *Die Burger* in the Cape Province and the *Volksblad* in the Free State, the new daily *Beeld* (established in 1974) was never designated as a mouthpiece or press organ of the National Party. From its inception, *Beeld*, while it supported the NP in elections, was no lackey. As its editor, I wrote: 'We respect the power of nationalism. Why then underestimate it among the people who constitute a majority in our country?'

With this approach, I endeavoured to enter into conversation with the black community. I wanted to acquaint myself with the everyday realities of the black population's lives and offer our readers an authentic picture in this regard.

When the hell of Soweto erupted in June 1976, we appointed the freelance journalist Jon Qwelane. Qwelane, who would become an ambassador under the ANC government many years later, was the first black journalist to work for an Afrikaans paper.[20]

Initially, a female journalist from *Beeld*, Nora Steyn, had blackened herself with shoe polish, along with a photographer, so that they could travel into Soweto in their Volkswagen for stories. It was brave of them, but perilous, and they were prevented from repeating this practice.

Khulu Sibiya, editor of *City Press* from 1988 to 2001, later wrote about *Beeld*'s reporting of the Soweto uprising: 'No white reporter could dare venture into Soweto during that period. Even black reporters survived only because they could easily mingle with the rest of the crowd.'

Sibiya was contributing stories to the *Rand Daily Mail* at the time and, since this paper already had many reporters on the scene, Qwelane asked him to write for *Beeld* too.

CONNECTING WITH OUR BLACK COMPATRIOTS

According to Sibiya, assistant editor Jack Viviers and I were appalled by their accounts of events in Soweto. 'Ton, even though he was shocked by our revelations of what was going on in Soweto, had a better understanding of the gravity of the situation. He instructed his senior editorial members to publish our stories as they were, and not to cut out anything. I was pleasantly surprised and impressed.'

In a contribution to a book published on the occasion of my seventieth birthday,[21] Khulu Sibiya wrote about the risks *Beeld* took to be able to offer authentic reporting about the situation in Soweto.

> I was to meet Ton Vosloo again in 1984, when Nasionale Pers bought *City Press*, *Drum* and *True Love*. As managing director of Nasionale Pers his task, among other things, was to reassure the staff of these publications of our total editorial independence and non-interference from the Nasionale Pers board.
>
> True to his promise, in my more than 20 years as a senior member of *City Press* there was never any interference from the board. The same cannot be said of the so-called English liberal newspapers that I worked for in the past.

The 1984 acquisition of the three black publications from Jim Bailey to which Sibiya refers above was, in fact, a continuation of the daring course *Beeld* had embarked on in the 1970s, with its exchange of articles with a black paper and the appointment of black journalists.

Also in the turbulent 1980s, when Nasionale Pers entered the pay-television market with M-Net, a variety of our publications and media services focused on the realities of South Africa as they were, not as they appeared to be from behind the ramparts of white domination.

By the time the new South Africa arrived, Nasionale Pers was a company that was already at home in the changed environment and interacted comfortably with the new actors, strictly according to business principles.

I cannot help thinking of Lang Hendrik van den Bergh's reproach in 1976 that *Beeld* was 'the world's biggest Afrikaans communist paper', when I read with gratitude what our first black president, Mr Nelson Mandela, wrote about our newspapers and about me.

Mr Mandela wrote the following, which was reproduced in the book *Ton van 'n Man*: 'The Afrikaans media adapted quickly and decisively to the new non-racial democracy which we South Africans peacefully negotiated amongst ourselves. Many – amongst whom ourselves – will argue that some of the best and most impartial reporting and commentary in the South African media is to be found in Afrikaans newspapers. As a leader Ton Vosloo played a very important role in achieving that.'

On 9 October 1997, President Mandela told a group of leaders from Nasionale Pers at a lunch how *Die Burger* had been a catalyst for great progress on the road to a negotiated constitution. A 'Dawie' column by editor Wiets Beukes, which appeared on 11 February 1989, had dealt with building blocks for the future. Beukes had advocated a radical reconsideration of laws such as the Group Areas Act, the Population Registration Act and the Reservation of Separate Amenities Act, because the new constitution had to be 'colour-blind'.

Mandela told our group that his point of departure in the negotiations had been that group formation should be freed from government interference and be allowed to happen spontaneously. At one of their first meetings, Mandela had drawn FW de Klerk's attention to the 'Dawie' column from 1989. According to him, President De Klerk had replied immediately: 'Well then, if that is what Dawie says, I'll tell my people we may just as well scrap those group laws.'

Mandela had been excited by this response. He reported back to his fellow leaders: 'We'll be able to work with this man.'

Hennie van Deventer, former editor of the *Volksblad* and later CEO of Nasionale Koerante, elaborates on Mandela's enthusiasm about the column in question. Beukes's column was written a week after the Afrikaner Broederbond had convened an important brainstorming session about South Africa's constitutional future. Beukes was a Broederbond member, and had delivered a paper on group rights that greatly interested the chair

Professor Pieter de Lange (also a director of Nasionale Pers), among others. A week later, Beukes converted his paper into his legendary 'Dawie' column.

Beukes, an extremely modest man, told Van Deventer that, even if this had been his only contribution, it would have made his career worthwhile.

The significance of President Mandela's account at that lunch is that it gave Afrikaans newspapers and their role in South Africa's political reform a different complexion from the negative picture that was painted of us in testimony before the Truth and Reconciliation Commission (TRC). Mandela showed deep appreciation of Nasionale Pers, indeed.

CHAPTER 10

Leadership

On 26 July 1990, Nasionale Pers Limited celebrated its 75th anniversary. A commemorative volume was launched to mark the occasion: *Sonop in die Suide: Geboorte en groei van die Nasionale Pers 1915–1948* (Sunrise in the South: Birth and growth of Nasionale Pers 1915–1948). Professor CFJ Muller had been tasked with writing the book.

At the launch, our chair, Professor Piet Cillié, presented me with copy number three. Cillié's words of praise reminded me of the great expectations the group had of my leadership on the road ahead. The inscription (in Afrikaans) on the front flyleaf read:

> *To Ton Vosloo*
> *With the firm confidence that he will fully realise the promise of his first, successful years as chief executive of our company – that he would become one of the great leaders of the Pers – in this last and critical decade of the twentieth century.*
> *– From his fellow directors of Nasionale Pers on our 75th anniversary.*

Having been CEO for five years, I was flattered by Cillié's favourable appraisal of my performance. The high hopes the company had of me when it came to the future, however, did not escape me. I could only speculate about how the critical final years of the twentieth century might unfold. But I had every intention of giving my all for Naspers in the coming decade.

As the leader of a large and diversified company such as Naspers, you have to judge yourself every day by where you are leading the group to. Leadership means questioning yourself, but without succumbing to indecisiveness.

Over the years, I purposely resolved never to become complacent. 'Show me a contented editor and I'll show you a bad newspaper,' Arthur Christiansen, former editor of one of the largest British newspapers, the *Daily Express*, once said. I nailed this adage to my mast as editor and also as chief executive. As chief executive, I did not indulge in self-satisfaction if I could help it.

My leadership had been formed in my journalistic years. It was a huge responsibility, but also exciting, to advance from general news reporting to sport, and to be an observer and reporter from 1958 to 1970 in the scrum of our politics, the House of Assembly.

Those parliamentary years were worth their weight in gold. Besides getting to know political leaders, I was also afforded a helicopter view of national affairs as they unfolded.

It was when I became editor of the young daily *Beeld* in June 1977 that I first tasted the full meaning of the loneliness of leadership. You and you alone had to take the reins, lead the editorial staff and forge your colleagues into a cohesive team. Moreover, in the prevailing circumstances you had to coach them not only to outperform the group of rival papers in the market, but also crush them politically.

I introduced my first team talk with a joke: a zoo crossed a tiger with a parrot, I said. *Beeld* went to investigate, and the reporter asked the zookeeper, 'What do you call this thing?' The zookeeper replied, 'I don't know, but when it talks, we listen.'

I continued: 'I hope I'm not the product of such cross-breeding, but I'm afraid I'll have to be listened to when I talk.'

These were some of the points I made:
- We're going to tighten the screws that need to be tightened.
- Quite a few shibboleths will go out the window.
- *Beeld* will be a lively, fresh, sparkling paper that reflects its environment, that speaks with authority and that, in the interest of its readers, will never back down or throw in the towel – a paper with which the public would like to associate itself because it is decent.
- We'll hit the big news story hard. Focusing our energies on the top story of the day will be our great offensive weapon. (This was indeed what *Beeld* did.)

With regard to leadership, I promised the editorial staff that in the production process I would be a visible, contactable and accessible editor.

This plan was executed successfully. By the end of 1982, *Beeld* was the Afrikaans market leader in the Transvaal, and its dominance led to the demise of all four of our rival Afrikaans dailies in 1983.

As editor, I wrote a daily memo to the editorial staff. One such memo, on a pink slip of paper and which is still my possession, made the following point: 'What gives Beeld a "*gees*", and progressively so, is the local letters that are now beginning to arrive. Today's letters page is from the heartland of our readership area ... we are getting under the skins of our people. We are now three months away from our third birthday. Maybe we are only now starting to identify truly with our environment ... this holds enormous potential.'

I found the increasing number of letters from the local community heartening and valuable indeed. A newspaper gets to know its market in this way, and can deliver a product that is tailored to its readership.

Unfortunately, leadership also meant having to rebuke my own seniors at times.

In June 1977, I received a telex from our office manager in Pretoria, Piet Botma. In a column about Nasionale Pers, Dr Albert Hertzog's far-right paper *Die Afrikaner* had referred to an article in *Beeld*. The article was about a couple who had been attacked while buying bananas near the Kruger National Park. According to *Die Afrikaner,* readers could not conclude from *Beeld*'s article that the attackers had been black men; apparently, *Beeld* had referred only to armed robbers and men.

Botma added: 'The criticism may be valid. I think in our society and political situation it is important to talk about black men.'

I replied: 'We have decided to avoid the issue of colour in the introduction to articles. *Beeld* wrote that the tracks of the attackers had led to a nearby black village. Surely this indicated who the thugs were.'

My modus operandi as newspaper editor was also accompanied by clashes with the approach of some leadership figures in the National Party. My decision as editor of *Beeld* to exchange columns and editorials with *The World* editor Percy Qoboza, for example, did not find favour everywhere. Eventually, we had to look on as Percy's paper was banned and he was detained without trial for five months on Justice minister Jimmy Kruger's instructions.

It was a novelty for an Afrikaans paper to exchange articles with a paper aimed at the black community. *Die Burger* and the *Cape Times* did exchange editorials in the 1970s, and *Die Burger* also exchanged comment articles with the Dutch daily *Trouw* in those years. But I specifically wanted white and black readers to hear one another's voices. And they had to discover one another on an equal footing, in comparable articles that appeared in one another's newspapers. I sought to break through the mutual isolation of newspaper apartheid.

Looking back today, the amount of suspicion, bigotry and harshness with which the authorities would sometimes respond to articles by black journalists was astounding. Equally astounding was how much daring it required of me to seek to bridge the distance *Beeld* was supposed to maintain between itself and a paper such as *The World* in terms of government policy. Prime Minister John Vorster was implacable in his condemnation of Qoboza.

Qoboza was a newspaper editor and fellow South African who was entitled to a political discussion or debate in the pages of the two papers the two of us had to lead. He knew his market, and knew that the genie would escape from the bottle once the NP government started learning that the plug could not be kept in permanently.

Sadly, he died in 1988, at only 50 years old and on the brink of the new dispensation for which he had fought. Qoboza had to take many risks, and his lifestyle was unhealthy. The stress of his editorship in the seething cauldron of unrest and revolt in the 1970s and 1980s took its toll.

His family invited me to deliver a tribute at his funeral service in Soweto's Regina Mundi Catholic church. Among other things, I said that, with the passing of Percy Qoboza, South African journalism had lost one of its bravest personalities.

During his career, Qoboza was subjected to two gruelling tests in particular. The first was the dramatic shutdown of *The World* in 1976 and his five-month detention without trial. His courageous leadership led to this censorship and incarceration. History has proved him right, and today his imprisonment redounds to his eternal credit.

The other test came when Nasionale Pers acquired Drum Publications in 1984. All of a sudden, Percy's paper was owned by Afrikaner nationalists. He had to think carefully about his standing in his own community and his role within the greater South African dispensation, with all its conflicting tendencies and ruthlessness. Percy accepted the exceptionally tough challenge wholeheartedly. At his first meeting with us, he broke the ice by remarking: 'Don't expect us to wear safari suits and grey shoes.'

I formulated my own style as managing director of Nasionale Pers during the time I served as Lang David de Villiers's deputy while rehearsing for my new role. I explained my approach at the Pers's leadership conference in April 1983.

My standpoint was that Nasionale Pers could not rest on its laurels now that its projects had been firmly established. Every product in our group was being assessed daily, weekly or periodically by Joe Public. As any real person, he or she had whims, fancies, prejudices and tastes that shifted continuously. He or she might like you or loathe you; one day the public loves you, but the next, it shifts its affections to another newspaper, magazine or book. So, we had to focus on renewal, look ahead and display entrepreneurial daring.

LEADERSHIP

As leader, I wanted us to get down to adapting to the changing political landscape without further ado. We had to set our sights on the politics of tomorrow. The culture of narrow, exclusive nationalism had to be eradicated. We had to start cultivating a more inclusive South Africanness.

I also stressed the idea of service at the leadership conference: 'No organisation exists for any other purpose than that of rendering service to society.'

Three quotations from famous people had to help me get my standpoint and approach across that day. Newspapers still ruled at the time, in the sense that they were not yet at risk of being dethroned by digital technology. I quoted Napoleon: 'Four hostile newspapers are more to be feared than a thousand bayonets.' About my own troops, I expressed the wish of being able to say what the Duke of Wellington had said about his: 'I don't know what effect these men will have upon the enemy, but, by God, they frighten me.' And I quoted Giuseppe Mazzini, an Italian politician, journalist and activist who strove for the unification of Italy and headed the Italian revolutionary movement. He said: 'Slumber not in the tents of your fathers. The world is advancing. Advance with it.'

In a large group such as Naspers – which had expanded over time from print media to pay television, from pay television to cellphones, and from cellphones to a panoply of digital products to become a group that operated in more than 130 countries – there is no opportunity for a leader to tread water. I had to adapt myself to the fast pace of the times and of Naspers's growth, and indeed also had to facilitate this pace, in the spirit of Giuseppe Mazzini.

With the technical means available to communicate with anyone, anywhere in the world, at any time, you were contactable 24/7. Sometimes, we negotiated or concluded contracts by taking steps in different countries across the globe, over a period of perhaps 24 hours. When one team sent off contracts in South Africa, the team in America would be asleep, and it would be almost evening in China. The negotiation process could progress through the time zones so that, by the time you walked into your office the next morning, the results would be on your desk.

Leadership in such an organisation requires a team you can count on, and discussions to ensure that you stay up to speed. It also requires the ability to digest the advice of well-informed financial or legal experts, to be able to present a considered plan to a board. The board must have confidence in its executive leader, who in turn has to be able to rely on the dependability and competence of the team leaders lower down. Integrity is the watchword. Enormous sums of money are sometimes at stake.

When I became chair of *Rapport* in September 1988, my advice was: Type with a typewriter or computer, or write in your diary if you only have a pen, just one word – excellence. Strive for it every day. Strive to be first in everything – not merely the first to go home! Then *Rapport* will come out tops, a paper that is not only big in terms of its circulation but also great in terms of its output, its quality.

To make a success of a company such as Naspers, you not only had to innovate continuously; you also needed to tap the expertise and proficiency of professionals who had acquired an in-depth knowledge of their field over many years.

I could build on the experience of very good people. I am thinking of Jurie Naudé and Danie Krynauw (Magazines), Jan Prins (Newspapers), Calvyn Palm (Technical), Heinie Jaekel and William van der Vyver (Books), Danie van Niekerk (Tafelberg), Koos Human (Human & Rousseau), Hennie Conradie, Eric Wiese and Jas du Preez (Finance), and George Coetzee and Gillian Kisbey-Green (Secretariat). Later, there were Hennie van Deventer (Newspapers) and Salie de Swardt (Media24). With them, you could go into battle; leadership of this calibre was the envy of rival press groups. I have devoted a separate chapter to Koos Bekker. He was special, to put it mildly.

Leadership meant not only leading a team with diverse competencies, but also making unpleasant decisions at times. For instance, I had to ask two heads of the Boekhandel group, Gawie Rousseau and Piet Botma, to resign. We also had to fire Izak de Villiers, embittered after steering *Rapport* in a completely wrong direction at a critical juncture in the country.

The departure of *Fair Lady* editor Dene Smuts was terribly unpleasant,[22] as was the dismissal of Wimpie de Klerk as editor of *Rapport*.

Sometimes, as a leader, you have no choice but to wield the axe. But such actions do not leave you cold. And the pain they cause the people who are affected may evoke reactions for which you, too, will suffer.

Leadership of a press group also demanded political leadership. The media deals with situations and events in public life; as I have already recounted in previous chapters, our newspapers occasionally published articles that would cause the highest political authority in the country to come down on us like a ton of bricks. PW Botha, in particular, was notorious for his outbursts. He was hot-tempered and bombastic, and would lash out with a venomous tongue. Even his so-called sympathetic nationalist press people were publicly berated as dirty swine. Thus, PW gradually alienated nearly all his friends.

As a leader, you serve on various professional bodies, such as the Newspaper Press Union in my case. You forge professional relationships with your counterparts in similar leadership positions in this way. At the time, it meant becoming acquainted with leaders of the opposition-minded English-language newspapers.

As editor, I was often critical of some newspapers, but as managing director I always endeavoured to build constructive relationships with press owners. The best example of how good relations of this kind could pay dividends was the investment in M-Net, which I managed to persuade the leaders of all the country's daily papers to do. The fact that the M-Net venture fell under Nasionale Pers's leadership reflected something of the respect and confidence we enjoyed within our professional field.

Tall trees catch the most wind, so the Afrikaans saying goes. Dr Danie Craven turned it around and said: 'It's the dogs pissing on the bottom of the trunks that cause the trees to topple.' I never saw myself as a tall tree, and preferred to operate behind the scenes.

One example of leadership behind the scenes relates to an incident at a meeting of Nasionale Pers's board of directors. Flip la Grange, former senator and arch-Bolander, slammed a book onto the boardroom table and objected in the strongest terms to our group's publication of a disgusting book.

He was supported by Billy van der Merwe, Super-Afrikaner, Broederbonder and senior lawyer. The book in question was *Jonkmanskas*, a collection of short stories by Koos Prinsloo. For its time, it dealt fairly openly with homosexuality and other issues that could offend conservative readers.

I was sitting next to Piet Cillié, and whispered to him to leave the matter to me. It is not the function of a board to assess manuscripts, I replied. We had highly experienced, professional publishers with good literary insight, people such as Danie van Niekerk and Koos Human. It would make fools of us as a board if we were to start assessing or censoring manuscripts.

If directors felt that a particular publisher was not worthy of his position, the board could discuss this – the heads of book-publishing operations were appointed by the board. But our publishers were held in the highest repute, and I did not believe that the matter merited further discussion. I was supported by Professor Elize Botha, former chair of the Suid-Afrikaanse Akademie vir Wetenskap en Kuns and esteemed scholar of literature; Professor Pieter de Lange, former rector of the Rand Afrikaans University (now the University of Johannesburg) and chair of the Broederbond; and senior director Jeff Malherbe.

I proposed to chair Cillié that we proceed to the next item on the agenda. The proposal was accepted. La Grange and Van der Merwe probably grumbled inwardly, but they were mature and decent people and we co-operated well in the team.

There had been a previous attempt at internal censorship, too. During chair Phil Weber's tenure, the board of directors had a letter sent to Schalk Pienaar via the secretary to convey their displeasure with *Die Beeld*'s reporting against the far-right Pretoria paper *Veg*. As political reporter, I had written the articles in question, in the heat of the *verkrampte* onslaught.

Pienaar was offended by this letter and complained to Weber. Weber apologised in writing, acknowledged that it was a mistake on the part of the board to dictate to an editor, and said that it would not happen again, affirming and strengthening editorial independence.

With the advent of the democratic South Africa, leadership was tested increasingly by the ANC government's policies on labour matters, competition and black economic empowerment. This required new adaptations.

From the outset, Naspers has contributed constructively to building our new society. Phuthuma Nathi, MultiChoice's extremely successful empowerment scheme, is a good example of this. The board allocated a large block of the listed MultiChoice shares to black people on the basis of a loan of R50 per share, of which the participant paid only R10. The shares had to be kept for five years and could not be sold to non-qualifying investors. The annual dividends reduced the loan debt and, as MultiChoice's share price rose, black participants benefited phenomenally from their investment. For a long time, it was the most successful empowerment initiative of its kind.

As a final word on leadership, I would like to refer to a speech I delivered to prospective entrepreneurs at Stellenbosch University. The title was 'Ton's Ten Lessons for Life'. Here is a brief summary of the contents:

1. Read and listen attentively.
2. Be curious.
3. Keep abreast of technology and changes.
4. Be social: work hard and play hard.
5. Maintain an open-door policy.
6. Dream big.
7. Embrace risk-taking and renewal.
8. Be known as a person of integrity.
9. Work with enthusiasm and stamina.
10. Believe in yourself.

CHAPTER 11

Broedertwis

One of the most intriguing stories about the rise and fall of National Party rule in South Africa lies in the role of the Afrikaner Broederbond (AB). From the 1960s onwards, the *verligte* movement in Afrikaner politics also impacted strongly and divisively on this organisation. As mentioned before, three newspapers spearheaded the articulation of the *verligte* perspective to a significant extent: the Sunday paper *Die Beeld* (1965–70); *Rapport*, the Sunday paper that emerged from *Die Beeld* in 1970; and the daily *Beeld* from 1974 onwards.

In the great '*Broedertwis*' (fraternal quarrel) – the division between *verligte* and *verkrampte* members of the AB, who were often also fellow members of the NP – the dominance of one side or the other could have consequences of historical import. The far-right faction of the National Party, which would have put South Africa's constitutional development in the 1980s and 1990s on a completely different trajectory, was narrowly thwarted when PW Botha was elected prime minister in 1978, for instance.

What characterised *verligte* journalists of Nasionale Pers was that they were supposed to support the policy of the NP government, but frequently used their opportunities and influence to question this policy critically or lobby against what they considered to be wrong.

Since the Party was dependent on the Pers for publicity, the latter could exert subtle or indirect – but, at times, also direct – pressure on the levers of power in South Africa. In any case, this pressure was more direct than the pressure that, say, a poet or writer could exert, who could easily be ridiculed or rendered harmless within the discourse of those days through of a slur such as '*volksvreemd*' (alien to prevailing conceptions of Afrikaner customs and values).

I do not for a moment underestimate the critical role of the intelligentsia, academics and creative writers and artists of all race and language groups throughout the apartheid era – nor the role of those AB members who strove to influence and reform their organisation from within through of 'loyal resistance'. Many resigned from the AB, with Beyers Naudé the best-known example.

The Afrikaner Broederbond was established in 1918 by a small group of idealistic Afrikaners whose aim was to help get their nation back on its feet after the South African War. The War had been followed by the Rebellion of 1914, which was nipped in the bud by the government of the Union of South Africa under the leadership of the prime minister, General Louis Botha.

In the wake of the South African War and the failed Rebellion, the Afrikaners were not only demoralised, but also politically, economically and culturally bereft, with widespread poverty a conspicuous phenomenon.

The AB, with its Protestant orientation, believed in a divinely appointed role and mission for the Afrikaners in South Africa. The organisation strove to restore and promote Afrikaner traditions and culture, including attachment to the church. The premium that was put on educational institutions and the publication of books, magazines and newspapers distinguished the organisation's approach at the time. The AB was an elite group of Afrikaner males; membership was secret. The idea was for the best from among the ranks of the devastated community to initiate and lead the restoration and reconstruction of the Afrikaner nation.

The cultural ideals of the AB were later converted into a nationalist ideology with a political aim. In 1934, this was formulated as follows by the chair, Professor JC van Rooy: '... the principal aim is for Afrikanerdom to reach its ultimate destiny of baasskap in South Africa. Brothers, our solution to South Africa's problems is not that one party or another would get the upper hand, but that the Afrikaner Broederbond would rule South Africa.'

The 1930s were a tipping point in Afrikaner history: the initial idealism of the AB was increasingly transformed into a nationalist pursuit of self-determination and power over South Africa during this time. True, the AB did not have a fascist takeover or government in view – at any rate, not after the Second World War. It was envisaged that an NP government would have the security, interests and upliftment of Afrikaners at heart. But such a government would need to win elections, and would have to do right by the other groups in the country. It would be fair to say that the AB sought to represent the cultured Afrikaner, but its ideal of Afrikaner *baasskap* was a problematic and ultimately unsustainable factor.

When the NP came to power in 1948 under Dr DF Malan, the AB achieved its ideal of a secret government behind the scenes. Dr Malan and the majority of his Cabinet ministers were Broeders. This was also the case in the governments of Hans Strijdom, Hendrik Verwoerd, John Vorster, PW Botha and FW de Klerk. In a way, the Broederbond *did* rule South Africa – for 46 years.

The Super-Afrikaners: Inside the Afrikaner Broederbond by Hans Strydom and Ivor Wilkins explains the hold of the AB over NP governments in detail. The government's policy decisions were discussed and cleared beforehand with the AB's leadership structure, the Bondsraad, and adjusted, if necessary. Successive prime ministers conferred in secret with the Bondsraad and discussed the steps they envisaged. The AB would subsequently circulate the planned changes countrywide through its organisational structures, and prepare the ground for their implementation.

In the 1960s, however, an intense battle started within the AB about the direction the country should follow. Within two decades of the end of the Second World War, the notion that Afrikaner or white *baasskap* over the black population could offer a solution foundered on demographic realities. Dividing the country into a so-called constellation of states, or into homelands in which the different races would develop separately but in parallel (as Verwoerd believed), or exorcising creeping black urbanisation by means of new labels such as pluralism, ultimately proved to be wish fulfilment. Verwoerd endeavoured to redefine 'white *baasskap*' as white *baasskap* over white people in their own country. But none of these manoeuvres could counter South Africa's demographic realities.

Within the AB, there was stubborn resistance to adjustments or concessions that could weaken the whites' monopoly on national government. This eventually led to a split in the AB and the breakaway of the so-called *verkramptes* under the leadership of a senior Broeder, Dr Albert Hertzog.

Beeld sniffed out the factional split within the AB at an early stage. By the end of the 1970s, the split was brought to a head by revelations about the secret workings of the Broederbond, not only in *The Super-Afrikaners* but also in Hennie Serfontein's *Brotherhood of Power: An Exposé of the Secret Afrikaner Broederbond*, which was published by Rex Collings in London in 1979.

In the 1960s and 1970s, the *verlig/verkramp* dichotomy, which also penetrated the Broederbond, tended to assume a strongly provincialist character. The difference between the South, or the Cape Province, which was home to the more liberal-minded wing of the National Party, and the North, represented by the Free State and notably the Transvaal, the home of *kragdadige* apartheid thinking, was reflected, among other things, in the difference in approach between *Die Burger* and papers such as *Die Transvaler* and *Die Vaderland*.

The rivalry between South and North also manifested itself in the country's prime ministers. In 1954, the Transvaler Hans Strijdom was chosen as new prime minister above Dr Malan's designated favourite, Klasie Havenga. The pattern repeated itself when the Transvaler Dr Hendrik Verwoerd was elected in 1958 above the Cape leader, Dr Eben Dönges.

Within this context, Nasionale Pers embarked on an onslaught on the Northern Afrikaans newspaper market in 1965 with the founding of the Sunday paper *Die Beeld*, as described in Chapter 7.

The board of the Northern Afrikaans newspaper stable, later known as Perskor, was packed with Transvaal Cabinet ministers, with Dr Verwoerd and Advocate John Vorster serving as chairs. Nasionale Pers, too, had its quota of ministers as directors – hence, both boards were well populated with members of the AB.

The North was dead set against Nasionale Pers's expansion of its newspaper operations beyond the Vaal River, as explained earlier. The massive press war that gradually got underway after the establishment of *Die Beeld* cost hundreds of millions of rands, and came to an end in 1993 with the final closure of *Die Transvaler* as a minor paper with limited circulation in Pretoria. This demise coincided with the end of any striving for Afrikaner *baasskap* within the Broederbond. In fact, the Broederbond accepted the new dispensation in South Africa and was formally dissolved that same year.

Die Beeld, under editor Schalk Pienaar and chief executive Dirk de Villiers, pointed out that any plan for white domination that the National Party had come up with in the course of its rule, or might still hope to concoct, would be unfeasible.

A good illustration of this approach was an article I had written as political reporter, based on a scientific study by the demographer Professor Flip Smit (then at Unisa) on the influx of black people into the urban areas of 'white' South Africa.

The government had held up 1978 as the year in which the ongoing stream of black people to the cities would start reversing. It hoped that, by that year, significant numbers of urban blacks would begin to return to their ethnic homelands as a result of improved socioeconomic conditions in those homelands brought about by its policy of decentralisation and the establishment of industries. Professor Smit's solid demographic projections shattered that hope.

His detailed analysis indicated that the reduction of numbers of black people in 'white' South Africa would not happen. Pienaar analysed these findings in an editorial, and stated that the NP policy was based on pure fiction. Race-based territorial separation was simply impracticable.

The emperor was shown to be naked. But instead of acknowledging that a gradual decline in the numbers of black people in 'white' areas was a pipe dream, the Vorster administration persisted, tinkering with its policies in only minor ways. The proponents of the supposed reversal of the flow of black people in 1978, people such as ministers Daan de Wet Nel and Sampie Froneman, continued punting the ideal. But their spin-doctoring convinced fewer and fewer people.

The contest between *verkramp* and *verlig* within the AB grew in intensity, and the divergence of opinion spread to Afrikaner institutions such as the Afrikaans churches, Suid-Afrikaanse Akademie vir Wetenskap en Kuns, the FAK, the ATKV, the Voortrekkers, the Rapportryers, youth organisations, and just about the entire spectrum of organised Afrikaner activities.

Rykie van Reenen mischievously referred to Professor Detlev Weiss and his wife Hymne as 'the Weiss Squad'. This *verkrampte* couple attempted to take the lead in all kinds of bodies in Pretoria. At times, their zeal – for instance, in advocating stricter literary censorship – led to embarrassment within the Akademie.

The internally divided AB walked on eggs in respect of the war between the two Afrikaans press groups. Schalk Pienaar was occasionally requested in a 'brotherly conversation' to temper his *verligte* pronouncements in *Die Beeld*. Discussions were also held with Dirk Richard, the editor of *Dagbreek*. The AB wanted peace to prevail.

Die Beeld, however, exploited the muddy situation with fearless journalism, to the provocation, political edification, or amusement of its readers on Sundays. Perskor's papers sided with the *verkramptes*.

Within the Perskor stable, the divergent political sentiments made for anomalies. Marius Jooste had established the daily papers *Oggendblad* and *Hoofstad* in Pretoria as part of the fortifications that were supposed to fend off the Nasionale Pers invasion. It became a divided fortress, however, when the *Oggendblad* editor Harald Pakendorf adopted a cautiously *verligte* tone, while Dr Andries Treurnicht, editor of *Hoofstad*, launched a *verkrampte*, far-right assault. The idea behind this ambivalence was evidently that Perskor was trying to offer a home to both left-wing and right-wing readers in its papers, to boost circulation.

On top of it all, Jooste was still a Transvaal *verkrampte*. Typical of his manipulations was a discussion he had on 10 March 1980 with *Rapport* editor Sakkie Perold, which Perold subsequently communicated to me. 'Perskor will have to go with Treurnicht in the event of a split,' Jooste said. 'It puts *Rapport*'s future in jeopardy.'

Jooste had been upset about a particular editorial in which *Rapport* had apparently put too much spin on the ball. *Rapport* had to remember that it had a Transvaal address, Jooste threatened, and he was quite willing to put the paper's future in jeopardy. He was *'gatvol'* with *Rapport*'s Cape-mindedness.

PG du Plessis, who was editor of *Hoofstad* at the time, told Perold that he and other Perskor editors had been called in. He was not allowed to attack Treurnicht: doing so would apparently be an unwise move in Pretoria, and could prejudice his future. PG was very despondent about the situation.

The press war led to other manoeuvres, such as Marius Jooste's purchase of *Die Landstem* so that he could incorporate it into the Sunday paper *Dagbreek*. Like other desperate, and even illegal, shenanigans to which I shall return, the move was intended to boost sales and generate more advertising income in the process. Nonetheless, *Die Beeld* gradually gained the upper hand in the battle against Perskor.

The press war confused the public and became so unsavoury in the eyes of NP politicians that John Vorster resigned as chair of Perskor to get out of the crossfire. He was succeeded by Ben Schoeman, another NP minister.

Nasionale Pers's directors included NP politicians such as PW Botha, Fanie Botha, Piet Koornhof, Nak van der Merwe and Senator Flip la Grange. Nasionale Pers's new chief executive was the eminent legal personality Advocate Lang David de Villiers. The chair was Dr Phil Weber, former editor of *Die Burger*. Both men were loyal Broeders.

With so many members of the same political club – the Broederbond – in positions of authority, engineering a compromise between the warring parties seemed possible. Under pressure from John Vorster, Ben Schoeman and Marius Jooste entered into an agreement with Dr Weber and Advocate De Villiers that led to the closure of both Sunday papers and the establishment of *Rapport* in November 1970.

Die Beeld's editorial staff were shaken to the core by this unnecessary compromise. After all, their victory in the press war was on the horizon. Schalk Pienaar in particular was deeply affected. He had suffered his first heart attack in 1967, followed by a more serious one in 1969. But the biggest blow to his messianic task of preparing Afrikaners for change came as a result of cancer, which prompted his early retirement at the end of 1970. His farewell speech expressed the emotional torment of being unable to continue with his work. In it, he quoted from Kahlil Gibran's *The Prophet*: 'It is not a garment I cast off this day, but a skin that I tear with my own hands.'

Pienaar was a tired and broken man in October 1970 when his colleagues said farewell not only to him, but also to the Sunday paper he had built up so successfully over five years, in order for *Rapport* to be launched.

He returned to Cape Town, and recovered to such an extent that in 1974 he could still help for a short while to get the daily *Beeld* off the ground as founder editor. He also occupied himself as a capable books editor of *Die Burger*.

Willem Wepener, aka Iron Man, had been assistant editor of *Die Beeld*. In 1970, he was appointed as *Rapport*'s first editor. In terms of the agreement, Nasionale Pers was promised the editorial side of the paper, while management would be in the hands of Perskor, with Duimpie Opperman as chief executive. This division made a *verligte* political outlook and tone possible.

The 50/50 marriage between the two former foes lasted until shortly before my retirement as executive chair of Naspers in 1997. In the last transaction of my career, I acquired the old Perskor's 50 per cent stake (then in the hands of Terry Moolman's Caxton) and put *Rapport* entirely in the hands of Nasionale Pers. This rectified a mistake from the past, in the opinion of *Rapport*'s editorial staff and in my own eyes.

From November 1970, *Rapport* maintained the *verligte* direction of *Die Beeld*. An exception was the period from 1991 to 1997, when Izak de Villiers was editor. He steered the paper to the right and disliked the steps taken by the NP government under FW de Klerk.

Among other methods, Perskor's dailies deployed the survival tactics of opportunistic *verkrampte* appointments and reporting, but also opportunistic *verligte* appointments and reporting. Editors such as AM van Schoor (*Die Vaderland*) and Carl Nöffke (*Die Transvaler*) aligned themselves with the *verkrampte* faction in the Transvaal NP and the AB, only to do a partial about-turn later when the tide started turning against them. Willem de Klerk was appointed as *verligte* editor of *Die Transvaler* in 1973, but the aim was clearly for him to serve as saviour of Perskor's flagship in the press war. In this fashion, Perskor muddled on.

A later editor of *Die Vaderland*, Dirk Richard, wrote that they had to fight the press war with 'one hand tied behind their backs'.

The political ambivalence with which Perskor sought to keep both *verlig* and *verkramp* happy in an attempt to boost sales was symptomatic of the company's desperation during the press war. The company reached its nadir when fraud was committed to inflate the Perskor papers' circulation figures artificially. Under Jooste's hand, thousands of copies of *Die Transvaler* and *Die Vaderland* were dumped down a mine shaft on the West Rand to make it seem as if they had been sold. Conduct of this nature changed the Afrikaans political landscape in the North.

I assumed my duties as news editor of the new Sunday paper *Rapport* directly after my mind-broadening experiences as Nieman Fellow at Harvard. So I approached the position with a fresh perspective on our country's situation.

By that stage of my career, I had attended twelve parliamentary sessions, got to know the politicians of the day, and acquired experience that was vital to a journalist.

As news editor of *Rapport*, I was in the fortunate position of leading a top news team. With colleagues such as Rykie van Reenen, Franz Kemp, Freek Swart, Jack Viviers, Eddie du Plessis, Coenie Slabber, Twakkies Laubscher and others, we were a formidable editorial team. The new paper kicked off with a bang. At one stage, *Rapport*'s sales figures topped half a million copies, which was unprecedented in South Africa.

Under Willem Wepener and his senior editorial staff, *Rapport* was unashamedly *verlig*. The paper egged on the widening rift within the NP, the

AB and the array of organisations that had been established in support of the Afrikaner cause. The white Afrikaans-speaking community was, indeed, starting to see the light.

As editor of *Die Burger*, the skilled wordsmith Piet Cillié could sometimes adopt a tone of refined reasonableness that may serve to illustrate the difference between Nasionale Pers's papers and those of the Perskor stable. An apposite example is the editorial he wrote in May 1975 on the death of the diehard communist Bram Fischer. The South African Communist Party was still a banned organisation at the time. The editorial says it all about Cillié's insight and empathy. The Afrikaans papers of the North would never have been capable of writing such a compassionate piece. A translated version of *Die Burger*'s editorial on Bram Fischer appears at the end of this chapter.

But back to the establishment of the daily *Beeld* in 1974. For four years, from 1970, *Rapport* had been Nasionale Pers's countrywide voice. But the company also had its sights set on making its voice heard on a daily basis in the North, and on entering the big reader market of the Witwatersrand and surrounding areas. This had been a long-cherished ideal.

The founding editor of the new daily *Beeld* was, again, Schalk Pienaar, with Johannes Grosskopf as his senior assistant. Still plagued by ill health, Pienaar handed the reins to Grosskopf after two and half months. At that stage, I was managing editor of *Rapport* under Willem Wepener as editor.

The founding of *Beeld* meant that Nasionale Pers had a daily in every province in the country except Natal. The papers could draw on joint resources, structures and equipment. An incredibly strong journalist corps, made of loyal and proud employees, was now established in all major centres of the country, with the exception of Durban.

With the launch of *Beeld*, *Rapport* immediately gave up a huge portion of its editorial staff, which illustrated the principle of mutual support and strengthening. I, for my part, could not wait to start my job as assistant editor at the new paper, along with seasoned colleagues from *Die Burger* such as Ebbe Dommisse, Bob van Walsem, Piet Botma, Salie de Swardt, George Boshoff, Johann Holzapfel, and Hannes van Zyl, the arts journalist.

There were *Volksblad* stalwarts such as Hennie van Deventer and Piet Gouws, and we were also joined by experienced colleagues from elsewhere: people such as the renowned sports editor and horse-racing expert Roelf Theunissen, Jack Viviers, and contributors such as Martie Retief-Meiring and Manie van der Schyff. Piet Muller joined the senior editorial staff, and we set up a strong bureau in Pretoria.

Perskor mobilised against this interloper with its Cape roots by launching two new papers in Pretoria. Thus *Beeld* was confronted with four competitors: *Die Transvaler* and *Die Vaderland* in Johannesburg, and *Oggendblad* and *Hoofstad* in Pretoria. The fortifications as a whole – the four morning and afternoon papers – succeeded to the extent that *Beeld* ran at a loss for ten years.

The first profit *Beeld* made after ten years came before Perskor's circulation fraud had become officially known. It is evident, therefore, that style, quality, substance and the verdict of newspaper readers secured this eventual victory. *Beeld* simply overshadowed the Perskor papers.

After he had long been kept in the dark, Johannes Grosskopf, later professor and second head of Stellenbosch University's journalism department, could finally have the satisfaction of knowing that, under his leadership, *Beeld* had overtaken *Die Transvaler* as far back as 1976.

From 1975 onwards, *Beeld* was gradually developed into the biggest Afrikaans daily in the country. Its circulation later surpassed 100 000. But it was definitely not plain sailing from the beginning. When *Beeld* started, we played a guessing game about the number of copies we would sell after the launch. I had eleven years' experience in the North under my belt – the rest of the team hailed from the Cape and the Free State.

My estimate was that our sales would come to 26 000 after the initial excitement. The first day's sales were close to 100 000. But once the dust of the publicity had settled, the figure stood at 21 000. I had been closest to the mark. This figure had a sobering effect on us.

The battle between the two press groups, however, was to continue until the end of 1982. Marius Jooste died in that same year. In 1983, *Die Transvaler* was moved to Pretoria, and in time all four of our rival papers closed down. This left *Beeld* as the only Afrikaans daily north of the Vaal River.

Perskor's circulation fraud, which became known as 'Syferfontein'[23] – a name that, to those in the know, was redolent of the idea of circulation figures that had been 'counted' honestly or dishonestly – led to a waggish message that I received as editor of *Beeld* from Stellenbosch on 23 December 1980. 'I suggest that you use the motto "The paper that counts" below your masthead,' Professor Christo Viljoen notified me with a wink.

The victory of the *verligte* papers, *Rapport* and *Die Burger* and others, also had an impact on the Broederbond. Its executive council under chair Pieter de Lange attempted to find a road out of the impasse into which the NP policy had driven the AB. Seminars were held countrywide behind closed doors, where participants discussed documents exploring the road ahead.

The leaders of the AB were ripe for change. As was to be expected, there was a backlash: the HNP faction broke away from the AB and founded its own, parallel organisation. Both organisations withered away as a new, emerging order in South Africa started depriving the old bastions of their influence and power.

In 1994, the Broederbond was replaced by the Afrikanerbond, which strives to maintain the language, culture, Protestant values and service-oriented involvement of Afrikaners in national affairs. All secrecy was lifted, however, and there could no longer be any question of governing behind the scenes. The organisation still exists; among other aims, it seeks to link up with other minority groups with a view to partnerships.

A final – spicy – story about Nasionale Pers and the Broederbond: I was initially unaware that the *verligte* Lang David de Villiers, who was managing director of Nasionale Pers for 13 years, was a member of the AB. A highly respected jurist, he led South Africa's legal team in the World Court case on South West Africa (now Namibia), which he won on a technicality.

Occasionally, he acted as a judge.

But all was not well with his marriage to Tink, more's the pity. When he entertained colleagues or friends at their double-storey home in Belvedere Avenue, Oranjezicht, she would stay upstairs and not even come down to greet the guests.

Her passion was the Thursday-evening symphony concerts in the Cape Town City Hall. The company's official car was at her disposal so that she could have her hair done in the morning before the evening's concert. As far as one could tell, this was the only way in which she was still connected to Lang David in her capacity as our MD's wife.

After my arrival in Cape Town as Lang David's successor, I discovered that, on some days, he would take a long lunch and only return to the office at about 16:00. Members of top management would then be called in for business matters at his discretion.

This situation had arisen because of his affair with Rae Golding, the wife of a Cape Town specialist. Lang David and Tink, however, stayed married until the latter's death.

After Tink's death, David and Rae decided to get married. She and her husband had divorced in the meantime.

David wrote to the Broederbond with a somewhat odd request. The AB did not allow members to marry non-Christians; Rae was Jewish. David requested that his decision to marry her be condoned, with retention of his membership.

The Bondsraad approved his request. The chair at the time was Professor Pieter de Lange, who was also a director of Nasionale Pers and an open-minded individual. According to my information, this was a rare decision on the part of the Broederbond.

After their marriage, the division of the AB of which Lang David was a member would meet regularly at his Oranjezicht home. Rae was endlessly amused by the secrecy and the rules that prohibited her from coming near the Broeders, yet required her to put out tea and biscuits for their 'comfort break'. The cups had to be waiting for them under a cloth, and Lang David would make the tea himself.

When a meeting was due to held at their house, Rae would make a

On 24 September 1980 *Beeld*'s sales surpassed those of its archrival, Perskor's *Die Transvaler*. Here I'm taking a sip from a bottle of six-year-old sherry to celebrate the occasion.

A cartoon from 1993 by Rufus Papenfus.

LEFT: The horseman. As a reporter in 1959, accompanying a delegation to open up the way to the inaccessible Die Hel in the Swartberg mountains. The horse dumped me after about 100 metres and I reached Die Hel on foot and footsore.

BELOW: The inauguration of M-Net in Randburg on 21 November 1985. Koos Bekker (left) and me with filmmaker Jamie Uys (centre).

RIGHT: On holiday in France in 2007.

BELOW: I am a passionate cricket fan and was an opening batsman with more ducks than fifties behind my name.

ABOVE: The Vosloo family in war-time, 1942. Johannes Vosloo in Egypt with the South African Police Brigade, and Hetta with Freddie (left) and me. Sister Joan was born in May 1944, four months after the sudden death of our father.

BELOW: Next to my mother, Hetta, with my sister Joan (left) and my daughter Nissa (second from the left) on the balcony of our home in Northcliff, Johannesburg, in my *Beeld* years, in 1978.

ABOVE: The 1970–1971 class of Nieman Fellows at Harvard University in Cambridge, USA. I am standing fourth from the right in the front row.

BELOW: In 1983 I handed over the editor's chair at *Beeld* to Willem Wepener (left). I receive a bottle of *mampoer* as a farewell gift from David Moolman (right) and Thys Uys (second from left).

LEFT: My parents Hetta Pienaar and Jacobus Vosloo on the occasion of their engagement in 1928.

BELOW: As the political climate changed, Nasboek increasingly published books by former political opponents. Here Piet Beukes receives a copy of one of his books on Jan Smuts. To his left is Harry Oppenheimer.

On the roof of South Africa House in London during my first overseas trip in 1962.

The serious young journalist, captured by a street photographer in central Cape Town circa 1960.

ABOVE: Five editors of Naspers papers on the beach at Uilkraalmond in 1985. From left to right: Chris Moolman, Willem Wepener, me, Hennie van Deventer and Wiets Beukes.

BELOW: Receiving an honorary doctorate from the chancellor of Stellenbosch University, Elize Botha, in 2001.

ABOVE: One of the most momentous days in the history of Naspers: the listing of the company's shares on the JSE in September 1995.

BELOW: *Die Oosterlig*'s rugby team in Port Elizabeth in 1957. I am standing on the far right at the back.

I present a gift to Nelson Mandela during a reception in the Naspers Centre in Roggebaai, Cape Town.

ABOVE: The board of directors of Naspers in 2014. Front: Fran du Plessis; first row, from left: me, Ben van der Ross and Don Ericson; second row: Rachel Jafta, Debra Meyer, Fred Phaswana and Steve Pacak; third row: Boetie van Zyl, Cobus Stofberg and Koos Bekker; at the back: Craig Enenstein, Roberto de Lima and Yuan Ma.

BELOW: As chair of the World Wide Fund for Nature I acted as host to Prince Philip, the then worldwide chair of this organisation.

Anet and I.

ABOVE: I receive the president of Poland, Lech Wałęsa, during a visit of the Naspers board to Poland in 2014.

BELOW: When *Beeld* finally won the Northern press war that lasted from 1965 to 1983, Fred Mouton drew this cartoon.

Chatting to politician Adrienne Koch who claimed in an unpublished book that she persuaded prominent cabinet minister Kobie Coetsee to change his mind and release Nelson Mandela.

This cartoon from 1985 depicts the antagonistic attitude of the SABC chair Christo Viljoen towards me and M-Net. The SABC was by far the biggest media monopoly in South Africa, and M-Net the fledgling competitor.

As a member of the under-13 relay team of the Laerskool Jordan in Uitenhage, 1949, the primary school champions of the Eastern Province. From left: Johannes Mulder, Robert Crouse, coach-teacher Johnny van der Merwe, me and Johannes Potgieter.

special trip to Sea Point in the morning and buy kosher biscuits for the Broeders at a Jewish bakery. She saw it as a fun way of getting her own back on the secret guests. This is how Lang David's son David, the conductor, told the story to the writer Amanda Botha.

Lang David later had a good chuckle when Rae told him how the Broeders had been treated to Jewish biscuits.

The directives regarding the suitability of lovers and marriage partners, a core principle of apartheid legislation, crumbled completely in the years preceding and directly following the election of 1994. It must have been a great shock and embarrassment to the AB, for example, when Dr Piet Koornhof, a chief secretary of the National Party and later a Cabinet minister and ambassador, openly embarked on an affair with a coloured woman, Marcelle Adams, and fathered the couple's twins. It caused a sensation. The old National Party and its government kept themselves out of the matter, however, as they were working on their own dissolution.

Die Burger, 9 May 1975. Editorial written by Piet Cillié on the death of Bram Fischer in May 1975 (translation)

Bram Fischer, the deceased leader of the South African Communist Party, had a colourful, tragic life that is worth pondering by fellow Afrikaners in particular.

In the febrile war years, the then leader of the Ossewabrandwag, Dr Hans van Rensburg – by his own account – was asked at a small gathering of supporters to give his candid opinion of [their main opponent] General Smuts. Van Rensburg surprised them by saying that Smuts had all the qualities of a great leader: the intellect, the experience, the magnetism … all the characteristics, except one: he was not on their side.

Bram Fischer was of the calibre that a nation, a movement, a party would have liked to have on its side. So many of his qualities, including his origins and family background, were 'right'. In his youth he had also nourished the belief that he would remain on the side of the Nationalist Afrikaners.

The change – and to this a conscientious biographer would devote meticulous attention – occurred in the late 1930s, when it was fashionable, as it has become again in recent years, for bright and idealistic young people in the Western world to be radically left, politically and socially.

For most of them it was a phase, a childhood disease like measles that one shakes off, having acquired immunity to it for the rest of one's life. But for a minority of intense and committed young intellectuals, here and elsewhere, their embrace of communism was like a real conversion which they were forever after unwilling or unable to exchange for the uncertainties and doubts that had preceded it.

All the dogged tenacity and brilliant acumen with which he would surely have served the Afrikaans-Nationalist cause had he remained on 'our side', Bram Fischer threw into his pursuit of a revolutionary transformation of South Africa according to communist dictates. He not only became the Communists' leader, he was arguably also their best mind.

Through his loyalty to the cause through thick and thin, he became one of their and their fellow travellers' chief martyrs. His death, while he was serving a life sentence, has instantly earned him a place of honour in their Pantheon.

With his passing, we who are of his blood but detest his politics cannot escape from a sense of great sorrow about a prodigal son who failed to return. Sorrow, mixed with concern. Because Bram Fischer was a supreme and extreme example of a type.

There are others like him, individuals who, for the sake of a vision and an idea, either false of true (who always knows for certain in such matters?), sever natural bonds and connections, endure exclusion and growing hostility, accept new and undreamt-of behavioural patterns, and welcome persecution and martyrdom, as it were, as vindication that they are indeed in the right.

They are seldom among the worst in terms of how humans measure virtue, and often among the best and especially the most intelligent among us. Who was it who said that with the fall of man into sin, it was the intellect that was most affected? The tree of knowledge was in any case the one that was eaten from.

A nation that wishes to keep its bright, searching children on its side and in its service would pray for the necessary wisdom and love to help preserve the connectedness and prevent total alienation. Perhaps it may then be spared the terrible self-reproach that is palpable in David's lamentation: '… My son, my son Absalom … If only I had died instead of you!'

CHAPTER 12

Turbulence at Nasionale Pers

In the election year of 1987, the Nasionale Pers board was rocked by the decision of former MD, Advocate Lang David de Villiers, to lend his support to Dr Esther Lategan, an independent candidate who was set to oppose the National Party MP, Piet Marais, in Stellenbosch. When I succeeded Lang David in 1984, he had been invited to serve on the Nasionale Pers board after stepping down as MD, as was customary. So, he was a sitting director in 1987.

The 1980s were marked by high political tension, and people were casting about for solutions to the crisis in the country. Another independent candidate – Dr Denis Worrall, formerly of the National Party – stood against the Cape NP leader Chris Heunis in Helderberg.

With his decision, Advocate De Villiers called into question the founding policy of Nasionale Pers: to support the National Party through its newspapers. Nasionale Pers as an organisation would only finally detach itself from its political partner about seven years later.

During his tenure as leader, De Villiers had striven to shift boundaries. Now, he would resign from the board – a consequence of his decision to support an independent candidate that was confirmed by the chair, Piet Cillié.

The scandal and painful ructions that accompanied this event have to be understood in the light of the Nasionale Pers history outlined in the preceding chapters.

On his resignation from the board, De Villiers wrote to chair Piet Cillié: 'As you are aware, I have long had misgivings as to whether it is in the best interests of Nasionale Pers, and the cause that it serves, that its newspapers should remain so closely attached to a political party.'

He continued: 'On the basis of the view you then put to me about the role and duty of Nasionale Pers and its newspapers in this election, I have to accept irreconcilability.' Lang David therefore stood by his decision.

He then motivated his action as follows: 'It is bound up with the quest for justice for all the people of South Africa over the years. Now that it has proved that the justice ideal is not attainable through apartheid and separate development, there is a call for a clear alternative policy whereby the ideal can be attained.'

In a civilised, respectful letter, Cillié associated this decision of De Villiers's with a form of betrayal, and praised the latest adjustments to the NP's policy. Cillié's reply reads as follows: 'Just this: No one is better aware than yourself of the leadership that emanated and continues to emanate from these newspapers in what you call "a quest for justice for all South Africa's people". Often this quest was pursued together with the National Party, sometimes in parallel with it, and, when we had to: also despite tension with elements of the party.'

Cillié continued: 'Must we now betray our tradition of fighting alongside the party for South Africa as comrades in arms and demonstrate our proud independence as a press group by helping to dismantle the National Party just when it is about to contest a vitally important election? We do not support the party because we are its slaves, as you know, but because now of all times it is so evidently the best, even the only, available instrument for security, reform and welfare in South Africa.'

Seven years later, National Party rule as 'the only available instrument for security, reform and welfare in South Africa' was a thing of the past. Nasionale Pers's papers left PW Botha's dispensation for what it was and, well before 1994, dared to take the kind of threshold-crossing step Advocate De Villiers had sought to take in 1987.

These arguments of Cillié's in 1987 do show how conscientiously Nasionale Pers dealt with its history. Realistically speaking, there was no way that the transition of Nasionale Pers to a future without the National Party, even to an institution that helped facilitate the dismantling of National Party rule, could have happened without turbulence and a degree of remorse.

Advocate Lang David de Villiers was later proved right. In Lang David, the board dispensed with a great man in exchange for the observance of an outdated rule, namely that the full board had to support the National Party in everything.

Another interesting aspect of the commotion surrounding Lang David's departure is that his decision showed how a *verligte* approach could lead to a hopeful alignment with a new South Africa.

In contrast to the decisive break with the apartheid regime on the part of Afrikaner dissidents such as Bram Fischer, Beyers Naudé and Breyten Breytenbach, *verligtheid* sometimes amounted to brinkmanship. A *verligte* Afrikaner had shaken off the putative narrow-mindedness and laager mentality of the traditional Afrikaner, and was open to change. But were all *verligtes* really ready for the full consequences of a black assumption of power?

In the case of Advocate Lang David de Villiers, apparently so. In his years as leader, De Villiers had endeavoured to shift boundaries. A true *verligte*, he encouraged editors to campaign for a more open society. Editors were spurred on through word and deed to open doors and windows to all communities in South Africa, and to the world.

While De Villiers was still managing director, PW Botha, as Cape NP leader, was a member of our board. The two of them clashed frequently. Their differences led to an outburst in 1983, when Botha won countrywide support in a referendum among the white electorate for the introduction of the Tricameral Parliament made up of white, coloured and Indian representatives.

Botha was over the moon. When *Die Burger* carried a report on its front page the day after the referendum on De Villiers's commentary that, while the referendum was step forward, the great keystone, namely the incorporation of black people into central government, was still missing, PW exploded.

To Lang David, the criticism was water off a duck's back. This kind of *verligtheid* carried him over the threshold in 1987 when he announced his intention to support Dr Esther Lategan's election campaign. It was this kind of step over the brink that was demanded of the white electorate as a whole in the referendum of 1992, when a decision had to be made about negotiations with the ANC.

The turbulence of 1987 was called to mind again in 2016 on the death of Dene Smuts at the age of 67. Smuts had notched up 20 years of service as an outstanding parliamentarian. But prior to her entry into politics, she had been a top journalist at Nasionale Pers.

The turbulence surrounding her own position had started with De Villiers's resignation from the board in 1987. The shock waves spread when Smuts resigned as editor of the women's magazine *Fair Lady*. The successor of Jane Raphaely, the founder of this consumer magazine, Smuts gradually started publishing articles on politically controversial personalities of the time, such as Winnie Mandela.

On 24 March 1987, I received a letter from PW Botha addressed to me as managing director that illustrated what a close watch the government's security apparatchiks kept on things.

He wrote: 'It has come to my attention that a certain journalist who is employed at *Fair Lady* is working on an article that is to appear in the magazine before the parliamentary election of 29 April 1987.'

The article would deal with extra-parliamentary groups such as the so-called Five Freedoms Forum. This forum, which was formally established on 17 March 1987, was made up of Nusas, Jodac (the Johannesburg Democratic Action Committee), the Justice and Peace Commission of the Roman Catholic Church, the Black Sash, the Detainees' Parents' Support Committee, the Young Christian Students, the Wits Academic Staff Association, Jews for Social Justice, the National Education Union of South Africa and Concerned Social Workers.

PW wrote: 'Most of these names have already been mentioned by me in Parliament as being members of Jodac, which has strong ties with the UDF.'

He continued: 'I really hope that *Fair Lady* is not going to move further in that direction. It would be a tragedy if the government should be forced to act against *Fair Lady* on account of manifestly left-wing tendencies that radiate from that magazine and about which I have been receiving an enormous number of complaints in recent times.'

PW concluded: 'Your kind attention and that of your management would be highly appreciated.' I did not dignify the state president's open threat of censorship with a reply.

Shortly before the 1987 election, Smuts saw fit to publish an article that extolled the virtues of Denis Worrall. As *Fair Lady* was a fortnightly magazine, there would have been no time to publish a reply to the political article, as could be expected in all fairness. Someone at the magazine printing works had sent a proof copy of the article to the head of Magazines, Jurie Naudé, who brought it to my attention.

To me, the article went against the grain of a consumer magazine for women. Ethically and in terms of journalistic balance, it would have been wrong to run it without Worrall's political opponent being afforded a right of reply.

I requested Smuts to come to my office for a cup of tea, and pointed out the objections. She stood her ground and refused to withdraw the article. In that case, she knew what to do, she said. An assistant editor, Erica Platter, resigned with her. (Ms Platter and her husband later gained prominence with their well-known wine guide.)

My view that the political articles jarred with the nature of *Fair Lady* as a consumer magazine was consistent with several discussions Piet Cillié and I, as the managing director of Nasionale Pers, had held with Smuts. Our standpoint was that she was steering the magazine in the wrong direction by increasingly politicising it, with adverse consequences for sales.

Smuts had barely left my office when reports started streaming into the world that she had been politically censored and had quit her job on principle. A storm erupted. Among other things, I was sent a cover page of the 27 May 1987 issue of *Fair Lady* on which 'Butcher Vosloo' had been written in big letters with a black koki. Shortly after her resignation, Dene Smuts described me in front of the Cape Town Press Club as 'a Ton of bricks'.

The English-language press admonished me and Nasionale Pers from a supercilious height, as if they themselves had not often axed editors with whom they differed in principle.

The poet Antjie Krog also entered the polemic. She commented as follows on my action in a letter that was published in *Die Burger* on 16 April 1987: 'This kind of Mafia-like conduct makes one despair of the quality of the people who are currently ruling the roost in this country.'

I replied to her in a footnote and wrote inter alia: 'Ms Krog should just try to imagine her own reaction if the editor of, say, *Huisgenoot* or *Sarie* had to publish an article, on the eve of election day and too late for a reply in the same magazine, in which Dr [Andries] Treurnicht or Mr [Eugène] Terre'Blanche was eulogised as a potential saviour of South Africa.'

In reality, we at the Pers liked Dene Smuts and people like her very much. Piet Cillié had interesting views about her that he shared with seniors at a leadership conference of Nasionale Pers. I quote excerpts from his speech: 'She was a brilliant student ... There was talk about her very liberal views at Stellenbosch. (But speaking of liberal views, you should have heard me and Schalk Pienaar at Stellenbosch!) ... I thought, and I still think, that she is one of the best female talents we have had at the Pers since Rykie van Reenen, and that is very high praise indeed.'

He continued: 'You know, if we have to ask everyone at Nasionale Pers whether he is a Nat, we will lose a lot of talent. We will lose some of our best people, because it is always the dissenting man who has brains. Or rather: he wouldn't be bright if he were not a bit obstreperous. We want obstreperous people, we have to integrate them. They *have* to be different. We don't want everyone to be the same, otherwise we will stagnate.'

But Cillié was scathing about Smuts's political slant with *Fair Lady*. 'The women of today want politics ... but she approached it in the wrong way. There is a way of practising politics, but then you need lots of experience and insight ... but Dene Smuts didn't know how to do it. She didn't have the right feel for it, and so we had trouble with her from time to time.'

Cillié referred to a resignation letter Smuts had written six months earlier. 'At her suggestion the two of us went out for a meal, and we sat searching each other's souls in the Mount Nelson's Grill Room for three hours. After the soul-searching she withdrew her resignation, and then came the Worrall episode.'

A postscript about Smuts: On 13 April 1987 I received a note from her predecessor, Jane Raphaely. I had sent her a copy of Smuts's article on Worrall. Jane wrote: 'I felt it was boring, badly written and a waste of *Fair Lady*'s space. No one would have read it to the end.' Also: 'She has done you and Nasionale Pers a lot of damage though and I'm very sorry about that.'

On 9 April 1987 I went to state my case about Nasionale Pers's standpoint in front of a *verligte* discussion group in Stellenbosch – a critical audience. About the political debate, I said: 'It does not mean we are not allowed to publish any views of or articles on people who are critically active on the battlefield. Personalities are the lifeblood of magazines. But the articles should be expertly done and not injudiciously drag the magazine into the debate. Good judgement and common sense are the yardstick. We believe in a healthy, developing South Africa where discrimination on the basis of colour increasingly has to give way to co-existence on the basis of merit.'

On reflection, and with the benefit of a fait accompli, I have to admit that Lang David and Dene correctly judged the situation that was unfolding in South Africa by 1987. Nelson Mandela was released from prison on 11 February 1990. Within two or three years of 1987, organisations such as the ones in respect of which PW Botha had threatened to act against *Fair Lady* were participating in the discourse from which the new South Africa emerged.

I was on the *verligte* road, open to change and renewal, but not yet ready to accept the full consequences of the jettisoning of separate development. Under my leadership, Nasionale Pers did step over the brink, as Lang David and Dene Smuts had done. The Pers took the right steps and prepared itself for the situation that would obtain after 1994. We did not do so because we trimmed our sails to the wind, as commentators have claimed. We did so because it was the right thing to do, and because it was our duty, as a media organisation, to prepare the way for our readers and viewers.

How should I have acted in 1987 in the case of Dene Smuts? The answer struck me later. One day, someone at our book-printing works sent me an anonymous envelope containing page proofs of poems from a collection by Antjie Krog that we were due to publish. The proofs were accompanied by margin notes commenting on the indecency of the poems, the distasteful words and phrases, the shocking tenor of the poems, and the immorality. Naspers dare not publish something like this!

I notified the head of the printing works that he had to inform his people that proofreaders or typesetters were not evaluators of poetry collections or books. This would amount to censorship after the books had already been approved for publication, and could severely embarrass the experienced publishers of our group. The practice of forwarding complaints about works that publishers had approved had to stop forthwith.

This was how I should have acted in the case of Dene Smuts. The proofs of the Worrall article had been sent by the head of the magazine-printing works to the head of Magazines. The latter – and then I – should simply have conveyed the message that a printing plant cannot exercise censorship over an editor. And then I should have thrown the complaint in the wastepaper basket. My failure to have taken that route proves that Smuts was right when she called me 'a Ton of bricks'.

For the sake of the historical record, here are translated versions of the letters of Lang David de Villiers and Piet Cillié.

DP DE VILLIERS QC, Huguenot Chambers, 40 Queen Victoria Street, Cape Town, 11 March 1987.

Dear Professor Cillié

It is with great regret that I hereby tender my resignation from my position as a director of Nasionale Pers.

The circumstances under which this is done are already known to you from our conversations over the past days. For the record, I outline these again briefly below.

As I informed you, Dr Esther Lategan, an independent Nationalist candidate in the constituency of Stellenbosch in the forthcoming general election, approached me with the request that I support her with advice and some other assistance. Subsequent to my first conversation with you, she elaborated further on the nature of the support she would like me to provide. It involves no active political career on my part. Something like that would not have interested me in any case. But if I were to lend her my support, it would obviously become known. That was why I consulted you, in particular from the perspective of my membership of the board of Nasionale Pers. I value the confidential, amicable and frank spirit in which we could discuss the matter.

You were firmly of the opinion that rendering support to Dr Lategan would not be reconcilable with the continuation of my directorship. On the basis of the view you then put to me about the role and duty of Nasionale Pers and its newspapers in this election, I have to accept irreconcilability. As you are aware, I have long had misgivings as to whether it is in the best interests of Nasionale Pers, and the cause it serves, that its newspapers should remain so closely attached to a political party.

This is not, however, the opportune time to go thoroughly into this matter. I have to accept the irreconcilability in the prevailing circumstances: and as I feel called upon to accede to Dr Lategan's request in spite of your appeal to me, which has weighed heavily with me, there is no honourable way open to me other than that of tendering my resignation. It was not a decision that was arrived at without remorse. Nasionale Pers has been good to me, very good, and I am deeply grateful for that. For its people, my colleagues over many years, I have only the highest regard. The friendships that have been forged are among the best one could hope for: hopefully they will remain intact. The co-operation with you yourself has been extremely enriching. I would not have traded my nearly 15 years as managing director for anything else. That my directorship should now have to come to this sudden end is therefore traumatic.

The reason for my conduct lies deep. The standpoint of the independent Nationalist candidate in Stellenbosch and her leading supporters there represents to me the best in the thinking and idealism of the Boland Afrikaners, of whom I am and will always be one to the marrow. It involves a quest for justice for all the people of South Africa. Long ago that same disposition led to a preference for 'apartheid' above 'segregation' because the former was accompanied by an upliftment ideal that was lacking in the latter. In the 1950s it led to a demand for recognition of the principle of self-determination, including independence, for black homelands - long before the Government's policy had arrived at it. At the beginning of the 1960s it was responsible for calls for a fundamental review of the policy that had brought about so much alienation between Nationalist Afrikaners and the Coloured population in the previous decade. In each case *Die Burger* understood this disposition well and went along with it.

Now, after it has long been apparent that the justice ideal is not attainable via apartheid and separate development, that same disposition is calling for a clear alternative policy by which the ideal can indeed be attained. The people in question in Stellenbosch, like the other independent Nationalist candidates, believe, rightly or wrongly, that the leaders of the National Party have not progressed as desired in this regard - neither in terms of substantive policy content nor in terms of urgency. And they wish to give the voters in the constituencies in question the opportunity to demonstrate that, as far as they are concerned, the Government may safely move ahead more radically and with greater speed on the path of reform. Viewed in this light, their aim in this election is therefore also not one of ousting or dismantling the National Party.

Particularly in light of intensive contact with a wide spectrum of moderate black and brown leading figures, over many years, my own convictions have for a considerable time now, rightly or wrongly, been in line with those of the independent candidates. In these circumstances, I cannot turn down a request for some advice and help. It would be untrue to my conscience and the principles in which I believe.

You and other directors are fully entitled to disagree with me. Let us do so amicably. In so far as my conduct may cause you or Nasionale Pers embarrassment, I can assure you of my sincere regret. But I do not have the feeling that I am leaving you or the Pers in the lurch - only that we are probably trying to pursue the same ideal, but along ways that unfortunately have to differ. Hopefully these ways will converge again.

Please receive once again my heartfelt appreciation to you and your fellow directors for your co-operation and friendship and support through all the years.

My wish for Nasionale Pers is that it will at all times, according to its best traditions, continue to serve the whole of South Africa and all its people.

With warm greetings
DP de Villiers

PS: I leave the announcement of the resignation to you. The letter is meant for you and the board; but you have my permission, if you think it appropriate, to publish the letter (or an apposite abridged version, in consultation with me).

PJ CILLIÉ, Nasionale Pers Limited, 40 Heerengracht, Cape Town, 13 March 1987.

Dear David

Your letter to me dated 11 March 1987 was served at an ordinary meeting of the board (all present, except yourself) this morning (13 March). As chair, I was assigned the grim duty of conveying our reaction briefly to you.

We appreciate the mixed tone of friendship, gratitude and regret in your letter, and your insight that it is the honourable way for you to rather resign from the board.

As board, we do not intend to enter into a separate election debate with you on the matters you broach in your letter. There will be ample time and opportunity for that in the coming weeks via other avenues. Like you, we also believe that now is not an opportune time to go into the question as to whether Nasionale Pers's newspapers should remain 'so closely attached to a political party'.

Just this: no one is better aware than yourself – as is even apparent from your letter – of the leadership that emanated and continues to emanate from these newspapers in what you call 'a quest for justice for all South Africa's people'. Often it was a quest pursued together with the National Party, sometimes in parallel with it, and, when we had to: also despite tension with elements of the party.

But must we now betray our tradition of fighting alongside the party for South Africa as comrades in arms and demonstrate our proud independence as a press group by helping to dismantle the National Party just when it is about to contest a vitally important election? We do not support the party because we are its slaves, as you know, but because now of all times it is so evidently the best, even the only, available instrument for security, reform and welfare in South Africa. You acknowledge this yourself (albeit that you contradict it in the same breath) by saying that your friends' 'aim in this election is therefore also not one of ousting or dismantling the National Party'. What else are they doing by rallying the voters against leading reformists such as Minister Heunis and Mr Piet Marais?

We respect your wish to be true to your conscience and principles by complying with 'a request for some advice and assistance' for a Stellenbosch candidate in the upcoming election. We fear, however, that you might soon be dragged into a countrywide vortex of anti-Nationalist hysteria by forces outside of your control. I tried in vain to spell out the painful consequences for your name and reputation.

Be assured nonetheless that, when all is said and done, we shall never forget your excellent service as chief executive of our company over fifteen historic years. You were an initiator and builder of admirable and lasting things for which we say thank you once again at this moment of parting.

We also like to keep a light burning in the window for those who have left us but who may wish to return home someday.

With kind regards

PJ Cillié
Chairman

CHAPTER 13

Shock waves, a tsunami and ongoing ripples

No overview of my long association with Naspers would be considered adequate if I failed to refer to our experience with the Truth and Reconciliation Commission (TRC).

The TRC was instituted with the agreement of the majority of the political parties to uncover and address human rights violations that had occurred during the apartheid era. The sessions of the commission lasted from 1995 to 1997. Prosecution of all suspects was an impossible task. In the spirit of reconciliation following the 1994 election, it was decided to grant amnesty to people or institutions who testified and disclosed the truth about human rights violations during the apartheid years. Hence it would be in perpetrators' and suspects' own interest to testify before the commission. Victims would also be afforded the opportunity to testify, with a view to the restoration of their human dignity. Testimony about human rights violations on the part of both the apartheid government and the organisations that had fought against the apartheid regime would be heard.

It turned out to be a commission that sent emotional shock waves – and then a traumatic tsunami – through the country, with ongoing ripples that have continued to impact on our national psyche.

In a collection of essays that appeared in 2015 in Naspers's centenary year,[24] Tim du Plessis and I, two main actors in Nasionale Pers's dealings

SHOCK WAVES, A TSUNAMI AND ONGOING RIPPLES

with the TRC, both gave an account of the events. What follows is a more detailed version of my own contribution, as it appeared in the book.

On 30 April 1997, I received a letter in my capacity as executive chair of Nasionale Pers that was to cause me endless problems. The matter still haunts me after 20 years.

The letter came from Advocate Denzil Potgieter, chairperson of the media and communications committee of Archbishop Desmond Tutu's Truth and Reconciliation Commission.

I provide this account as a post-mortem and because it deserves a place in Nasionale Pers's history that spans more than a hundred years. All formal documents, letters, representations, contentions, criticism and countercriticism are on record. Historians can thrash out the whole affair in greater depth one day.

In Advocate Potgieter's letter, the media and communications committee of the TRC invited Nasionale Pers, like other press groups, to testify before the commission about the role the media had played in South Africa from 1960 to the election year of 1994.

I replied on 26 May 1997 that we would like to obtain clarity about certain aspects of the TRC's intended handling of the matter. Advocate Potgieter referred, for instance, to 'violations' that had to be pointed out and the TRC's aim to gain 'as complete a picture as possible of the nature and extent of such abuses'. This wording, I wrote, 'makes us uncomfortable, since Naspers wants to make it abundantly clear that it does not consider itself guilty of any violation of human rights or other concordant abuses'.

Advocate Potgieter replied reassuringly – there was no intention to engage in a witch-hunt.

I notified the commission that Nasionale Pers's role in our national history was available in full in the publication *Oor Grense Heen*[25] (Across Borders), which detailed the company's history over a period of 75 years. Furthermore, everything we had said about our national situation was available in our daily newspapers' archives.

I made a string of recommendations, at the request of the commission, on how the press could play a decisive role in future in helping to ensure a stable and just society.

Other press groups were obliging and testified before the commission. The Independent group (the old Argus group that was owned by the Irishman Tony O'Reilly at the time[26]) admitted that they could have done more, especially with regard to the treatment of their own staff and the representation of certain incidents during the apartheid years. The group offered its 'regrets' to all South Africans.

Then, the *Cape Argus* took a malicious swipe at us in an editorial on 16 September 1997: 'Conspicuous by their absence, however, are the actual allies of the apartheid regime, the Afrikaans press, which, in essence, has told the TRC to "go to hell". We hope the TRC will make a special note about this section of the press.'

The heat intensified when about 150 journalists and former journalists from our newspapers and magazines, acting in their individual capacities and not on behalf of Nasionale Pers, made a submission to the TRC in which they apologised for their role in maintaining apartheid.

So, Nasionale Pers – and I as head of the group – stood isolated as a bully who refused to testify. I had kept the board of directors informed throughout. They unanimously supported my standpoint and that of our senior newspaper editors.

In his book *A Rumour of Spring*,[27] Max du Preez cites Hermann Giliomee, who claimed that Nasionale Pers's board was unsure and could not decide whether to accept or decline the invitation to testify. Jeff Malherbe, a director with many years' experience in the courts and of the frailties of human nature, apparently persuaded the board with these words: 'Never bat on your opponent's pitch.' In other words, in the case of incriminating confessions the TRC is seeking to elicit, don't play along with the opposition.

As chair, I cannot recall whether Jeff, our senior director at the time, said these words. It was a favourite saying of his during discussions. If he did use it on that occasion, it would have summed up the board's unanimous sentiment.

My defence against appearing before the TRC was based on one word: loyalty. Loyalty to my present and past colleagues, our staff, our writers, both full-time and freelance, and to talented experts with diverse skills who were or had been in the employ of Nasionale Pers. Many people had made their mark on history through their contributions to Nasionale Pers publications, or through books we published.

Did I have to go and apologise on behalf of my colleagues who had driven the *verligte* movement, let alone the writers and poets whose books we had published? How could I implicate the work of luminaries, architects of the Pers, mentors and forerunners such as Piet Cillié, Schalk Pienaar, Rykie van Reenen, Willem Wepener, Danie van Niekerk, Koos Human, Maria Elizabeth Rothmann (MER), Alba Bouwer, Dirk de Villiers, Phil Weber, Willie Hofmeyr and Dirk Opperman, to name but a few, in an investigation into the violation of human rights, of all things?

This was a critical question. In the new, inclusive democracy, newspapers with capable and experienced journalists would be vital. Media that keep a close watch on the powers that be and think critically are indispensable to a viable democracy. Public hand-wringing about opinions that had been overtaken by time was not in keeping with the role the rapidly transforming Nasionale Pers was playing in the reformed South Africa.

Moreover, with its starting point of 1960, the TRC would take into account less than 50 per cent of Nasionale Pers's role in the history of South Africa. Nasionale Pers had formed part of a freedom struggle against the British colonial legacy that was not so radically different from that of other liberation movements in Africa. The entirety of Afrikaner aspirations that Nasionale Pers had actively elaborated from 1915 onwards needed to be assessed, not only a selected period. The TRC did not want to know about the Pers's contextual background.

Did I now have to keep silent about the spirit of loyal resistance prior to 1960, as formulated by Van Wyk Louw and put into practice by Nasionale Pers?

All these considerations contributed to my decision to make the studies that were on record and the archived files of Nasionale Pers's publications freely available to the TRC, but not to appear before the commission cap in hand.

Today, 20 years later, and after individual employees of Nasionale Pers have submitted their personal confessions and regrets about the past to the TRC, I have reconsidered my own line of argument and would like to make the following points:

The TRC highlighted many wounds and abuses through its investigations, and its approach led to healing.

I have said in many speeches since then that apartheid, as implemented by the National Party, had degenerated into an inhumanly cruel policy and deserved to be consigned to the dustbin of history.

It was wrong of us as a company and newspapers to have supported the policy for so long.

Today, I am saying loudly and clearly that we have to admit the error and apologise to our fellow South Africans.

We have to express appreciation to the leaders of Nasionale Pers, both on the management and editorial sides, who in critical years resisted unacceptable and sometimes horrendous aspects of apartheid.

Had it not been for the promotion of a *verligte* mentality and loyal resistance, FW de Klerk would never have been in the position to help lead South Africa to an inclusive democracy in February 1990.

Because of the previously mentioned factor, Naspers can stress anew the value of independent newspapers within a democracy.

Today, Naspers's company philosophy supports and serves an inclusive democracy. This should remain its governing principle in future.

The decision of the board that Nasionale Pers would not testify before the TRC in the manner requested by Advocate Potgieter had repercussions within the group itself. A number of the younger journalists in our group disagreed with my views and mounted a counteroffensive. The ringleader was Tim du Plessis, to whom I had long been a mentor.

I now give snatches of the piece Tim du Plessis wrote in Naspers's centenary year, with minor adaptations or additions where necessary.

According to Du Plessis, the 'TRC thing' – the dispute between top management and younger Naspers journalists – was probably destined to be hatched in *Beeld*'s newsroom in Johannesburg. While *Beeld* was a paper in the Nasionale Pers stable, it was also 'different'. The main difference was that, unlike *Die Burger* and *Volksblad*, it had never been an official mouthpiece of the National Party.

For years, numerous non-NP-supporting Nasionale Pers journalists had simply looked the other way. After all, the newspapers offered much more than the political commentary they carried. As apartheid grew increasingly intolerable, the traditional relationship between Nasionale Pers papers and the NP became problematic to more and more journalists.

The next major watershed after the 1994 election was the TRC's investigations into human rights abuses that lasted from 1995 to 1997. The TRC presented an opportunity for such violations to be settled conscientiously and without prosecution. Journalists at *Beeld* wished to seize this chance. They launched an initiative that cohered with *Beeld*'s tradition of making its voice heard at critical junctures. Their initiative obviously applied specifically to the investigation into the media's accountability.

Towards the end of 1996, the TRC announced its intention to hold a series of sessions that would focus on the role of the media during apartheid. Johan de Wet, a former editor of *Volksblad,* was editor of *Beeld* at the time. He would later also become editor of *Rapport.* De Wet headed what was arguably one of the most politicised newsrooms in the country. The intense workplace discussions about the TRC and other political issues were continued in the evenings and over weekends when colleagues socialised.

It was in this climate at *Beeld* that the TRC rebellion germinated. De Wet described the zeitgeist as follows: 'And when the TRC started talking about media participation, things naturally started buzzing at *Beeld*. The atmosphere was charged with suspense about how Nasionale Pers would respond.'

A part of the drama took place in a forum with the obscure name of the 'Kennis-legger'. This was a file in the editorial text system Nasedit that had been created as an electronic noticeboard, as well as a platform for editorial staff to exchange views on matters that affected the paper. Everyone had access to it.

The discussions spread to other editorial offices, although they never reached the same magnitude and intensity there as they did at *Beeld.*

It was clear that a significant number of Nasionale Pers journalists and ex-journalists – but quite possibly not a majority – believed that their company, given its ties with the NP, had an obligation to say something to the TRC, and that the sessions the TRC envisaged on the role of the media would be the right forum for doing so.

Du Plessis writes:

> Things came dramatically to a head on Friday 25 July 1997. We knew that out of the public eye, Nasionale Pers's top management and the TRC were engaged in a dialogue. We also knew that the board had discussed the matter, and had heard that the final decision about a submission to the TRC had been left to Vosloo's discretion.
>
> In his final reply, Vosloo wrote that the commission's assurances, 'together with our own standpoint that Nasionale Pers does not consider itself guilty of any violations of human rights or other concordant abuses, confirm our view that we have no confession to make or apology to give'.
>
> Vosloo's letter caused a huge stir, particularly among *Beeld* journalists and colleagues in other centres who felt Nasionale Pers was duty-bound to make a submission. The matter was fiercely debated in the 'Kennis-legger', in the cafeteria and at social gatherings.
>
> In September 1997, at a Nasionale Pers leadership conference at the Victoria Falls, Vosloo appeared for the last time as chief executive of the group. That evening an informal reception was held in a giant boma. During the pre-dinner drinks, Vosloo spoke to me and Lizette Rabe, then editor of the magazine *Sarie*. The conversation soon turned to Nasionale Pers and the TRC. I remember Vosloo said that not even Frederik van Zyl Slabbert thought it was necessary for Nasionale Pers to appear before the commission.

'It shocked me,' Du Plessis writes, 'because I attached much value to Slabbert's views. But I replied that it was all very well for Slabbert to talk; his record under apartheid was different from that of Nasionale Pers. Vosloo reiterated all the reasons why Nasionale Pers was opposed to participation.

SHOCK WAVES, A TSUNAMI AND ONGOING RIPPLES

Our conversation became heated, with Rabe trying her best to keep the peace – without success. Vosloo and I parted unamiably.'

He continues:

> To me personally, this was the first moment of quite a few as the drama unfolded. More such confrontational moments would follow, all equally intense. Vosloo had been my editor at *Beeld* for five years. More than that: he was also a mentor and a father figure – one of the finest people I knew. Knowing that you were at loggerheads with him was hard.
>
> Even before I was back in Johannesburg, however, I realised there was no turning back. Something would happen; no one knew what.
>
> The next moment, there was a proposal that we sell our Nasionale Pers shares and donate the proceeds to the TRC's 'restitution fund' – never mind that such a fund did not exist. Suddenly there was a practical option on the table.
>
> In 1994, when Nasionale Pers listed on the Johannesburg Stock Exchange, employees could buy shares at a discount. The proposal was that the 'donation' of our shares to the TRC's assumed restitution fund would be accompanied by a letter in which the donor stated: 'My company refuses to say anything about Nasionale Pers's past, but as employee: here are a few rand from my Nasionale Pers shares. This is my way of accepting responsibility for the past.'
>
> I told De Wet about our plan. I recall that he warned me in a fatherly tone of the implications, also as far as my career ahead was concerned. Yet he never left the impression that he repudiated us and our actions.
>
> De Wet was in an awkward position. He had worked with Vosloo for decades and was particularly loyal to him. But he was sitting with strong-willed members of his editorial team – including his two deputies – who disagreed with Nasionale Pers's approach.
>
> In an undated letter to Vosloo, presumably a few months later, De Wet wrote: 'The more I think about the issue, the more I realise that we should not be ashamed to say that we had made mistakes. Our newspapers *did* serve as cheerleaders of the NP, we *did* follow the

NP's lead for too long. And this *was* to our detriment.'

Weeks before the TRC media hearings were due to start, De Wet wrote in a column: 'But *Beeld* will also have to go and testify that it indeed committed occasional errors of judgement; that it indeed failed to inform its readers adequately at times; and that quite possibly it did contribute to a climate in which human rights abuses could be perpetrated.'

When asked about these views in July 2014, De Wet replied: 'What the journalists concerned did was their democratic right, even though I did not think the action they took was right. After all, some of the signatories had only started working at newspapers after the advent of the so-called New South Africa. Surely they could not have been co-responsible for what their journalistic predecessors did, or failed to do, in the name of apartheid.'

The question of loyalty towards Vosloo as an individual and Nasionale Pers in general was an additional, very important factor.

'With hindsight,' De Wet said, 'I realised that *Beeld*'s editorial approach – for which I had final responsibility – erroneously led the "petition" writers to believe that I would stand by them through thick and thin. This was a mistake.'

De Wet was also directly responsible for the next turn of events. He reported the 'share-selling plan' to top management, where, according to our information, it was noted with alarm.

De Wet then started acting as an intermediary between the dissidents and top management. During this process, a 'concession' was negotiated: Nasionale Pers journalists would be allowed to make submissions to the TRC as individuals, but they were not permitted to speak on behalf of the company.

We considered this a step forward, but soon realised that a miscellany of statements by individuals, most of whom were young and relatively unknown, would have no noteworthy impact. The 'concession' also failed to deal with our conviction that Nasionale Pers as a company had to accept responsibility for its role in the previous dispensation.

Du Plessis writes: 'From all the discussions, the idea emerged to draft a single submission that all those who wished to participate could endorse with their signatures in their individual capacities. It read as follows:[28]

> I, a journalist from _____, which forms part of Nasionale Pers, wish to make the following submission in my individual capacity and not on behalf of Nasionale Pers or any of its publications.
> I believe
> Reconciliation between and the just treatment of the different groups of people in South Africa are essential to nation-building in our country, and that disclosure of our past is an essential part thereof;
> Although the Truth and Reconciliation Commission is not perfect, it creates a much-needed process to deal with our divisive, unjust past as part of the transition to a fully fledged democracy based on justice, respect for human rights and the supremacy of the law;
> Since early this century a close relationship developed between Nasionale Pers and the National Party, with our newspapers acting as NP mouthpieces;
> Nasionale Pers's newspapers formed an integral part of the power structure which implemented and maintained the system of apartheid through, for instance, the support these influential newspapers gave the National Party running up to elections and referendums;
> The efforts Nasionale Pers made to change and oppose apartheid should also be acknowledged, as should the efforts to prepare whites for and persuade them to change and reform. This, however, does not diminish or neutralise the efforts to support apartheid;
> Although I was not personally or directly involved in gross human rights abuses, I regard myself as morally co-responsible for what happened in the name of apartheid because I helped maintain a system within which these abuses could occur;
> I, like many others, was blind and deaf to the political aspirations, anger and suffering of my fellow South Africans;
> I, like many others, and given the context in which I worked, did not properly inform readers of the injustices of apartheid, did not oppose

these injustices vigorously enough and, where I had knowledge of these injustices, too readily accepted the National Party government's denials and reassurances;

To all those who suffered as a result of this, I offer my sincerest apology and fully commit myself to prevent the past from being repeated.

The statement was printed on a page without a letterhead. Each signatory wrote his or her home address by hand at the bottom of the statement. The document was copied and circulated for a few days.

There is considerable confusion about the exact number of Nasionale Pers journalists and former journalists who signed the statement. It was generally accepted that there were 127 signatories. Professor George Claassen from Stellenbosch University's journalism department compiled a list of just over 80 names. The National Archives in Pretoria, where the TRC's records are kept, has a record of about 40 statements.

In the fallout from the submission bombshell, it was suggested that the more senior journalists in particular had lobbied for signatures and even put pressure on juniors. De Wet opined: 'As far as I can guess, the two deputy editors of *Beeld*, Tim du Plessis and Arrie Rossouw, cracked the "petition" whip. Peet Kruger, an assistant editor at the time, was presumably equally active behind the scenes, but was less prominent in public.'

By the time the statements were ready to be submitted, the TRC's sessions on the role of the media had been concluded. Christi van der Westhuizen, now a professor, and Adri Kotzé, a *Beeld* journalist who covered the TRC, were delegated to hand over the statements to the TRC.

Du Plessis sent a separate letter on a sheet of paper without a letterhead from his home address to Archbishop Desmond Tutu, in which he wrote inter alia: 'It should be emphasised explicitly that all the statements are made in an individual capacity. No one has been authorised to speak on behalf of Nasionale Pers or any Naspers publication. I would like to put on record that no employee of *Beeld* or of Nasionale Pers was threatened with dismissal if he or she were to make a submission to the TRC.' He signed the letter as 'Tim du Plessis, journalist attached to *Beeld*'.

Christi van der Westhuizen writes about the submission: 'I had to sign a document in confirmation of the handover. The administrative process confirmed the official status of the moment, which gave it an air of solemnity. Adri was with me, and I think both of us felt that a little bit of history was made that day.'

Within hours, Tutu issued the following statement:

> The Truth and Reconciliation Commission today received the submission which follows this statement, signed by 127 journalists from Nasionale Pers newspapers and magazines.
>
> The submission has been endorsed by journalists, in their individual capacities, from *Beeld*, *Die Burger*, *Rapport*, *Volksblad*, *Insig*, *Huisgenoot*, *Sarie*, *You* and *Fair Lady*, as well as a number of former Nasionale Pers journalists. We understand that more are expected to sign.
>
> Their submission is an extraordinarily powerful statement, and I welcome it on behalf of the commission and of victims of apartheid. While I understand they are not under threat of losing their jobs, I want to commend the journalists warmly for following their consciences in the face of very considerable opposition. Theirs is a very significant contribution to reconciliation and the process of healing our land.

The statement had barely been issued on SAPA when Du Plessis received a call from Hennie van Deventer, then head of Nasionale Pers's newspapers. 'He was furious about the uniform statement and that we had abused the concession to make individual submissions. You broke your word, was his accusation.'

Du Plessis writes: 'The following day, Saturday 27 September 1997, Vosloo said in a statement that was published in full in *Die Burger*:

> It is a great pity that some journalists were unwilling or unable to grasp Nasionale Pers's standpoint. In our discussions with the protesting editorial members, room was left for individual action. This is what has now happened. About 127 employees out of a staff complement of 7 000 felt compelled to confess.
>
> The action is of course welcomed by Dr Desmond Tutu and the

unbalanced TRC, because the individual petitions are virtually all identical and the document is completely one-sided in its silence on, for instance, ANC atrocities. Also, far from being individually driven, the action was orchestrated, and there is information about undue pressure on colleagues.

The document is a repudiation of great and honourable names in Nasionale Pers's long and proud journalistic tradition, and is regrettable.

In its conduct, the board of Nasionale Pers played its traditional role by forming a bulwark between its newspapers and vindictive politicians, and our colleagues could not or would not grasp this standpoint.

They have now achieved their goal, and the proof of that is the avid embrace of their standpoint by the TRC.

As far as Nasionale Pers is concerned, this matter has now been aired sufficiently.

Du Plessis continues: 'On 29 September, the following Monday, Vosloo brought up the issue at a lunch in Cape Town. Among other things, he said: "Also in my last week in the executive position I had to experience the pain of thoughtless disloyalty towards a great institution. It was a personal disappointment. But that was what I signed up for when I accepted the position, to experience the sweet along with the bitter."

'Yet the proverbial silence after the storm descended remarkably quickly. Soon all the rebels were again hard at work producing newspapers and magazines. None of the participants with whom interviews were conducted about this piece of Nasionale Pers history thought that they had acted incorrectly.'

Du Plessis writes that he has been asked on occasion whether, given the realities of present-day South Africa – endemic corruption, abuse of power, inefficient administration, defective economic policies, the arrogance of the ruling party, etcetera – he does not think that the dissidents made a mistake.

The answer is no. The new dispensation's mistakes, even transgressions, do not change anything about the injustice of the previous one. That was what had to be addressed. The two cannot be offset against each other.

SHOCK WAVES, A TSUNAMI AND ONGOING RIPPLES

A very important point that must be noted is that there were no reprisals against the 'rebels'. On the contrary: no one has any knowledge of signatories who were victimised. Three years later, Kruger and Rossouw became the editors of *Beeld* and *Die Burger* respectively.

Four years later, Du Plessis was appointed editor of *Rapport*, and subsequently also became editor of *Beeld*. Esmaré Weideman, who was co-editor of *Drum* at the time, not only became editor-in-chief of Media24's family magazines, but is now chief executive of Media24. Michelle van Breda became editor of *Sarie*. Many of the other 'dissidents' were promoted to important positions such as deputy editor, assistant editor and news editor. Ruda Landman was later appointed as a director of Media24.

Here and there, relations had become strained, but there was no lasting animosity. Du Plessis writes: 'This can be credited mainly to Vosloo's leadership and broad-mindedness. He is no ostraciser. He gathers people and binds them to a greater idea.

'In June 2014, when my employment contract at Media24 ended, Vosloo told *Rapport* we had indeed disagreed about the "sins of the fathers" with regard to the TRC. "We resolved that dispute, although my standpoint at the time still haunts me. Tim the Younger probably proved a point (or did a favour?) to Ton the Elder with his attack that has been common among humans and animals through the centuries: the youth challenging the elders," Vosloo said.'

Du Plessis concludes: 'Nasionale Pers's wrestling with the TRC was ultimately an important customs point and passport stamp signalling its departure from an old order, on a journey towards a new one.'

As a situation becomes further removed in time, it becomes possible to attach all kinds of skewed interpretations to it. A good example of such retrospective gimmickry can be found in a book on the supposed sins of the predecessor of the ANC government.

In 2017, an activist and director of a movement called Open Secrets, Hennie van Vuuren, drew attention with what he described as the private sector's economic crimes and human rights violations.

His 'revelations' appeared in a book, *Apartheid Guns and Money*. Here he reveals for the first time, according to publicity for the book, 'key donations by the private sector and companies to the National Party. The sponsors include individuals and organisations such as Christo Wiese, Johann Rupert, Nasionale Pers, Barlow Rand, Sanlam, Eric Samson (Macsteel), Bill Venter (Altech/Altron), Basil Hersov, Bertie Lubner (PG Glass) and others.'

To me, as former chair of Nasionale Pers and Sanlam, this is not news. There was a time during the sanctions years, for instance, that South Africans, both Afrikaans and English speaking, collaborated across a broad front to keep the South African economy afloat. Nasionale Pers was a supporter of the National Party from its inception in 1915. Over the years, the group's publications supported and built the NP with a political ideal in mind. There were also financial donations.

Sanlam did the same, because the Afrikaans-nationalist movement as a whole could not get going unless it had a supportive business base. All of this is ancient history, not secrets that are now being exposed 'for the first time'.

When the inclusive democratic system was at hand, I realised that more political parties than just the National Party deserved financial support. Nasionale Pers's Chairman's Fund started making new donations. The following conditions were set: parties that applied for support had to follow a healthy, open policy and subscribe to the Constitution. This included the endorsement of freedom of speech, an open economy and the concept of a multiparty state.

Parties that subscribed to these principles have received donations from us over the years. They include the NP until its demise; the old Democratic Party; the Democratic Alliance; the ANC; the Vryheidsparty; Bantu Holomisa's United Democratic Movement; and Mosiuoa Lekota's Congress of the People.

Do we have to apologise for these donations, too? Naspers had to come clean about its history. But we may as well be spared books which parade alleged sins long after the event, and which attest to the author's ignorance and misapprehension.

CHAPTER 14

Presidential tempers

When I think back on the presidential tempers I have experienced in South Africa, PW Botha tops the charts – ahead by the proverbial mile. I was one of many who got the sharp edge of his tongue.

One person who understandably denied that he had a short fuse was his first wife, Elize. In the biography *PW*,[29] Elize says, in reply to a question by the authors about his bad temper: 'Oh, those stories ... quick to react, yes. Strict, even implacably strict, yes. But can't people tell that when he sounds so cross, it is done deliberately? He does it for effect.'

Yes, Mrs Botha. Maybe your husband only sounded cross for the sake of the effect it was supposed to have. But with all due respect to you and your deceased status, do you have any idea of some of the consequences of his irascibility and uncontrolled outbursts?

PW Botha flipped his lid more often than was good for him (and for others). He would haul people over the coals and yell at them. In the end, he alienated almost all of his close friends. His explosive temper may even have led to the stroke that was to end his career.

Here is one example of the damage his uncontrolled outbursts could cause. In 1986, a group of people were lunching at Groote Schuur at the president's invitation. Politicians and diplomats of the so-called Big Five Western powers were being hosted. They were visiting South Africa to negotiate about the independence of South West Africa, now Namibia, and about South Africa's domestic policies. The overseas delegation had apparently made fairly good progress with the South African team headed by Foreign Affairs minister, Pik Botha.

Spouses had also been invited, and a convivial atmosphere prevailed. PW's clergyman was on hand to say grace. All went fairly smoothly until about halfway through the meal. Suddenly, Elize turned to PW and told him in Afrikaans that the guest on her other side, an American diplomat, was critical of our internal policies, or something along those lines.

PW saw red and confronted the diplomat half across Elize. The altercation became increasingly heated, PW's voice becoming louder and louder. Everyone fell silent except PW and the visitor. Things deteriorated to such an extent that the clergyman at the far end of the long table jumped to his feet and started praying for peace.

The lunch ended in chaos. Pik Botha was speechless, for a change. The foreign diplomats sat stunned. The Big Five took their leave unceremoniously; that same afternoon, it was announced that they were flying back home and the talks were off.

The negotiations had to be cobbled together again laboriously. This was but one of many occasions where PW's temper cost our country a lot of goodwill.

In his book *The Cape of Storms*,[30] former *Cape Times* editor Tony Heard describes Botha's outburst directly after Tsafendas had stabbed Verwoerd to death in the House of Assembly:

> An extra shock was also in store for Helen Suzman. Immediately after the attack, the lone Progressive MP was confronted angrily by Cabinet Minister PW Botha. In her own words to me, 'he came down the aisle of the House, stopped opposite the front bench in which I was sitting, wagged his famous finger at me and shouted: "It's you liberals, now we will get you all; you did it", and went storming out of the House'.

Mrs Suzman reported the incident to the secretary of Parliament, RJ McFarlane, who discussed it with the speaker, Henning Klopper.

Heard writes: 'Botha most ungraciously apologised to her in the presence of the speaker, saying: "In terms of the rules of the House I apologise."'

This high-handedness was not only reserved for PW's political opponents. One of PW's old friends, Dr Andreas Wassenaar, an Ossewabrandwag comrade of his at the start of the Second World War and later chair of Sanlam, wrote two bestsellers about the Nationalist government's poor economic and financial policies in his mature years. One was titled *Assault on Private Enterprise*.[31]

Wassenaar made an appointment to visit PW in Tuynhuys in order to present him with a signed copy of the book. The conversation started off jovially, Wassenaar told me. But PW grew increasingly irritable about the criticism, and he rejected Wassenaar's views.

PW became so incensed that Wassenaar gave up and said despondently: 'I think I'd better leave. But here is a signed copy for you.' Whereupon PW exclaimed: 'You can stick the book up your arse!'

According to Dr Connie Mulder, a fellow Cabinet member and, in 1978, a rival of PW's for the prime ministership, he had heard that PW was a *laatlammetjie*, considerably younger than his siblings. His mother had let him do as he pleased, as on the occasion when he rode his horse into the kitchen of the *bywoners* (tenant farmers) on their farm. When he was reprimanded by the people in the kitchen, his mother protected him. So, the young PW had been allowed to ride roughshod over others.

But the most vituperative dressing-down dished out by PW that I was involved in happened at the Union Buildings in Pretoria on 22 November 1983.

The two Afrikaans press groups, Nasionale Pers and Perskor, were very concerned that the state-controlled SABC had obtained the right to broadcast advertisements on its television service. The percentage of advertising per broadcasting hour was gradually increased, and newspapers were starting to fold because of the loss of advertising revenue. M-Net, which would later enable the press groups to benefit financially from television advertising, had not yet been established.

Our chair Piet Cillié, our managing director Lang David de Villiers, I as deputy MD and Jan Prins, head of our Newspapers, went to see PW, along with Perskor chair Willem van Heerden and CEO Koos Buitendag. It was supposed to be a friendly discussion.

To our great surprise, at the Union Buildings we were shown to the Cabinet room and found ourselves faced with almost the entire Cabinet. Owen Horwood, Pik Botha, FW de Klerk, Dawie de Villiers and Barend du Plessis were there. Also present were PW's secretary General Jannie Roux as well as his colleague Dr Daan Prinsloo, a former SABC journalist who later wrote a hagiography[32] of PW.

PW kept us waiting for a while. When he entered the room, we could see he was furious. He got straight to the point and started tearing into Lang David. The reason for PW's wrath turned out to be an article in the magazine *Leadership*. A few weeks earlier, Lang David had voiced his views about the dire situation in which newspapers found themselves in an interview with *Leadership*. The article had been published shortly before our discussion with PW. De Villiers had thought it fit to send copies to PW and to Pik Botha as minister in charge of the SABC with the idea that the article would familiarise everyone with the issue.

PW launched into a tirade and accused Lang David of having embarrassed the government by arguing the press groups' case in public before he had availed himself of the opportunity of a friendly discussion with PW. Perhaps PW thought that the interview was meant to put pressure on the government in advance. After reading the interview in *Leadership*, he had immediately ordered that our friendly discussion become a formal one. He had also asked the ministers with an interest in the matter to sit in on the meeting.

None of the ministers said a word.

De Villiers tried to explain to PW that his view of the situation was incorrect. By sending the article, he had merely wished to brief the president beforehand so that everyone would be prepared for the discussion, to save time. Both Cillié and Van Heerden also attempted to get the discussion about our concerns back on track in a calm and composed manner.

But PW kept ranting on against Lang David and all of us from the press. The discussion was summarily cut short. As leaders of Nasionale Pers and

Perskor, we were supposedly friends of PW and the National Party. It was of vital importance to the NP that our newspapers survived. We left the Cabinet room dismayed and disillusioned.

Outside the Union Buildings, I said to Jan Prins, a former rugby man, who was standing next to me: 'Jan, I'm reminded of the 1951 tour of the Springboks when they thrashed Scotland 44–0 and a Scot said afterwards: "We were lucky to get nil."' This was exactly how PW Botha had made us feel, mauled by his explosive temper.

Back in his office in Cape Town, Piet Cillié wrote a sharply formulated letter to PW Botha, his friend of long standing. Botha was a former director of the Pers and Cillié his fellow combatant in the Afrikaner cause. This letter of Cillié's is Africana, also in terms of its restrained yet stirring use of language. (See the translation of Cillié's letter at the end of this chapter.)

Botha wrote back, with no chance of a conciliatory tone.

On 1 December of that year, I summed up the letter as follows in my diary: 'In his reply, PW is surly and unfriendly towards Cillié. Rebukes him about a personal attack, yet leaves the door open for a personal conversation between the two of them.'

Among other things, PW had complained in his letter about the scant regard Nasionale Pers had for him after he had done so much for the Pers without compensation. The note on this in my diary read: 'He is lying, he donated his director's fee voluntarily and as a gesture to the National Party. And, as Cillié says, what didn't the Pers do for PW – we made him prime minister.'

I think Botha felt sorry about his behaviour: a few months later, in February 1984, he backtracked in a discussion with me and Cillié. He said he had been seriously offended by Lang David's article in *Leadership*, and also that we had handled the meeting clumsily – firstly, by raising the article that had stolen a march on the supposed friendly discussion. Lang David had spoken for too long. Moreover, Lang David has insulted members of the Cabinet and officials by saying he hoped the figures he mentioned would remain confidential.

Cillié retorted: 'Yes, but you had rattled him beforehand, so he was put off his stride.'

They did tease each other good-naturedly about their exchange of 'friendly' letters. PW said that, although he was annoyed at the time, he had decided that he and Cillié were too old and close to death to be enemies.

The matter was settled with a proposal that the SABC CEO Koedoe Eksteen and I hold talks and try to find common ground. Then we could submit a proposal to PW for discussion in the Cabinet.

In November 1984, PW vented his spleen about articles our newspapers had been publishing about public servants' remuneration. As a shareholder of Nasionale Pers, PW demanded information from me about the remuneration and fringe benefits of our top management. He probably wanted to be able to prove how much better off the private sector was.

I provided PW with the full details. He did not respond directly, but tore into us about an editorial in *Beeld* of 3 December 1984. After a by-election in Primrose, Germiston, in which the NP had lost ground to the new Herstigte Nasionale Party, *Beeld* wrote an editorial titled: 'Just a little humility'. The editorial concluded with this sentence: 'Our politicians would do well to remember that you cannot yell at people until they vote for you. Just a little humility (or even a little love) would yield much better results.'

PW's whims and outbursts could blow over, however, and did not always lead to irretrievable relationship breakdowns. This is illustrated by an invitation to Piet Cillié to attend a function of the Bible Society where PW was to be the host.

Cillié's sharp letter to PW after our visit to the Union Buildings on 22 November 1983 was still hanging in the air. If, in light of the letter, PW did not want him to attend the gathering of members of the Bible Society, Cillié wrote to PW, he would understand and register an apology. Cillié showed me his letter. He subsequently tore it up and attended the function anyway. No offence had been given or taken, Cillié told me later.

Another example of PW's irascibility follows. As in the previous case, it shows that his anger was sometimes short-lived and could subside, but often after the damage had already been done.

In response to a 'Dawie' column in *Die Burger*, PW phoned me and said he had had it with *Die Burger*'s editor Wiets Beukes. 'I won't phone him again. I'm going to ignore him. My wife and I were about to donate R1 000 to *Die Burger*'s Christmas Fund, but not any more, my heart is troubled.'

But the very next day, 4 December 1984, I received a positive letter from PW with an appendix consisting of the announcement by Pik Botha that the government would appoint a task group to consider the introduction of a pay-television service. This step led to the founding of M-Net in 1985, a development that, for years, immeasurably assisted the owners of daily papers in South Africa to hold their own against the electronic media.

In October 1985, however, our papers came in for another round of insults. PW called me on a Sunday morning and said he wanted to get a few matters off his chest. He was fed up with *Rapport*, and his office was now closed to its editor Wimpie de Klerk. How could he rely on us? *Rapport* was now just an old 'Sap' paper. Furthermore, he said, he had always made time for our other editors such as Wiets Beukes (*Die Burger*) and Willem Wepener (*Beeld*) and given them background information about national affairs in a good spirit. But at the first opportunity to defend him, they criticised him instead.

He added: 'If the pay-television decision had been on the Cabinet agenda a few days later, I would have wrecked it myself.'

Getting into his stride with accusations and insults, he also hit out at academics at Stellenbosch University. 'I didn't want the chancellorship. I was forced into it. I was begged. People came to me with petitions. People came personally to ask me, like Piet Cillié. I'm now a bitter man. When I go, I'll make all these things public so that people can see how hypocritical the Stellenbosch people are.'

How did I react to this outburst at the other end of the telephone line? My notes read: 'I to-ed and fro-ed, but PW worked himself up more and more. What I always tell myself after such conversations is that getting things off his chest probably has therapeutic value for him and he most likely feels better afterwards.'

The following incident may have indicated the effect that PW's explosive temper had on his health. It looked, in any case, like a prelude to his later stroke. On 30 August 1984, a State Bible was solemnly handed over at a ceremony in Cape Town. The Bible (number one) had 24 pages at the front on which the state president's oath was printed in both official languages. Special goatskin paper, guaranteed to last for 500 years, had been used for this section. It was the only State Bible in the world in which a state president confirmed his oath of office with his signature, along with that of the chief justice.

I was at PW's side at this event. When he had to sign his name, I noticed that his hand was shaking badly and his signature resembled a mangled scrawl.

A few days later I received a call from Martin Koekemoer from Botha's office. He asked to see me in confidence, and arrived with copy number one of the State Bible. PW had botched his signature because he had signed the Bible in a stooped position, Koekemoer explained. He requested that the problem be fixed urgently.

I took the matter up with our printing works and the calligrapher. They cut out the spoilt page and replaced it within an hour. PW appended his 'correct' signature. Everything had to be done in great haste because the chief justice was due to fly overseas that evening, and his signature had to be obtained again as well.

Martin Koekemoer addressed a request to me: 'It should never leak out that PW botched his important signature.' Well, I have leaked the story here anyway, after 33 years.

Among PW Botha's predecessors, HF Verwoerd stood out as a prime minister who never lost his temper. A frosty glare from those ice-blue eyes was enough.

John Vorster could grumble, sometimes in an overly touchy manner. But he never launched into undignified outbursts. Towards South Africa's English press, however, he was extremely hostile. He referred to them as the 'English pest'.

The era of PW Botha was followed by the leadership of FW de Klerk. Then came the settlement with the ANC and the rise of Nelson Mandela,

Thabo Mbeki and Jacob Zuma. The new heads of state I would get to know on another level, as my involvement in journalism was far in the past by the time they assumed office.

I got to know FW de Klerk at an early stage of his career in my capacity as a political reporter. Prior to his parliamentary days, he was national chair of the Junior Rapportryers movement and not yet the *verligte* mind that would lead South Africa's white electorate towards an inclusive democracy. In the Transvaal, the Junior Rapportryers was an organisation that inclined in a far-right direction at times. Among their ranks were young men who later revealed themselves as staunch *verkramptes*, fellows who would throw their weight behind Albert Hertzog and Jaap Marais.

In 1967, I represented *Die Beeld* at a Junior Rapportryers congress. I reported on the organisation's contentious decisions and was criticised for 'inaccurate' reporting. FW as chair made an appointment with my editor Schalk Pienaar to complain about the matter.

Pienaar called me in beforehand and asked where I stood. I showed him my notes and said I was convinced that my reporting had been spot-on. That was Pienaar's style: always acting as a shield for his reporters, but also making a point of establishing whether your facts checked out. Woe betide anyone who failed to report truthfully.

FW de Klerk got a civil reception in Schalk Pienaar's office. But he left unsatisfied. Years later, FW told me that Pienaar had a least written a nice, positive report about him as a young leader.

My encounters with De Klerk were invariably courteous and civil. That is the kind of person he is. Because our papers supported his *verligte* political direction, there were never any unpleasant clashes. Izak de Villiers's right-leaning leadership at *Rapport* was the only problem.

President Mandela was equally courteous and dignified in his dealings with us. My interaction with him started after his release when, in my capacity as company chair, I invited him to a breakfast with our editors and seniors in Johannesburg.

I organised a breakfast at a Johannesburg restaurant for 08:00. Just after 07:00, I went to check whether all the arrangements were in order. And there was Mandela, dressed in a grey suit, sitting ramrod straight on a couch in the foyer! He laughed and said he was accustomed to a prison schedule, which meant getting up at the crack of dawn.

At the breakfast, I asked him what he wanted us to order for him. Every kind of breakfast food was available. 'I would like some fresh fruit and then mieliepap.' The embarrassed restaurant staff told me they only had cold cereals, no cooked porridge. It was my fault; I should have asked Mandela beforehand about his dietary preferences.

He told me that, since his prison years, he had only some porridge and a cup of tea for breakfast. This was his morning diet, and it kept him healthy.

We subsequently organised another meeting with Mandela, at a restaurant in Pretoria's Fountains Valley. Our group's head of public relations, Anet Pienaar, put a great deal of effort into arranging the lunch and forum event, with many guests.

Then, a telephone call: Mandela notified us regretfully that he had to cancel his attendance. His divorce case with Winnie Mandela was being heard in the court that morning, and his presence was required. The disappointed guests had to eat without the guest of honour.

On another occasion, he came to eat with us as our guest at the Naspers Centre at 40 Heerengracht in Cape Town. The news spread like wildfire through the building. The foyer and every corridor were crammed with employees and outsiders who wanted to touch the great man.

In our dining room on the 18th floor, Mandela turned serious and he lambasted us as an institution and our newspapers for supporting apartheid. He was quite icy. But then he became cordial and told our directors and senior executives how a 'Dawie' column by *Die Burger* editor Wiets Beukes had helped him cut through a knot with FW de Klerk and his team.[33]

I replied to him as host, and dealt cautiously with the issue of our institution's association with the previous regime and our comrades-in-arms relationship since 1915.

One treasure that hangs in the corridor of the Naspers head office is a framed letter that Mandela wrote. During his years as a prisoner on Robben Island, he had studied and read widely; Afrikaans literature was among the topics he studied. He had written a letter to Tafelberg Publishers in which he requested certain collections of poetry. As a gift, the publisher Danie van Niekerk, a refined gentleman, sent Mandela the *Groot Verseboek* anthology of Afrikaans poetry that included poems by Ingrid Jonker.

Mandela thanked Van Niekerk in excellent Afrikaans and mentioned the impact that a poem by Jonker had had on him. In his inaugural parliamentary address as new president, Mandela quoted Jonker. The reports on his speech flashed around the world, thereby introducing Ingrid Jonker to the international community.

I suspect that the Cabinet secretary, Professor Jakes Gerwel, had a hand in the reference to Jonker's poem in the speech. Jakes was an Afrikaans literature scholar, and later joined the Naspers board at my invitation. He was an excellent director and later chair of Media24.

A further word about Jakes: In earlier years, I used to bump into him frequently at airports, even overseas. I knew he was studying for a doctoral degree in Brussels. We both hailed from the Eastern Cape, and we got on very well and forged closed ties. Only much later would I discover that Jakes had been a courier for the ANC on the sly, carrying messages to comrades overseas.

After our initial meeting, Mandela and I often got together at Mandela's request. At times, he was very lonely in his Cape Town residence. He would then call out of the blue and invite me to visit him for a light lunch and a chat. Included in these memoirs is an article I wrote for *Rapport* about a day trip with the former president across the Cape Province.[34] I salute him: a remarkable human being.

I met former president Thabo Mbeki on various occasions, with or without Afrikaans leaders and businesspeople. He was always courteous and an excellent listener. He had a good understanding of the Afrikaans heritage and Afrikaners' contribution to the new South Africa. Among his greatest confidants were Afrikaners such as Professor Willie Esterhuyse from Stellenbosch. Esterhuyse writes extensively about the behind-the-scenes encounters that preceded the formal negotiations for a new dispensation in his book *Eindstryd*,[35] which was published in English as *Endgame*. A movie with the same title was made about these secret talks in 2009.

I met Jacob Zuma twice, while he was still deputy president. On one occasion, Van Zyl Slabbert, Hermann Giliomee and I went to see him in Luthuli House in Johannesburg about the issue of Afrikaans and Afrikaans universities. He smiled good-naturedly, called in younger colleagues who made notes, and promised that we would hear from him. In the case of both meetings, there was never any follow-up communication from his side afterwards.

I conclude this chapter with the letter Piet Cillié wrote to PW Botha in 1983. This was Cillié's hand-written version, which his secretary would have typed up neatly.

Letter from Piet Cillié to PW Botha, November 1983

Dear PW

I write to you in a highly personal vein, friend to friend, about Tuesday's discussion in Pretoria. I do so in order to clear the air and mend the relations. If my letter is not conducive to that, tear it up and forget about it.

I requested a confidential discussion with you and a few key ministers on behalf of Nasionale Pers because we wished to have a heart-to-heart conversation with you as political comrades in arms about the implications of an increasingly pressing problem for our joint cause. It is the strangulation of especially daily newspapers by the growing encroachment of TV on the total advertising market, beside a few other concerns.

This is of course a national problem that affects the entire newspaper and magazine industry, but the Afrikaans-Nationalist Press in particular. For that reason it is also of vital importance to the Government and to our Party.

The general problem has already received considerable airing in broad outline, and is by no means confidential in nature. I broached it in my latest chairman's report, and when Nasionale Pers was asked by the President's Council to give evidence on the role of the press in the new dispensation, it was one of the points that were extensively addressed in a public submission by the three officials who accompanied me to the discussion in Pretoria: David de Villiers, Ton Vosloo and Jan Prins. Their evidence was widely covered in the press at the time, without causing any sensation.

The article David wrote for *Leadership* was nothing other than a mere summary, on request, and already submitted months ago, of what has been said before in public from our side. It was by no means written with a view to our discussion, which in fact had not even been arranged at the time. We decided at a late stage to provide the government participants in the Pretoria discussion with copies beforehand to orientate them briefly, with the idea that from this basis they could explore a fruitful future course together with us.

None of us, nor Perskor's men who had joined us, detected any offence to either you or the government in the article. After all, it is the most natural thing in a living society that there are constantly problems arising that need to be brought to the attention of the authorities because they necessitate new thinking and policy making or policy co-ordination.

We (and Perskor's men along with us) were therefore stunned and dismayed by your reaction as it was shown at the meeting. We did not in the least expect an atmosphere of hostility and confrontation in which reasonable discussion and mutual influencing would become practically impossible.

You chose David's article as the particular target for your painful remarks, but in this matter Nasionale Pers stands united, with the result that the four of us who were there all carry the wounds of the blows you struck. They hurt all the more because it happened in such a broad circle, few of whom could have been properly aware of the give-and-take and the frank clashes that sometimes occur in our relations and that we have learnt to process over the years. Some of those who were present might well have gained the impression that Press and Party (or Government) live in a state of full-scale enmity. Some of your colleagues were visibly embarrassed and concerned.

In the two-hour discussion, not a word of friendship or goodwill towards Nasionale Pers was heard, only disparaging remarks such as that the Pers come to ask you for 'kado'tjies' (your word) [handouts] in a time of war, and an insulting suggestion (help me if I misunderstood) that from now on you won't be prepared discuss an urgent joint problem with the Managing Director of the Pers. Even if we had wanted to fight (and, once and for all, we did not want to) the terrain was such that out of courtesy and respect we could not do so.

If we were to convey our honest impressions of the event to the Pers's people (which I shall try to prevent at all costs), and the SABC's men were to do the same in their circle (which I cannot obviate), there would be nasty repercussions for all concerned.

It is a great pity that the subject that was under discussion, and which in the judgement of our delegation is vital to the national interest, could not enjoy the constructive attention it deserved. What we got instead was misrepresentations that all is well and going swimmingly. I think your experience has taught you that such complacency in the face of problems is always a danger sign. When has Nasionale Pers ever, either publicly or confidentially, brought a problem situation to the Party's or the Government's attention where we were seriously mistaken?

Therefore I am glad and grateful that you have held out the prospect of further engagement, on your initiative.

You know how much hope and faith I personally and the Pers in general put in your leadership of South Africa. You have grown in your office to a stature that is increasingly becoming comparable to that of your greatest predecessors. Hence it upsets us exceedingly when things occur that fall short of our high opinion and expectations of you. On my part, I always allow for the unknown pressures, tensions and irritations under which you have to live. For the rest I can only pray, for what it is worth, that you may be preserved from all conduct that is unworthy of you.

Kind regards, and strength to you,
Piet Cillié

CHAPTER 15

Hit the big story hard!

Nasionale Pers's daily in the North, *Beeld*, was launched on 16 September 1974. From the outset, the paper was distinguished by its fresh and direct news presentation. The political orientation of the editorial team, led by Schalk Pienaar for the first three months, was unashamedly *verlig*.

Expectations were high that the paper would swiftly gain ground in the market. But the rival papers pulled out all the stops in defending their territory, including 'Syferfontein'. Under this name, Perskor's circulation fraud created a misleading picture of the difference between the circulation figures of *Die Transvaler* and *Beeld* and became a big story in its own right in 1980. It took quite a few years before *Beeld* finally managed to gain the upper hand over its rivals – or so it appeared because of Perskor's deception.

Beeld's journalists had ample opportunity to hit a big story hard. What this journalistic outlook comes down to is a paper's energetically focusing its attention, time and human resources on a big breaking news story. If it is a developing story, a paper that goes all out in this way can scoop others with the best information about a topic that causes public excitement.

A paper that hits big stories hard stimulates interest and makes its readers sit up. This approach need not detract from the thoroughness, reliability and value of the information in its reporting – on the contrary.

In a fiercely competitive market with several rivals, we had to find a strategy that would enable us to pip our rivals at the post. In practice, hitting the big story hard meant working smarter and harder, and co-operating better, than the competition. As my good newspaper friend, the late Koos van der Merwe, used to say: it's that fleck of foam on the racehorse's nose that wins it the race. In our race for superiority, we consistently caused that fleck of foam, the effect of committed exertion, to appear on the horse's nose. This modus operandi became part of *Beeld*'s DNA.

When a big story broke, the entire *Beeld* team would roll up their sleeves. No one would dream of leaving the office by 17:00 or 18:00. You would call home to announce that the editorial staff would be burning the midnight oil; put the food in the warming oven, darling. These words, which I borrow from Marita van der Vyver, aptly epitomise 'hitting the big story hard'.

Like a rugby team that keeps mauling towards the try line, over a period of ten years we competed against four Afrikaans newspapers in a circulation war. Ten years after *Beeld*'s founding, I could at last declare proudly: 'I think *Beeld*'s record speaks for itself.'

Our modus operandi is well illustrated by the case of David Protter – Dave Protter, as he is more commonly known.

On the morning of 28 April 1975, news editor Hennie van Deventer received a tipoff that a siege was in progress at the Israeli consulate in Fox Street in the Johannesburg city centre. South Africa was extremely security conscious in those years. A crisis at the Israeli consulate immediately raised the spectre of terrorism. Jack Viviers, head of our crime team, had his contacts in the so-called security community. He notified us that this was a story that would spread internationally.

We activated a formidable team. Our journalists and photographers went all out to get as close to the action as possible. The horse ran, foam on its nose.

The story comprised dramatic events, a nail-biting two-day wait for the resolution of the crisis, tragic consequences and the involvement of prominent people, including foreign political leaders. It was a sensation, with a variety of facets that our team could investigate and follow up.

Beeld's issue of 29 April 1975 carried the banner headline: 'Hel los aan Rand' (All hell breaks loose on the Rand). That day, we sold 102 402 copies, a record figure.

What happened was that a security guard at the consulate, David Protter, had taken employees hostage. He demanded to speak personally to Israel's prime minister, Yitshak Rabin, about the lax security at the consulate. He also wanted to advise the premier about how to deal with Israel's political problems. He was clearly a mentally disturbed individual, someone who lived in a world of his own.

Protter held 21 staff members of the consulate hostage for 17 hours, shot a security guard dead and fired at people in the street with his Uzi submachine gun. At the end of the two-day siege, four people were dead and 82 injured. Dave Protter, who was 27 years old at the time, was taken into custody.

The response of our security services was naturally part of the drama, and therefore part of the news story we could hit hard. The South African Police deployed its counterinsurgency team. General Lang Hendrik van den Bergh, the renowned chief of the Bureau for State Security and a flamboyant publicity hound, arrived in person.

What followed after Protter's arrest extended the life of the big story. He was charged with murder and attempted murder, but the judge found he was a psychopath, on the basis of expert evidence, and sentenced him to 59 years in jail. Protter served 15 years of his sentence before his release in 1991 after a panel of experts decertified him as a psychopath.

Remarkably, David Protter recently made the news again, from a fresh angle. Owing to a capable journalist's open ears, sharp eyes and good nose for a story, *Rapport* was able to disclose brand-new facts about Protter on 14 August 2016.

Thanks to Hendrik Hancke, who reported on Protter's later life in *Rapport* on 14 August 2016, we know that, in the years since his release, the deranged terrorist of 1975 has morphed into the 'armed hero' of Tzaneen. Protter owns a rapid-response security company. He has an arsenal of weapons at his disposal. Addressed as 'Colonel' Protter in that neck of the woods, he is the go-to guy in the event of serious trouble.

According to the article, Protter has received high praise from former police officers. Retired superintendent Willie Willers said they were grateful that Protter was helping to bring criminals to book. Once, he even defused a highly explosive taxi war.

In 2002, when she was still a councillor for Tzaneen, the DA parliamentarian Désirée van der Walt wrote: 'It is but once in a lifetime that one has the privilege of meeting someone whose life revolves around saving lives in his community at all costs.'

A news story that is hit hard, and thus also followed up to wherever it may lead, can be a journalistic gift that keeps on giving. This is undoubtedly true of the story of Dave Protter, the erstwhile killer who ended up making a name for himself as a protector of lives.

'I have been working hard in this community for 25 years in an attempt to make up for my actions in 1975,' Protter told Hancke.

And about his conduct at the time: 'Nothing I can do would compensate for the people who lost their lives as a result of my actions. Nothing. Still, I have no option but to try and make amends for that by continuing to provide a much-needed service to the community.'

Beeld's hard-hitting coverage of Protter's gruesome act in 1975 enhanced its reputation as an alert reporter of newsworthy events and a lively, highly readable paper. On top of that, it made for a day of record sales, proving *Beeld*'s potential to become the biggest Afrikaans paper in the North. After 42 years, the story of David Protter lives on, with an astounding twist. It exemplifies how far good journalism can reach.

The assassinations of NP politician Robert Smit and his wife Cora in the run-up to the general election of 1977 is another example of a big story. Smit and his wife Cora had been shot at their home and then stabbed, and the words 'RAU TEM' had been sprayed on the wall with red paint. *Beeld*'s competent coverage of the horrific story considerably boosted our sales. These politically motivated murders were never solved, and have remained a mystery to this day. Numerous rumours and speculative theories about possible culprits and scenarios have emerged over the years.

I became editor of *Beeld* in 1977. During my tenure, our paper kept growing its sales by striving, through diligence and teamwork, to extract everything from important news events that would inform readers but also grab their interest. By concentrating on cutting-edge stories and presenting the news in a lively, contemporary idiom, we steadily made headway.

Accordingly, we continued hitting the big stories hard. The bonfires of joy and excitement burnt high in *Beeld*'s reporting when our own Miss South Africa, Anneline Kriel, was crowned Miss World in November 1974.

Then came less happy news that nonetheless also called for powerful, hard-hitting journalism – and received it from *Beeld*: the Soweto uprising of 1976. The Information Scandal of 1978 that led to the fall of the Vorster government. The turbulence that preceded PW Botha's election as prime minister. The Laingsburg floods of 1981 that claimed the lives of more than a hundred of the town's residents. Each of these landmark stories was powerfully portrayed in terms of news coverage, photos and commentary.

After my years, *Beeld* continued its tradition of hitting the big story hard. Think of the time of terror, when a car bomb was detonated in front of the Air Force offices in Church Street, Pretoria, killing 19 people and injuring 188. In 1985, a school bus drove into the Westdene Dam in Johannesburg; 42 learners from Vorentoe High School drowned. In November 1987, the *Helderberg*, a South African Airways Boeing, crashed into the sea, killing all 159 people on board. In 1988, Barend Strydom, a former police constable, fired randomly at black people on Pretoria's Strijdom Square, causing fifteen deaths. Events such as these were conveyed by means of news coverage, illustrations, typography and commentary that did justice to their dramatic force and significance.

Beeld is still the leading Afrikaans newspaper in its distribution area. It continues to present the news that matters in a way that inspires readers' trust. It documented South Africa's transition to a full democracy in 1994, for instance, in full. *Beeld*'s archives are an important database of detailed knowledge about that era.

A final general remark about 'hitting the big story hard': *Beeld*'s sister papers, notably *Die Burger*, tended to react rather snootily to what was seen as *Beeld*'s sensationalist approach. Of relevance here was the difference between the South and the North, in terms of the kind of readership to which an Afrikaans paper had to adapt.

The Boland was a place of green landscapes and blue sky where old families, old farms, old schools and universities, and large middle-class communities had long been established. It was a scene of tranquil rural towns and relatively affluent urban areas. Many of its people were acquainted with one another on a social or public level. The region was a far cry from the hard, impatient North, with its fast pace, its mineworkers and factory workers, its huge contrasts between socioeconomic classes and ethnic groups, and its barren winter landscapes.

I provide one example of how this difference could influence the content and style of a paper in my years as a newspaper man.

In those days, *Die Burger* used to devote a few columns of space every morning to 'in memoriam' notices. It was as if the Boland comprised one big extended family, as if everyone knew of and was interested in one another. In the old Transvaal, where I was editor of *Beeld*, one had diverse and dispersed Afrikaans communities in Johannesburg, on the East and West Rand, in Pretoria, and elsewhere in the countryside.

We tried hard, but failed, to get readers to send us death notices, because the Transvaal contained a heterogeneous Afrikaans community. But gripping, hard news, such as stories about Dave Protter, appealed to readers across the board. Hence it made sense to give coverage to such events, rather, and to hit the story hard.

Behind *Beeld*'s success story is its early years of blood, sweat and tears. I have already dealt with the press war of those days in earlier chapters. One of the big stories about the South African press industry at the time was the 'Syferfontein' scandal, which I describe in Chapter 11. In brief, Perskor committed circulation fraud by dumping unsold copies of *Die Transvaler* and *Die Vaderland* down an abandoned West Rand mine shaft at night. The aim was to create a rosier picture of the paper's circulation for advertisers. By adding the phantom figures to their actual circulation figures, Perskor papers could charge a higher rate for advertisements. In the process, Johannes Grosskopf, editor of *Beeld*, gained a negative impression of his own paper's circulation. This misleading impression weighed heavily on him. It was only in 1980 that a Perskor official spilled the beans about the whole scam.

A particularly poignant aspect of Grosskopf's battle to get *Beeld*'s circulation up to par was that he would only discover in the final phase of his career as a journalism professor at Stellenbosch (1984–1993) that, under his leadership, *Beeld* had already surpassed the sales of *Die Transvaler*. I am glad that in 1984 I was in a position to recommend Grosskopf for the professorship.

Ultimately, Perskor's circulation trickery led to the inglorious end of Marius Jooste's career and the closure of all four Afrikaans dailies of this press group.

My appointment as editor of *Beeld* in 1977 happened against the backdrop of the board's dissatisfaction with the leadership of Johannes Grosskopf. Grosskopf was a highly intelligent but aloof editor. He had failed to weld the team together into a fighting force that could push forward and take on the rival papers effectively. The board reckoned I might be able to achieve that. Grosskopf was transferred to Washington.

I sat down and worked out my strategies. One plan was the rolling-up-sleeves approach that required everyone to give their full commitment and co-operation. While such an approach demands much, it can yield profound job satisfaction and great success.

Another resolution was to concentrate our outputs on cutting-edge news, the most important or interesting news of the day. I also resolved that the news had to be presented in a fresh and lively way. The paper had to take into account what its readers could stomach. But it would be fearlessly *verlig* as far as its political approach was concerned.

There were also two secret weapons that helped give *Beeld* an advantage. One was a game I devised, a 10-point crossword puzzle called the Minipot.

It appeared weekly, and the following week the winner would be rewarded with a substantial cash prize. The other was a jackpot bet on Rand horse races, where participants had to predict the top three horses in a particular race, as well as the winner's winning time. The latter was, of course, quite tough to determine.

These two competitions attracted thousands upon thousands of entries. I used to drive home on Friday evenings with a car filled with plastic bags stuffed with entries. My daughter Nissa and her schoolfriends would spend just about the entire Saturday combing through the entries to pick out the winners.

Besides the excitement that accompanied the competitions, they generated thousands of new buyers for *Beeld*. Our rival, *Die Transvaler*, woke up very late. Once it had cottoned on, however, it copied our Minipot, with even bigger cash prizes.

The competitions turned into a kind of lottery. More people than ever started buying Afrikaans dailies. The main benefit for us was the new exposure *Beeld* got. We added thousands of regular buyers to our circulation, because readers liked the young, innovative paper. *Die Transvaler* could not count on a similar upsurge of interest in the paper itself.

'Hitting the big story hard' was, and still is, a recipe for successful newspaper journalism. But as in the case of the competitions with cash prizes, it was also a strategy to produce the most appealing paper within the context of the press war that was waging in the North.

The press war, with its strategic manoeuvres, had started even before the launch of *Beeld* on 16 September 1974.

As a daily of Nasionale Pers in Johannesburg, *Beeld* would be outspokenly *verlig* in its political orientation – *verlig* on the basis of sincerely held convictions. The *verligte* mindset of the Sunday paper *Die Beeld* would be continued in the *verligte* inclination of *Beeld*.

Marius Jooste and his fellow combatants at Perskor saw the new, competing daily's predictable political orientation as a market-share grab at particularly the *verligte* readership segment of the Afrikaans newspaper market in the North.

To counter the threat, a plan was devised to recruit someone with a high profile and a reputation as a *verligte* thinker – Professor Wimpie de Klerk of Potchefstroom, inventor of the *verlig-verkramp* terminology – as new editor-in-chief of *Die Transvaler*. After all, the North had Perskor's afternoon paper *Die Vaderland* to cater for its conservative readers. The idea could also have been sparked when it came to Jooste's knowledge that De Klerk was being considered for a position of assistant editor at *Beeld*, which was soon to be established.

However the idea originated, the appointment was made in 1973 and *Die Transvaler* could scoop *Beeld* with a *verligte* approach even before Nasionale Pers's paper hit the streets in 1974.

In the first months of 1973, Wimpie de Klerk was still a theology professor at Potchefstroom University. Carl Nöffke, De Klerk's predecessor as editor-in-chief of *Die Transvaler*, branded him a liberalist and reviled him in his paper. So, it was sheer strategic opportunism that led to De Klerk's appointment on 14 August 1973: a shifting of allegiance with no change of Perskor's political heart, a manoeuvre in the press war.

The appointment was accompanied by scheming that raised questions about how exactly Marius Jooste had arrived at his brainwave. Lang David de Villiers wanted to lure Wimpie de Klerk to *Beeld*. Jooste caught wind of what was afoot. His informant was most likely his board member Professor Karools Reyneke, rector of Potchefstroom University. The latter was aware that Nasionale Pers was making overtures to De Klerk. Jooste was then able to trump his press rival by offering De Klerk a more important position, namely that of editor-in-chief of *Die Transvaler*.

De Klerk's choice of *Die Transvaler* with its well-known *verkrampte* approach can be queried. He was probably given assurances that he would enjoy editorial freedom.

He joined the staff of Perskor, his appointment causing a stir. A gifted individual, he was welcomed in high circles as a celebrity and was a popular speaker at both men's and women's clubs.

Die Transvaler experienced an upturn under De Klerk's leadership. He received good reports from inner-circle contacts and even steered his paper in a *verligte* direction. The competition with *Beeld* spurred his own journalists on to produce their best efforts. Jooste, however, did not afford him full editorial freedom. De Klerk was pulled up short every now and again, also by leaders in the NP government. For those in the know, the slip of Perskor's allegiance to the right-wing cause sometimes showed under *Die Transvaler*'s new *verligte* dress.

It is assumed that Wimpie de Klerk was probably unaware of the circulation fraud that was committed right under his nose in respect of *Die Transvaler*. With his background as an honourable person of high repute, the possibility that he had known about it must have affected him painfully. After the revelation of the Syferfontein scandal in 1980, De Klerk was fired as editor of *Die Transvaler*. He was subsequently appointed at *Rapport*. Marius Jooste died in 1982.

Beeld was launched in September 1974, with Schalk Pienaar as the initial editor. In terms of our freedom to write openly, honestly and critically about political affairs, we were more than a match for *Die Transvaler* under Wimpie de Klerk.

But the intelligent, *verligte* approach of Wimpie de Klerk did mean that we were up against stronger competition. With people buying *Die Transvaler* because of De Klerk's editorship, and the falsification of this paper's circulation figures to boot, *Beeld* experienced tough years. I told the editorial team: let's do our job as well as possible and let Wimpie make speeches; we'll come out on top.

In 1981, I received a good testimonial for *Beeld* from an unexpected quarter. It came from Professor Koos Roelofse from Unisa's communication studies department. A former journalist at *Die Transvaler*, he was no fan of *Beeld*.

Roelofse had visited *Beeld* in search of study material. He wrote to me afterwards: 'I found the time I spent at *Beeld* instructive, notably because of visible innovations in an institution that is usually rather loath to change. To my mind, *Beeld* is today undoubtedly the leading Afrikaans paper, probably because it expresses and embodies the needs, interests and aspirations of the community better than any of its rivals (also its sister papers).'

HIT THE BIG STORY HARD!

I appreciated these words very much. For what was one seeking to achieve, after all? To provide a valuable service to others.

A story that is hit hard arouses interest because of the concentrated attention that a team of talented journalists devotes to it. There are, of course, also stories that generate their own impact, for example, a polemic article that lands vicious punches by means of satire and ridicule. In my journalistic career, I sometimes evoked sharp reaction with my articles. One of the most gratifying instances was in July 1968, in co-operation within NP van Wyk Louw.

Louw was scathing about the numerous ministers of the Dutch Reformed Church who were involved in a group that was part of the *verkrampte* onslaught in Pretoria. Louw wrote: 'Thus a Synod decided just like that - apparently without much discussion, but under the guidance of the Holy Ghost (presumably that is still the case?) - to approve a resolution of the Afrikaans Literary Society under the guidance of its leader SI Mocke. It was directed against [Etienne Leroux's novel] *Sewe Dae by die Silbersteins*. One wonders whether the two "guidances" did not get mixed up? Was it the Holy Ghost that had discovered Mr Mocke? Or was it a small Transvaal "pressure group"?'

In the ensuing polemic, Louw named the members of the group: Mrs Hymne Weiss and her husband Professor Detlev Weiss, at one stage chair of the Suid-Afrikaanse Akademie vir Wetenskap en Kuns. Others were the theologian Professor Ben du Preez, the Reverend AP Potgieter, secretary of the organisation Christelike Kultuuraksie, the Reverend Dan de Beer, chair of the Transvaal DRC's synodal commission for public morals, and Gert Beetge, head of the white construction workers' union, secretary of the National Council against Communism and loyal supporter of Dr Albert Hertzog. They comprised 'the Weiss Squad', as Rykie van Reenen had dubbed the lobby group.

Louw wrote in an extensive polemic in *Die Beeld*: 'Pretoria is riddled with groups and grouplets ... why Pretoria, in particular? Hot, moist conditions cause all kinds of bugs to incubate: are people in Pretoria too close to the glow of governmental grace? ... It is said that ... Pretoria's ultimate status symbol is: being able to count on at least two cabinet ministers to attend your party, and being able to say of a minister or a minister's wife: "We greet each other with a kiss" – this is where heaven and earth meet.'

I was commissioned, with Louw as co-author, to reply to the question: what, apart from its jacarandas, makes Pretoria so different from every other city in South Africa? I pointed out that only about 700 of the city's white residents made Pretoria what it was – in many respects our country's caricature city.

Louw's article appeared on the same page as mine, and his carried the headline: 'Só broei hulle mekaar warm'. Jaap Steyn, who provides considerable background information on the poet's skirmishes with the 'small pressure group' in Pretoria in his biography of NP van Wyk Louw,[36] writes about our co-operation: 'These were extremely interesting articles that would get readers talking.'

Impactful articles of this nature, often written to expose the behind-the-scenes machinations of conservative lobby groups, formed part of the battle between *verlig* and *verkramp*. History ultimately designated the winner.

CHAPTER 16

Verwoerd sinks our sport

It was a peaceful Saturday afternoon in July 1965 at the Loskop Dam campsite near Middelburg, in what is today Mpumalanga. The weather was pleasantly warm in the Middleveld. The Transvaal youth wing of the National Party, the Jeugbond, was holding its congress, and the guest speaker later that evening would be Prime Minister Hendrik Verwoerd.

Parliament was in recess, a time when Cabinet ministers and MPs worked their constituencies, parties held congresses, and politicians made ample use of the opportunity to engage in game hunting.

Within a few hours, the tranquil atmosphere at the campsite was to be shattered by a policy statement that would shoot around the world and make South Africa fall into disfavour with all and sundry.

I was the only journalist on the scene, in my capacity as political reporter of the Sunday paper *Dagbreek en Sondagnuus*. Verwoerd was chair of the press group that owned the paper, the Afrikaanse Pers Limited, and about half of his Cabinet ministers were directors.

The Jeugbonders braaied meat and made mieliepap with 'sheba' (braised tomato-and-onion relish), the standard fare at such events. The premier sat with his back against a tree, surrounded by a circle of acolytes. They were talking politics.

At some point, the chief secretary of the Transvaal NP, Jack Steyl, arrived with a copy of *The Star* under his arm and told Verwoerd: 'Just look at what Dr Craven says about the Maoris.'

The lead story in the Saturday edition of *The Star* came from New Zealand, where the Springbok rugby team was touring at the time. Whether or not Maori players could be included in an All Blacks tour to South Africa was a big debating point in South Africa. According to the article, Dr Danie Craven, president of the South African Rugby Board (SARB), had said in an interview that Maoris were welcome to tour to South Africa as part of an All Blacks team.

It was a daring statement on Craven's part, as in 1965 the South African government upheld a policy of absolute racial segregation of sporting competitions in South Africa. There had been various attempts to circumvent the law – for instance, a proposal to divide our team for the Olympic Games into contingents in order to participate 'separately but together'. Naturally, this did not convince anyone.

Verwoerd said nothing that was audible to me where I sat outside the circle in the company of his bodyguards and private secretary, chatting to random congress-goers. That evening, the recreation hall was packed with enthusiastic Jeugbonders. Verwoerd was received with clamorous applause and songs of praise.

As usual, he spoke without notes. After the initial platitudes, he let fly and said it had come to his attention that Dr Craven had made a policy statement to the effect that Maori players would be welcome to tour with an All Blacks team to South Africa.

The next All Blacks tour to South Africa was only scheduled to take place five years later, in 1970. But Verwoerd deemed fit to repudiate the internationally respected Dr Craven summarily, in front of the Transvaal youth. Doc Craven was, of course, not only president of the SARB, but himself a famous ex-Springbok, the coach of the Springbok team, and a renowned figure among younger people. He was a great educator; at Stellenbosch, he had a hand in coaching the famous Maties rugby teams.

It is possible to give a (translated) verbatim account of the section of Dr Verwoerd's speech that pertained to the Maori issue: the South African Political Archives of the University of the Free State prepared a tape recording made at the event for publication. The prime minister put his point of view as follows:

> At the moment we have the argumentation on the terrain I would rather not have talked about, namely with regard to our rugby team in New Zealand, but I am forced to talk about it because in recent times so much has been said and written openly on that topic in the opposition papers, which obliges me to state my and the government's standpoint very clearly and unambiguously. Here we have a team from South Africa, which, according to our custom, is a white team, going to another country where there are also non-whites, non-whites we don't look down upon, non-whites of quite a high level, non-whites whose traditions we can also have respect for, but in any case, here we go to another country in which there are both whites and a sizeable minority group of certain non-whites, the Maori people.
>
> In that country, because of the conditions that prevail there, a form of integration has developed. I don't wish to judge it, nor do I wish to criticise it. It is that country's own affairs, it is that country's customs, to which it is fully entitled. It is their business and not ours, and in terms of our basic principle stance, we say that when you go to another country and you are the guest of that country, then you conduct yourself in accordance with that country's conditions and in accordance with its expectations. And therefore our team goes there and we will play against white New Zealanders, or whites and Maoris, or Maoris, however New Zealand chooses to organise it. It is their business, because the fact that we accepted the invitation to go to that country means that we must be willing to adapt ourselves to that country's customs.
>
> And it is right that we do so, because it is in accordance with our great ground rule on which our entire battle for survival is based, namely that we don't interfere in another state's affairs, which then also includes the converse, namely that we don't allow any other state to interfere in ours. (Applause.) And hence our standpoint is that, in the same way we subject ourselves to the other country's practices and customs without hesitation, without criticism, we happily expect that

when other countries visit our country or send representatives, they would conduct themselves in the very same way, namely that they would refrain from interfering in what are our affairs and adapt themselves to our customs. (Applause.)

And now it turns out that while we are still guests over there, journalists keep posing questions to people such as Dr Craven and Mr Kobus Louw, manager of the team, about what would happen if the New Zealand team should come here. I don't know exactly what replies they gave, but what I do know is that what our local opposition papers concluded from their answers, and then stated openly, is that we are willing to receive mixed teams here, and from that they then conclude that once we have received teams with Maori members here, what would also then have to follow as a consequence (applause), and I would like to add to that … and we all know what that is.

There was a single public telephone at the hall. I made a beeline for it to phone my report through to *Dagbreek*'s editorial team in Auckland Park. An editorial secretary took it down and typed up the article. I constructed the article to the best of my ability. The big news was in the first paragraph. A journalist knows that the information that is likely to have the greatest impact should be mentioned first. And I *knew* this article would cause an uproar.

While I was composing the article, I knew at the back of my mind that the minister of Sport and Home Affairs, Senator Jan de Klerk (father of FW and Wimpie), had had a discussion with Craven prior to the Springbok tour. Craven had been left with the impression that, if he handled the issue diplomatically, the door could be opened for Maori players.

As I read out my article to the secretary, the call was interrupted by the *Dagbreek* editor Dirk Richard, who asked me what exactly the drift of the article was. I told him brusquely that he could read it himself; it did not require any interpretation.

Dirk had always been a coward and probably only wanted to cover his own backside in the event of repercussions. I had had ample experience of that in the course of our working relationship.

Presumably Dr Craven, in contending with a hostile press and public loathing of the apartheid system in New Zealand, had gambled too strongly on Senator De Klerk's remarks and put his case too confidently. But the die was cast.

News agencies picked up the *Dagbreek* article and spread it around the world. The following Monday, our newspapers testified to the consequences of the speech. Verwoerd had slammed the door shut for South Africa as far as international sport was concerned.

The incident instantly provided ammunition to the campaign for an international sports boycott against South Africa. In London, the South African Non-Racial Olympic Committee (SANROC), which had been founded in 1962, must have jumped with joy at this stroke of luck.

Dennis Brutus, SANROC's organiser, was a South African activist, educator, journalist and poet who had gained renown with his campaign to get South Africa expelled from the Olympic Games. To Brutus, Verwoerd's policy statement, which he had made without consulting his Cabinet or caucus, was like manna from heaven.

The predictable result of the Loskop Dam speech was indeed that the noose of sanctions was tightened. Political and trade sanctions, as well as sanctions against arms sales and mineral exports, were enforced more stringently. We became increasingly isolated as a country.

This situation prompted 'Dawie' to remark controversially in *Die Burger* that our country had become 'the polecat of the world', particularly in the wake of the Sharpeville tragedy. This description also flashed around the world and became common currency. Nelson Mandela would later promise that South Africa would 'never, never and never again ... suffer the indignity of being the skunk of the world'.

As sports and other sanctions intensified, the South African government would seek to counter our sporting isolation by various means. The All Blacks toured South Africa as the Cavaliers and played unofficial tests. The minister of Finance obtained Cabinet approval to dish money out lavishly in order to facilitate sanctions-busting on various terrains. So, we had so-called rebel sports tours and visits from artists whose careers were past their prime. Celebrities and dignitaries of all kinds were lured to our shores in an attempt to give credence to our image as a 'normal' country.

This deformed setup continued until the negotiations between the South African government and the ANC led to the lifting of sanctions and the advent of genuinely normal conditions.

The *verkrampte* and downright foolish way in which the National Party government sometimes dealt with racial questions is illustrated by a speech Prime Minister John Vorster delivered in Bloemfontein in 1967. In the audience was Professor Owen Horwood, vice-chancellor of the University of Natal. Vorster announced that he was including Horwood as an English speaker in his Cabinet, along with other English speakers, namely Alf Trollip (minister of Labour) and Frank Waring (minister of Sport). The news was received with enthusiasm.

What raised the roof of the City Hall, however, was when Vorster pointed out that the England cricket selectors had included a former South African, the coloured player Basil D'Oliveira, in their team that was due to tour South Africa. That could not be allowed to happen, Vorster said. There would be no tour if that was the case.

As expected, the English cricket bosses, the MCC, summarily rejected the attempt to impose South Africa's colour discrimination on their own team selection. The tour was called off. As in the case of Verwoerd's impromptu speech at Loskop Dam, Vorster's attempt in Bloemfontein to 'show them who's boss' did enormous damage to South Africa's image and to South African sport.

Basil D'Oliveira became one of England's best all-rounders of his era and was knighted by Queen Elizabeth. Vorster, after a brief spell as state president, had to resign in disgrace because of the Information Scandal. In the 1990s, a building that Stellenbosch University had named after him as former chancellor was renamed, partly because it stood on land from which coloured people in the town had been evicted in the past.

VERWOERD SINKS OUR SPORT

It was widely known that white South Africans set great store by sport and took pride in the Springboks above all. The international sports boycott hit sports fans hard, and our sports policy became a hot potato.

The Transvaal NP leader Ben Schoeman was known as a straight talker. Shortly before the French rugby tour to South Africa in 1971, this former stoker and train driver, dubbed 'Blunt Ben' by the English-language press, delivered a speech in Innesdal, Pretoria. The area was the right-wing stronghold of the MP Jaap Marais.

The French rugby team that was due to tour South Africa included a coloured wing, Roger Bourgarel. Blunt Ben took on the critical audience. France, he said, was resisting the international arms boycott against South Africa and selling essential military aircraft such as the Mirage and Alouette helicopters to our defence force. This was vital equipment for protecting our country against communism and attacks from north of South Africa's borders. 'Must we now put the safety of all of you at risk because of one coloured wing?' he said in hammering home his view.

The audience did an about-turn and gave him a standing ovation. Bourgarel was part of the French touring party, and arrangements in this regard increasingly became looser.

The heavens would not have fallen had Verwoerd conceded in 1965 that Maoris would be allowed to play in a visiting New Zealand squad five years later. Nor if Vorster had been prepared to accept a coloured South African in an England cricket team in 1967.

How could we know that this would not have caused a catastrophe? I had previously written a report about a Maori player who had toured South Africa with Fred Allen's All Blacks in 1949. He was the lock Harry Frazer, who later married a South African woman – information I had received from Dr Craven. But this report was vehemently denied from New Zealand.

The exclusion of three Maori players from the 1949 All Blacks team, in compliance with South African legislation or customs, is, however, an acknowledged sore point of New Zealand's rugby history.

It is recorded somewhere that, as far back as 1928, a Maori player or two had been included in the New Zealand team that toured South Africa. It seems that not many people noticed any difference this had made to their lives.

CHAPTER 17

St Nelson and me

In 1999, I undertook a day-long 'road trip' in the company of our country's first democratically elected president. It took place shortly before he was due to retire as state president in June of that year. The trip started and ended in a small jet aircraft. The two of us were scheduled to perform all kinds of good deeds in poor communities. I would discover before long where I had been earmarked for a good deed. That day, I witnessed how skilfully St Nelson, South Africa's own patron saint, endeavoured to look after the needs of the lowliest among his people.

President Mandela had invited me to visit Calitzdorp and Carnarvon on this memorable day. Prior to his retirement, he paid visits to a string of places where the need among disadvantaged communities was most acute. On the basis of a pre-compiled list, businesspeople were invited to accompany him on these visits. On their arrival at the selected destinations, their arms were twisted to donate a school, a clinic, or anything else that could help uplift the community.

That day, it was my turn. We flew from Ysterplaat to Oudtshoorn in a fast little jet. Mandela, a TV team from the SABC and several staff members had departed from Waterkloof at 6:00 that morning to pick me up in Cape Town.

We were accompanied by the well-known educationist Franklin Sonn, already finally back from his term as the first South African ambassador in Washington after the 1994 election.

A flight attendant from the South African Air Force brought Mandela a small woollen blanket. The president took off his shoes and stretched his legs out on his leather seat. He asked for his glasses, and first read *Die Burger* and *Cape Times*. On the earlier leg of the trip from Waterkloof to Cape Town, he had already perused *Beeld*, the *Citizen*, *The Star* and the *Sowetan*. Mandela was an avid newspaper reader.

In between, we talked enough to fill books. In an article about the day trip I wrote for *Rapport* at the time, I stated that it would be a breach of trust to pass on everything Mandela had said about the De Klerks (FW, as well as his now late wife Marike), PW Botha, Bill Clinton (then still the controversial US president), the British queen, Kabila, Savimbi, and Arab kings and princes. But while Mandela was a fount of stories, I added, he was not malicious, and did not engage in unkind gossip.

On our arrival in Calitzdorp, a crowd of thousands awaited us on the rugby field in Bergsig, the coloured town on the opposite side of the Nels River. People cheered and shouted as our green Mercedes, reinforced with armour plating and bulletproof glass (Mandela had inherited it from PW), drove through a guard of honour formed by drum majorettes.

They yelled: 'Viva Tata!', 'Viva Madiba!', 'Viva Mandela!' And as he emerged from the vehicle: 'Jive for us!'

Mandela did not jive. He had been informed that we could spend only 45 minutes here before hurrying back to Oudtshoorn. From there, we were due to fly to De Aar in our jet. A smaller turboprop aircraft from the defence force would then transport us to Carnarvon, where an equally large crowd stood waiting in the sun and dust.

And what did Mandela do next? He thanked the crowd for their attendance, but disappointed them by remarking that he would not be saying much more. Instead, he wished to introduce them to an important man, one of the wealthiest men, someone who could buy the whole of Calitzdorp without blinking an eye. And this man was now going to tell them about everything he intended to do for them.

I was totally unprepared for a speech, let alone for being introduced as the community's mega-rich prospective benefactor! St Nelson had wrong-footed me good and proper. Speaking off the cuff, I stammered that I was actually only a salaried employee of Naspers. And besides, who was I, after all? The people of Calitzdorp knew about *Huisgenoot*, *Die Burger*, *Rapport* and M-Net, but not about Ton Vosloo. Nonetheless, I said, we would devise something to help address the needs of learners.

The crowd cheered, and in a quiet moment I thought how strikingly the event resembled the Nats' gatherings from thirty, forty years earlier. The dominee was present to open the proceedings with a reading from Scripture and a prayer, the choir got their turn, the boutonnière was pinned to the lapel, the gifts were handed out, and there was a long list of acknowledgements – all in robust Afrikaans. These were my people ... people who had been pushed out and humiliated by their white compatriots for so long.

Back in the aircraft, I heard about relations with the prison warders on Robben Island, at Pollsmoor and at Victor Verster. How the Reverend Scheffler's visits as spiritual guide were terminated abruptly after Mandela gave him a guava as a gift for his wife. Or how the Reverend Mehl's visits later resulted in the security police following his car in secret to see which address he stopped at: he was suspected of being a messenger for the ANC.

We talked about the roles of Kobie Coetsee, Pik Botha and Niël Barnard in the delicate negotiation process, and about how Mandela became exasperated with FW at Codesa and let fly at him about the NP's suspicion that the ANC was negotiating in bad faith, which nearly wrecked Codesa. Mandela later phoned FW; on the resumption of the negotiations, he conspicuously walked over to FW and shook his hand to restore trust. (At the end of the chapter is a postscript in which I recount some details of the first, secret, meeting between Mandela and PW Botha.)

President Mandela also told us in the plane that the new Mrs Mandela, Graça, was overworking herself in her commitment to upliftment projects. In reply to a question, he said he harboured no bitterness about his 27 lost years. 'In prison we gave an undertaking that once we were free, all of us, the older people and the young ones, would devote our lives to constructive contributions to society.'

On the way to Carnarvon, I remarked that he might get some mutton as a gift pack. In the north-west part of the country, I explained, people were meat eaters; if you asked for vegetables, they would give you a pork chop. In Calitzdorp, it had been port. Calitzdorp was, after all, our country's port capital.

To be sure, on our arrival in Carnarvon, Mandela was presented with a gift of wrapped meat. He was not very keen on meat himself. Over the whole day, he drank only mineral water and ate only two minuscule sandwiches after the flight attendant had informed him in response to his question that they had no peanuts on board.

We were warmly received at Carnarvon, and I was again introduced as the man who could buy the town without blinking an eye. I promised the community that we would consider a computer centre that Naspers might sponsor jointly with MWEB and M-Cell.

The choirs of all three schools in the town started singing. The little ones reached out their hands. The women, too, reached out to Madiba. And then he started jiving. He grabbed the Northern Cape premier, Manne Dipico, to join in. You could see and feel that this was a politician of note, a man in total harmony with his people.

At Carnarvon, I was able to witness the Madiba magic firing on all cylinders. I attributed this magic to different aspects of his personality. All his qualities were observable at that event in the Northern Cape. He was unpretentious, yet as astute as they come. He could mingle with kings and commoners with equal ease. Everyone felt he was interested only in them. He radiated old-world warmth and spontaneity. He was genuine.

His release was seen worldwide as a personal moral victory over South Africa's racial policy. The martyr status his incarceration had added to his exceptionally endearing personality had indeed turned him into a secular saint, from the dusty streets here in Calitzdorp and Carnarvon to the gilded receptions at which he was honoured in Stockholm, Washington, Tokyo and Paris.

We boarded the plane for the return leg to Cape Town with dust-coated shoes. Mandela's were collected and polished to a shine. He sat with his feet raised and drank water, and we talked frankly and at length. A journalist's dream.

At times, my eyelids threatened to close, despite the fact that I had not had to get up as early as Madiba that morning. The octogenarian opposite me did not stumble over a word, did not repeat an anecdote, and kept me and Franklin Sonn spellbound with incredible inside stories. The man had stamina that wore me out.

Mandela had not only stamina, but also steely determination. The old Afrikaner expression for a good and true man, a man 'with a heart of gold and a will of steel', came to mind.

When his government cut the defence force's budget by R700 million in its first year, he showed his true mettle. He had requested a helicopter to fly somewhere. The helicopter at his disposal broke down shortly before the flight. On another occasion, it had to turn back after five minutes in the air, ostensibly as a result of engine problems.

'This was the defence force's way of signalling to me that they were unable to maintain their aircraft if we cut their funds,' Mandela told us on the return flight. He had to show his steel. As commander-in-chief, he summoned the Defence minister, Joe Modise, and requested a report on what was wrong with the choppers. Matters had improved drastically since that time; the two aircraft in which we travelled that day were both in top-notch condition.

At nearly 82 years of age, Nelson Mandela himself was in top-notch condition, maybe as a result of the self-discipline that was evident during the trip from his healthy eating habits alone. His plane dropped Franklin Sonn and me in Cape Town and then headed back to Waterkloof. He still had a journey of an hour and a half ahead of him. For us two much younger men, it was the end of an exhausting but joyous day in the company of an unforgettable man.

A few months later, at the turn of the millennium, Mandela was declared one of the 100 most influential people of the twentieth century by *Time* magazine.

Postscript: Meeting between Nelson Mandela and PW Botha
Dr Niël Barnard was head of the National Intelligence Service during the 1980s. He was PW Botha's right-hand man. In his book *Secret Revolution:*

Memoirs of a Spy Boss,[37] Barnard reveals details of the top-secret talks between him and Nelson Mandela in 1988 and 1989, while the latter was still in prison. These initial talks, held at a time when PW Botha was still executive president, would eventually result in Mandela's release in 1990, the unbanning of the ANC, and the subsequent political transformation. Dr Barnard also lifts the lid on Mandela's first face-to-face meeting with President PW Botha in Tuynhuys, Cape Town, on 5 July 1989.

I had known about this historic meeting from as far back as 26 years before Barnard's disclosures. My informant was the late Alf Ries, our group's political editor. The two of us had had a close relationship since our years in the parliamentary press gallery, and used to share confidential information. For both of us, this relationship contributed significantly to the range of our knowledge and the reliability of the information we were able to convey in political articles.

A confidential report Ries had sent me on 27 July 1989, based on a conversation with Niël Barnard, provided me with background knowledge that pertains to Barnard's story. I kept the information to myself at the time, as the confidentiality of the contact between Mandela and PW Botha was in the national interest.

Barnard was not unknown to me. He used to visit me fairly often at my office in Johannesburg. The aim was not to share secrets, but to cultivate sound relations. I got to know him as a strong individual with an even stronger ego. He was frustrated by the secrecy that went hand in hand with his position because of its attendant lack of recognition.

From Alf Ries's confidential report, read with Barnard's memoirs, I know that Mandela had regularly expressed the wish to meet PW Botha. PW was to him the symbol of authority and leadership among the 'Boere'. He was of the view that any peaceful settlement would have to be negotiated principally between him and his people on the one hand, and the 'Boere' on the other hand.

During the drive from Victor Verster to Tuynhuys on 5 July 1989, Barnard cautioned Mandela against aggression. He had to keep in mind that Botha had had a setback, and that the meeting would be purely a goodwill visit.

They drove openly through the security gate at Tuynhuys. None of the guards had caught wind of anything out of the ordinary, because visitors from Africa were a common occurrence.

The meeting went off successfully. Mandela greeted Botha in Afrikaans, and the two men chatted about this and that for about twenty minutes. Then Mandela said he wanted to use to opportunity to state that, if there were to be a settlement, the setting of preconditions for negotiations would have to be ditched. He specifically referred to the precondition that the use of violence had to be renounced.

Botha handled the statement well, and said they should drop the issue and concentrate on peace.

Botha never held another discussion with Mandela; the negotiations were conducted between FW de Klerk and Mandela with their respective teams.

It is debatable whether we would have reached a settlement had Botha still led the government after 1989. The interesting factor here is that PW Botha's irascibility would have been pitted against Mandela's disarming ability to make friends and influence people. PW would probably have tried to hold out against surrendering power to a majority government based on universal franchise. But was Mandela not, perhaps, the one person who may have been capable of mollifying PW?

Kobie Coetsee was the first NP politician to meet Nelson Mandela, before PW Botha had. When Mandela was admitted to hospital while in prison in 1985, Coetsee met him there, on neutral ground and out of sight of his normal guards.

Niël Barnard is largely dismissive of Coetsee's role in the negotiations. In his second book about his career,[38] Barnard writes about Coetsee's periodic attendance at the talks and the about-turns during the negotiations. Perhaps the answer lies in a text that reached my desk in 2016, written by Adrienne Koch, a mistress of Coetsee. She claimed that it was her influence that made Coetsee, a conservative, Afrikaans, Nationalist political leader, into one eager to negotiate with Mandela. She asserted that she had had the decisive influence on Coetsee's view on the matter.

Koch became the dynamic mayor of Paarl at 27 and, later, a member of the senate and the presidential council. She belongs to the well-known Waring family. Her father, Frank Waring, was a Springbok rugby player who became one of the first English Cabinet members appointed by John Vorster – as minister of Sport and Tourism. Her mother, Joyce Waring, was known nationwide as a columnist for Sunday papers.

Koch's unpublished memoirs, *An Adulterer's Prayer*, is an interesting footnote to the politics of the time. It describes an intensely physical relationship that started long before Coetsee became a Cabinet member, as well as a woman's frustrations in politics. In addition, it is one of many examples of how politicians and ordinary people were able to find meaning by making their life story part of a long journey, with Madiba as a guiding star.

CHAPTER 18

Robert Mugabe and John Vorster

Among the most interesting political interviews I conducted as a journalist was one with Robert Mugabe.
In 2017, 37 years after he had taken office in 1980, the army finally forced him to step down as Zimbabwe's political leader. On reflection, what is fascinating is how consistently he has adhered to his standpoints over nearly four decades. At the age of 93, his views are still essentially the same. He may not always have asserted his principles in honest and successful ways – the opposite may even be true – but the principles, as such, he still proclaims today.

The interview took place in Harare on 18 August 1982. I was editor of *Beeld* at the time, and could submit a series of questions to which Mugabe would respond. In 1982, he was not yet president of Zimbabwe, but prime minister with executive powers. The first post-independence president, Canaan Banana, had played a largely ceremonial role. In 1987, the powers of the prime minister were transferred to the presidency. Thenceforth, President Mugabe was able to determine the course of his country without insurmountable complications up until 2017.

In the second part of this chapter, I recall a conversation I had with John Vorster in 1977, with the help of the notes I made at the time. In doing so, my aim is not to eulogise Mugabe by holding up Vorster as an antipode. Mugabe caused great damage in Zimbabwe. But I would like to compare the clarity of vision and the detailed ideals and intentions of Mugabe, a man who in 1982 was riding the crest of the political tide in southern Africa, with Vorster's situation and attitude a few years earlier. As the Information Scandal revealed, Vorster resorted to police-state security measures in attempting to safeguard the South Africa of the National Party and keep it afloat on a dangerous political tide. In addition, the outdated apartheid system was defended with the dirty tricks and subterfuge of a propaganda war. In Vorster's case, this approach was accompanied by a cynical attitude towards the same kind of African people to whom Mugabe gave hope. This is the impression that the two conversations create when one compares them today.

My interview with Mugabe took place about two years after the brutal guerrilla war against Ian Smith's white minority regime had come to an end. In South Africa, PW Botha's NP government was in power at the time, with no intention of going down the same path as the former Rhodesia.

The political orientation of the ZANU party, which Mugabe had led in the struggle years, was characterised by African nationalism, Marxism and later aspects of Maoism. ZANU had strong ties with China both before and after the struggle for Zimbabwe's independence. The African equivalent of Maoist socialism would eventually become known as Mugabeism. This ideological orientation shines through in my interview with Mugabe, albeit that, on assuming power, he had accepted the existing capitalist system in Zimbabwe and, ostensibly, free democratic elections.

Mugabe's connection with Maoist China in the years of the guerrilla war may explain his attempt to eliminate physically, or suppress through brutal intimidation, the supporters of the rival, Russian-supported ZAPU movement led by Joshua Nkomo, a member of the Ndebele tribe. The massacre of at least 20 000 supposed dissidents in Matabeleland by the North Korean-trained Fifth Brigade certainly indicated Mugabe's inclination and willingness to take radical action.

The militant appropriation of agricultural land at a later stage, glorified as a people's movement and an essential step towards decolonisation, was also in keeping with the Maoist-Mugabeist pattern. The same, in fact, applied to Mugabe's president-for-life career – if need be, notwithstanding democratic elections.

Mugabe would increasingly rely on his security services to stay in power, and ultimately ruined the country economically because of the expropriation of white farmers' farms and the development of a corrupt patronage system. The majority of skilled whites left the country; subsequently, an enormous number of black Zimbabweans, too, were forced to seek refuge in South Africa for economic reasons.

Despite all this, Mugabe's charisma never waned. What many white South Africans fail to grasp sufficiently is that the picture of Robert Mugabe as a demon without redemption, painted in the Western world on account of his shocking behaviour, is not necessarily shared by these South Africans' black compatriots. On the contrary, he is extremely popular among many supporters of the ANC and certainly those of the EFF. Mugabe is, after all, an icon of the struggle against the colonisation of Africa by the West. The obduracy with which he taunts the Western world actually contributes to the status he enjoys in South Africa.

This admiration is not always shared by Zimbabweans who have found refuge in South Africa, but one should not underestimate the support for Mugabe in South Africa.

Initially, Mugabe followed relatively moderate social and economic policies. His first steps, such as strengthening medical care and education, were quite benign. At the beginning of his rule, there was merely talk of benevolent socialism. Hence, radical developments still lay in the future when I was granted an interview with him. In South Africa, there was nonetheless great unease because Mugabe was known as the most radical head of government the new Republic of Zimbabwe could have chosen in its first election.

Below is a translated version of my interview with Mugabe, as it was published in *Beeld* on 19 August 1982. What is apparent from the interview, among other things, is that what Mugabe expected of the government of PW Botha was eventually realised with the acceptance of an inclusive democracy by FW de Klerk's government in 1994.

Zimbabwe stands by its policy that it will not allow any camps of the South African ANC and PAC, and the continuation of trading links and expansion of economic contact are encouraged.

These are two of the points the prime minister of Zimbabwe, Mr Robert Mugabe, made yesterday in an interview.

Owing to the time factor, I had to share my interview with five editors from the Argus group. In the course of the 65-minute conversation, Mr Mugabe said inter alia: 'As was decided at the time of independence, there can be no ties with South Africa in the prevailing circumstances. It would be of no use to have a meeting with Mr PW Botha.

'A solution in South West Africa could contribute to a change in attitude in so far as it would remove an existing problem. But it wouldn't change anything about Zimbabwe's view that South Africa's real problem is internal.'

According to Mr Mugabe, he fails to understand why South Africa and its agents harass Zimbabwe by sabotaging its trade routes or by destabilising the country. Mr Mugabe spoke broadly about his own policy and what he described as the success thereof, his plan for the socialisation of the country, internal unrest and detention.

On the relationship with South Africa, Mr Mugabe said: 'Our relations are not good.' He repeated the principles his government had decided on at the time of independence two and a quarter years earlier: no political and diplomatic contact, but acknowledgement of economic relations.

Regarding the possibility of a meeting with Mr PW Botha, he said: 'It would then become a political issue. We follow the definition of no contact, and there is no possibility of such a meeting taking place. A meeting would only serve the purpose of providing South Africa with propaganda, as was the case with meetings in the détente era.

'I believe the best thing that can happen is for South Africa to talk to the recognised leaders in South Africa. It has to thrash things out with Mandela, Tambo and several others. They have to form a joint front to solve South Africa's problems.

'Until such time, South Africa will constantly have to act to defend its system against the systems of neighbouring countries.'

When I pointed out to him the forces of white and black nationalism in South Africa, Mr Mugabe said there were models one could follow, and South Africa had to work out a model based on the existing realities. But he would expect, and Africa would expect, the basic principles of a democracy to be taken into account.

'That is for South Africa to decide. But we will be delighted if that model is democratic, in other words, based on majority government. I am convinced the whites will be able to accept it. They will lose political control, but the whites have the ingenuity and economic resources to sustain themselves.

'Maybe colour is a stronger factor in your case than in ours. With us it also used to play a role, but as a political factor it is now losing the battle. If you regarded all your groups as South Africans, I don't see how it can be detrimental to South Africa. People work out political recipes based on the supposed fears that groups have of each other.

'I realise that it will take time for South Africa to adapt, but the principles for political progress include non-racialism; that the people of South Africa have to form a unit; and that majority government has to be attained.

'The issue of diplomatic relations depends on whether there is an improvement in the political position of the majority in South Africa.'

What Mr Mugabe understands by his policy of socialism is the necessity of putting the resources of the country at the disposal of the population as a whole.

'All the resources belong to all the people. In that philosophy, we see a moral approach that will enable us to live together as equals. It is wrong, immoral and unjust to leave the resources in the hands of individuals. Capitalism is a curse.

'But that said, we recognise the reality of the capitalist system. You cannot ignore it or convert it overnight. Where the transformation is possible, we will tackle it. Herein lies a contradiction, but it can be reconciled. We will ensure that private enterprise remains viable because it contributes to the economy and to job opportunities for people.

'This partnership between two systems will continue to exist until we have completed the changeover. Our aim with socialism is state ownership of some components; joint ownership between the state and the people of other activities; collective farming on the part of peasant farmers; and the preparation of workers for participation in the management of industries.'

Zimbabwe's growth rate was 12 per cent in the first year of independence, and 8 per cent in the second year. Mr Mugabe said it was levelling out, as was the case worldwide, but the growth rate would still be positive in the current financial year.

He believes that the Zimbabwean peasant farmers will play a big role in the country's continued economic prosperity. 'Our African people are regarded as good agriculturalists across the continent, and with the envisaged state support things can only improve,' he said. The flight of skilled people was to be expected. About them, namely people who can't or won't adapt themselves to the new situation, he said 'good riddance'.

'Of course we want to retain the skills. Everyone who wants to make a contribution is welcome to come here. We must acknowledge each other as allies rather than enemies.'

Mugabe obtained his first degree at the University College of Fort Hare in the Eastern Cape.

Those years made a big impression on him. Along with other foreign students, he used to listen to Duma Nokwe (an ANC activist) talking about resistance against apartheid. They discussed the ideal that Africa as a whole needed to undergo a revolution. India, which gained its independence in 1947, was the model.

Mr Mugabe said he had joined the ANC Youth League. The plan of passive resistance was born at that time.

In those years, he said, apartheid was not so noticeable. He travelled in racially mixed buses, and the old Park Station in Johannesburg did not yet have separate sections.

'But on the train through the Free State to the Cape Province I noticed that South Africa had two worlds, the world of the Free State and the rest.' Mr Mugabe laughed heartily and added: 'I'm sorry that I didn't get to see Natal.'

ROBERT MUGABE AND JOHN VORSTER

> Mr Mugabe displayed no outward signs of any grudge about his years in South Africa.

So that was my interview with Mugabe in 1982. While doing research for these memoirs, I also found among my documents my notes on a discussion I had had with John Vorster. This conversation took place on Friday 2 September 1977, a year before the Information Scandal of 1978 that forced Vorster to resign as president.

On rereading these notes, I was struck by Vorster's self-assurance and arrogance, and how dismissive he was of people of colour within our political dispensation. In 1982, Mugabe was describing an idealistic project geared to the welfare of his country's population, specifically the black population. Vorster, on the other hand, was occupying himself with the politics of calculation, manoeuvring and manipulation within a situation that was gradually becoming intolerable.

This conversation in 1977 was confidential and not for publication, but here are some of my notes nonetheless:

> Vorster told me that he had advised 'Smit' (which was how he pronounced Ian Smith's surname) against summarily rejecting the British proposals with a view to a settlement. 'Let Nkomo and Mugabe do it. If "Smit" wants to break, then rather break on the issue that he has to hand over his security forces to the terrorists. The world will show understanding of that decision.'
>
> Then, Vorster added: 'In South West our breaking point will also be the issue of the withdrawal of our troops. If need be, we will revise the Turnhalle constitution and give South West Transkei status.'
>
> On the Jimmy Carter administration, Vorster said: 'America is reluctant to come down hard on us. It could have internal repercussions for Carter. The appointment of Andrew Young (an African-American appointed as US ambassador to the United Nations) is the best thing for us, and a white backlash is building in America. He should appoint more Negroes [sic].'
>
> Vorster remarked during the discussion that the world would not

implement effective sanctions against us – they needed too much from us.

Then he said: 'About the nuclear bomb, America knows exactly what we have, what we are capable of. They want you never to detonate the thing, or to say that you don't have it.'

On sanctions and the threat of an oil boycott, Vorster said: 'We have oil supplies for two years, longer with rationing. We can get it from international companies as long as Iran "pumps it into the dam". He added that Indonesia was also making overtures, and that we could even get oil from Saudi Arabia.

We talked about the cautious road towards a new constitutional dispensation – the tricameral system that was later adopted. He said the majority of the coloured Labour Party might accept the proposals. 'Hendrickse [the Labour Party leader, the Rev Allan Hendrickse] won't – he has Indian blood. Middleton would like to, but his mother is Zulu and he doesn't want to turn against his mother. Sonny Leon has Chinese blood.

'We'll build a middle class – the Indians are willing but they want to keep their options open, and complain about the urban blacks that are left out.'

With regard to the urban blacks, Vorster said: 'I want to create higher communication channels for them than town councils, but they have to start somewhere. I want to tie down their revolutionary urges with better housing and living conditions.'

With hindsight, I draw two conclusions from the above: Mugabe had correctly read the zeitgeist and the big powers' handling of southern Africa in the years that were to come. And John Vorster, and PW Botha after him, had been too devoted to the existing order of retaining white control and suppressing resistance to it to offer South Africa a chance of a good future.

CHAPTER 19

Entry into a wider world

My overriding passion in the ten years prior to our listing on the Johannesburg Stock Exchange in 1994 had been Nasionale Pers and its subsidiaries: our group's products, services and business success. Following my appointment as managing director in 1984, I focused my attention and energies 101 per cent on the success and interests of our company. I dedicated myself to expanding the group.

As Nasionale Pers grew increasingly successful, interest in the group mounted. This led to the listing in 1994. Subsequently, the company found itself in a larger, more diverse environment. I had to step out into a wider world. It was a change I had already experienced and foreseen during the preparatory work for the listing.

I received more and more requests to serve on other boards, deliver speeches, and open art exhibitions or conferences. I tried to confine myself to matters that related to the greater cause of communication.

All work and no play makes Jack a dull boy, as the saying goes. But at Nasionale Pers, known as Naspers from 1998, there had been no shortage of occasions to socialise and relax with colleagues. Given its array of newspapers, magazines, publishing imprints and printing houses, and with pay television added to the mix, the group provided more than enough opportunities for breakaways and celebrations of milestones.

Now, however, I would start moving outside the Naspers circle.

At a relatively early stage in my new career as business leader and managing director, I was able to live out two new interests outside of Naspers's offices. In one case, I accepted Dr Anton Rupert's invitation to serve on the board of the Southern African Nature Foundation, which later became the World Wide Fund for Nature (WWF South Africa). Our country's fauna and flora fascinated me. It was a pleasure to expand the nature reserves through the agency of the WWF. These initiatives subsequently led to the Transfrontier Parks.

There were two people whose dedication to nature conservation struck me in particular. One was Frans Stroebel, who had represented South Africa at the European headquarters of the UN in Geneva in the 1970s and later became Dr Rupert's right-hand man. As chief executive of the Nature Foundation/WWF, he did outstanding work in obtaining conservation status for our natural heritage.

The second person was the former MP for Saldanha, Piet 'Weskus' Marais. He had pleaded and begged for, and propagandised, a West Coast National Park with indefatigable fervour. Marais' zeal was rewarded with the establishment of this beautiful coastal park.

The park was created in co-operation and agreement with the owners of the Postberg reserve area. It was the first nature reserve based on a new concept, one in which the state partnered with private owners in a conservation project. Piet Marais has not been given nearly enough recognition for his unquenchable enthusiasm and efforts to preserve the natural heritage of the West Coast.

Dr Rupert's far-sighted objectives for the Nature Foundation were thwarted by sanctions, and South Africa had to relinquish its membership of the International WWF in Switzerland. As the SA Nature Foundation, we retained associate membership, however, and South Africa remained one of this global organisation's mainstays.

On the adoption of inclusive democracy, South Africa was readmitted as a full WWF member. I had the privilege of serving as chair of WWF South Africa for five years, a time in which I officially received the WWF's international president – Prince Philip, Duke of Edinburgh – and showed him some of our natural treasures.

ENTRY INTO A WIDER WORLD

While I was still editor of *Beeld*, my interest in nature saw the introduction of a regular column on outdoor life, written by Professor Manie van der Schyff. On account of this interest, I became a director of the former National Parks Board (later SANParks). I served for 11 years, and resigned after one year of a third term because I was not prepared to put up with provincialist antics that did not have conservation as their primary goal.

At that time, I crossed swords with Hernus Kriel, who served as the first premier of the new Western Cape province from 1994 to 1998. The Western Cape government had nominated me as its representative on the Parks Board, which was constituted on a provincial basis; I soon discovered that the provinces were quite envious of one another.

On one occasion, we adopted a resolution that I had supported. According to Hernus Kriel, however, it did not serve the interests of the Western Cape. He summoned me and made his dissatisfaction known. I answered him with one sentence: 'In the business world it is a principle that when you serve on a board, you wear the hat of that board and not that of outside interests.'

Kriel became exasperated. My resignation was probably a godsend to him, too, as he could appoint a more biddable person.

But probably the biggest step in my business career after assuming important positions at Naspers was my acceptance of Sanlam's invitation to join their board in 1989. Our group's policy – which still applies – was that its employees were prohibited from serving on the boards of outside institutions. Exceptions to this rule were the boards of charitable organisations such as the WWF, the Parks Board or the Cape Philharmonic Orchestra.

One of the reasons for this policy was that Naspers, with its extensive business activities, had a duty to be involved in work-related organisations such as the former Newspaper Press Union. These organisations deserved the attention of our top management, and kept us very busy, in fact. For instance, at one stage I was chair of the Newspaper Press Union and led the South African delegation to the conference of the World Association of Newspapers in Prague, where South Africa was reinstated as a full member after the sanctions years.

I mulled over Sanlam's invitation over for a long time, as I was aware of the restrictions Naspers imposed. Life insurance would also be new terrain for me.

I discussed the invitation with the Naspers board, which made the concession that I could accept it by virtue of the close ties between our group and Sanlam, the biggest shareholder in Naspers. There were also historical ties: Nasionale Pers's first chair in 1915, WA (Willie) Hofmeyr, had also been the founder of Santam and Sanlam in 1917 and 1918 respectively. In addition to being chair of Nasionale Pers, he was chair of Sanlam for many years.

So, with the permission of the Naspers board I served as a member of Sanlam's board for 16 years and was chair for two and a half years, from January 2002 to June 2004. According to Sanlam's archives, I was a director from 15 November 1989 to 5 May 1998, then deputy chair from 6 May 1998 to 31 December 2001, and chair from 1 January 2002 to 2 June 2004. I was the first person after Willie Hofmeyr to chair the boards of both organisations.

Speaking of other organisations, there was one invitation I never told the board of Naspers about. I can now let this cat out of the bag.

The National Party began to fall apart in the 1990s. FW de Klerk had let Marthinus van Schalkwyk become the party's leader. A delegation of Western Cape MPs and MECs led by Kleppies Heyns, a senior MP, came to see me and invited me to become the leader of the New National Party (NNP) in the Cape.

To persuade me, they stressed the historical bond between Nasionale Pers and the National Party in the Cape Province, Dr DF Malan's leadership of the party and editorship of *Die Burger*, and Willie Hofmeyr's leadership of the Cape National Party in its formative years.

The invitation left me gobsmacked. I hope I succeeded in turning down the opportunity to lead the National Party out of the wilderness after the ANC's takeover with sufficient tact. My reasons were that I was not a politician and had no aspirations to hold public office. The gentlemen took their leave, and that was the end of the story. Thank heavens.

But back to Sanlam, which was a new field for me. I thought I should start off by alerting the board and management to the realities of the new South Africa that were beginning to take shape.

Pretoria had always been Sanlam territory, I explained. The thousands of predominantly Afrikaans-speaking civil servants, members of the army and the police, the Afrikaans-language colleges, universities and businesses, all provided a ready market for Sanlam. The other insurance companies had struggled to make headway against the Afrikaans mindset of numerous large institutions.

This situation was set to change radically, I warned. Sanlam needed to transform its entire image. The company had to prepare itself for the reality that the new civil servants and the new employees in traditionally Afrikaans institutions would not be well disposed towards Sanlam.

Selling this message to the Sanlam bigwigs at their Bellville headquarters was hard going. In those days, the board was structured in an incredibly hierarchical fashion. This was evident from its practices and conduct. The chair, flanked by his managing director and the company secretary, would sit facing the directors, who were arranged in a semicircle in front of him. Directors took their seats within the semicircle according to seniority, and this seating procedure was sacrosanct.

The board members within the semicircle were not fully informed about sensitive issues. For example, they were told one December that the managing director, Pierre Steyn, had had a melanoma removed from his leg during the holidays, that he was in good health, and that everything was going well. Steyn died three months later.

The dynamic Marinus Daling then took over as managing director and also as chair. Marinus was a real go-getter. He would make major decisions and only inform the board after the event, but he was an intelligent leader.

His major gripe was that, as a young chief executive, he had been sent to Johannesburg in the sanctions years by the chair, Dr Fred du Plessis, to expand Sanlam as a business conglomerate. In this way, Sanlam moved into other sectors such as the motor and mining industries, and became the majority shareholder in General Mining (now Billiton). Other companies such as Anglo American, Anglovaal and Barlows were similarly expanded into conglomerates.

Then the wheel turned, and diversified conglomerates suddenly fell out of fashion and favour with analysts and 'the market'. Marinus was instructed to dismantle what he had built up, and bring Sanlam back to life insurance, its original business. With hindsight, one wonders whether that was a wise decision. By walking away from Billiton, for instance, Sanlam wiped out capital of billions of rands. Sanlam would have been a global giant today had it held onto the most important interests in the conglomerate.

I became a senior director and chaired committees such as remuneration and human resources. Later, I served as deputy chair. When Marinus was suddenly felled by cancer, the mantle of non-executive chair was passed on to me.

In those years, one of my main pillars of support on the Sanlam board was a perspicacious engineer and fellow Naspers director, Boetie van Zyl. Another stellar director was the former head of General Mining and later minister of Finance, Derek Keys. He was one of the most intelligent forward thinkers I have ever known. When Sanlam took the lead with demutualisation under Daling's leadership, Keys's advice was invaluable. In the process of demutualisation, Sanlam's policyholders became shareholders. When one looks at the share price today, it was undoubtedly a step forward.

The dynamic Daling decided to split his position of executive director and chair so that he could become non-executive chair of the board with a managing director at his side to lead Sanlam. Daling egged those of us on who served on the human resources committee to get hold of the young Leon Vermaak of Santam as managing director. We also considered three of Sanlam's chief executives, but none of them inspired excitement.

Though Vermaak hit the ground running, it soon became apparent that he was not as familiar with the life-insurance market as he had been with the short-term insurance market, which had been his speciality when he was in charge at Santam.

In my position as non-executive chair after Marinus's sudden death, I had to make weighty decisions – quickly. I had the tough task of letting Leon go. Fortunately, he went on to make a great success of the short-term insurer Auto & General in Johannesburg.

For the position of managing director, Boetie van Zyl and I picked

ENTRY INTO A WIDER WORLD

another Santam man: Dr Johan van Zyl, former vice-chancellor of the University of Pretoria and an agricultural economist with international exposure. His powerful presentation of his plans for Sanlam had impressed us.

Johan proved to be an enormous asset to Sanlam and expanded the company immensely. Under his leadership, Sanlam shook off its reputation as a company controlled by the 'Boere van Bellville' and became one that was representative of South Africa as a whole. Under Johan's leadership, Sanlam entered into a partnership with Ubuntu-Botho, mining magnate Patrice Motsepe's black-owned investment group. The alliance developed into one of the most successful black economic empowerment deals in South Africa and greatly benefited all shareholders of Sanlam.

In 2004, I stepped down from the position of non-executive chair and was succeeded by General Roy Andersen, Chief of the Defence Reserves of the South African National Defence Force. As a former CEO of Liberty Life, Roy was well acquainted with long-term insurance.

Johan van Zyl retired after a hugely successful career, but was earmarked to return as chair after a cooling-off period.

After the Sanlam years, I refocused my full attention on Naspers and systematically reduced my outside interests. I resigned from the board of the WWF and also stepped down as chair of the Cape Philharmonic Orchestra, but stayed on as trustee of the orchestra's investment fund.

In the meantime, there had been other interesting developments. In 2008, I was approached out of the blue to make myself available as the 13th chancellor of Stellenbosch University. Though I felt flattered, I turned down the offer. I know my limitations, and a chancellorship would have made me feel inadequate.

My supporters then recommended Dr Frederik van Zyl Slabbert, who was appointed to the position. This brilliant individual's career had been marked by a certain changeability, but as an academic and someone who represented Stellenbosch's desire to transform, he was an appropriate choice. Sadly, he suffered a heart attack at the end of 2008 and had to resign as chancellor in September 2009 for health reasons. He died on 14 May 2010.

Among my extramural activities, one initiative in particular has been hugely successful: the arts festivals, primarily the Klein Karoo Nasionale Kunstefees or KKNK (Klein Karoo National Arts Festival).

In the old South Africa, white and coloured Afrikaans speakers were assured of the protection and cherishing of their mother tongue and of the promotion of Afrikaans as a language of culture. Initially, it was unclear what the fate of Afrikaans would be after the changeover to an inclusive democracy.

Like many other people, I realised that the new dispensation had to be approached in such a way that Afrikaans speakers would not experience an excessive sense of loss. Light was needed to dispel the gloom, and hope had to be created. A bright idea in this regard was the proposal from Nic Barrow, a businessman from Oudtshoorn, that a festival be held there. Nic discussed his idea with Andrew Marais, Naspers's head of public relations, and the two of them came to see me about it in 1993.

The idea of an Afrikaans cultural festival, with a small 'c', attracted me. I felt that fellow Afrikaans speakers should be able to socialise without the barriers of the past or the traditional formality and stuffiness that tended to characterise theatrical and musical performances. This idea subsequently took shape in the form of the KKNK. The first festival took place in 1994. On my recommendation, the board of Naspers donated what was a generous amount in those days – R250 000 – as a nest egg.

The KKNK immediately gained acceptance, and its popularity grew when Karen Meiring took over its management. She was managing director of the KKNK from 1999 to 2007. Karen and Naspers's PRO Anet Pienaar formed a top team that led the KKNK from one high-water mark to another.

Media24's many publications and other media, such as the Afrikaans radio station Radio Sonder Grense and M-Net – and, later, KykNET – enthusiastically supported the festival. The new outdoor and travel magazine *Weg*, under the leadership of Bun Booyens, was successfully launched in Oudtshoorn. *Die Burger* and its offshoot *Krit*, the festival's paper, became indispensable partners.

This festival far surpassed its original aim of cheering Afrikaans speakers up during the transition to an inclusive democracy. It stimulated an unprecedented upsurge of interest in Afrikaans literary and non-fiction writing, theatre, panel discussions and debates, music, and other forms of cultural expression. Employees of Naspers were involved, inspired and part of the creativity and the fun. And this was only the start of a countrywide movement that has seen Afrikaans as a creative medium flourishing at arts festivals.

Through the festivals, Anet and I deepened our collegiality. This led to friendship – a friendship that resulted in our marriage in 2001. At the time of writing, we had been through 23 KKNKs together.

With the success of Oudtshoorn in mind, I asked one of my fellow board members, Neil van Heerden, why the North could not embark on a similar festival. Neil still lived in Pretoria at the time. He was a former director-general of Foreign Affairs, South Africa's ambassador to the Federal Republic of Germany and the European Union, as well as executive director of the South Africa Foundation: a refined man of culture.

Neil took the initiative, and the successful Aardklop festival, based in Potchefstroom, was born. Again, Naspers was a founding sponsor; with *Beeld*, *Rapport* and Media24's magazines, we could introduce the new festival properly as far as publicity was concerned.

Anet later launched initiatives in Kimberley and White River. The Diamantfees moved to Bloemfontein, where today it has become the successful winter Vrystaat Arts Festival, with *Volksblad* as its publicity anchor. In the Lowveld, White River has given way to the popular Innibos festival in Nelspruit (Mbombela).

Dr Dorothea van Zyl and her Maties team started the Woordfees in Stellenbosch in 2000. In 2015, the dramatist Saartjie Botha took over from her as festival director. The Woordfees has become extremely popular, a gem of a festival. The annual Tuin van Digters (Garden of Poets) poetry festival in Wellington also deserves special mention. With Jakes Gerwel on the board of Naspers and as chair of Media24, the Suidoosterfees was launched in 2003. Jake's formula to make it a 'seamless' Afrikaans festival has ensured that it has become a great success.

A quarter-century of festivals followed the establishment of the KKNK, developing a chain of stages and platforms that continue to create opportunities and spaces for artists from all genres to express their talents. Thousands upon thousands of Afrikaans-minded people socialise here annually. The festivals have also started liaising with one another, co-operation that has made it possible to embark on expensive initiatives such as staging high-quality productions. Platforms have been created for good books, for magazines, for international participation from the Netherlands and Flanders, and, increasingly, for English-language participation.

Coloured people have shone on the stage, resulting in the launch of initiatives such as the Adam Small festival in Pniel. Schools, churches and charitable organisations have, to a growing extent, acquired a profitable share in venue rentals and catering, for example.

Naspers has gained other partners, with institutions such as Absa and the ATKV, and businesspeople from various regions, becoming sponsors. The Dagbreek Trust and the LW Hiemstra Trust, as well the Het Jan Marais Nasionale Fonds, have begun to give support. The story of these arts festivals illustrates the power of a good idea.

The KKNK's success has also had an unintended consequence. Many towns have traditionally hosted agricultural shows. Suddenly, these shows have morphed into arts festivals, often with little art and much noise. Inexperienced songsmiths have begun to deploy their talents. Something like trivialisation and cannibalisation has started eating into the success of others. Our country and the shrinking Afrikaans-speaking community can afford, at most, half a dozen festivals that are worthy of that name. Or maybe the attempt to give the festivals an informal, inclusive, convivial character gives rise to fringe phenomena that one simply has to accept as part of the bargain.

Nowadays, my reduced interests include being a trustee of the LW Hiemstra Trust, which supports the cause of quality Afrikaans books and poetry. And, out of sympathy, I let my arm be twisted to serve as a director of the Eseltjiesrus Donkey Sanctuary. This organisation runs a small farm outside

McGregor where abused, neglected and elderly donkeys can live out their lives with respect and dignity, thanks to charitable donations.

After my retirement in 2015, I was appointed as honorary professor in Stellenbosch University's journalism department. The three-year appointment comes to an end in 2018. It involves four lectures a year, and allows me to keep in touch with younger prospective media practitioners in the rapidly changing digital era.

I can look back on an eventful life, chock-a-block with innovations. But at heart I am still the ever-curious pressman. What also makes me profoundly grateful, however, is the service I have been able to render in functions other than journalism, often thanks to the confidence or support of other people. What you can give according to your abilities is what makes you happy in this life.

CHAPTER 20

Does Naspers still have a soul?

During a discussion about Nasionale Pers's identity at our annual leadership conference in 1987, Izak de Villiers, then editor of the women's magazine *Sarie*, said that, to him, the identity of the company was the fundamental question. 'If you start stripping everything away, what the company does and what it sells, what is it, really?' He also said: 'The company has set itself a certain task, one of upliftment, education and guidance. All this forms part of this company's soul, of its identity.'

Izak's concern about Nasionale Pers's 'soul', an aspect of a commercial enterprise's health that is not commonly examined by its stakeholders, could be explained by the background with which he had joined the Pers.

Before Izak became editor of *Sarie* (from 1983 to 1991) and subsequently editor of *Rapport* (from 1991 to 1997), he had been a minister of the Dutch Reformed Church. The prodigious writing talent that secured him top positions at Nasionale Pers had been devoted to matters of faith: he was an author of devotional books, a hymnist, a presenter of a religious radio programme and a writer of spiritual poetry.

It was from the perspective of this background that he had raised his concerns about the state of the company's soul at the 1987 leadership conference.

In 2009, years after the end of Izak's journalistic career – and with

DOES NASPERS STILL HAVE A SOUL?

Naspers oriented completely differently politically, technologically and commercially from how it had been at its inception in 1915 – he broached the issue of the company's soul again. Izak asked in his book *Strooidak en Toring* (Thatched Roof and Spire) whether the organisation that once had little money and lots of idealism now only had lots of money: whether Naspers still had a soul, or whether it had perhaps sold its soul.

Izak did not like the strongly *verligte* political direction of the later Nasionale Pers that helped bring the ANC to power. It was an important component of his concern and led, among other things, to *Rapport*'s temporary shift to the right under his leadership.

If a company does, indeed, have something like a soul, one could ask whether this soul would have any impact if the company does not achieve commercial success. An idealistically inspired company that fails to keep up with the direction and pace of the world – and, yes, to make money – ultimately offers precious little value to anyone. On the other hand, a media organisation that exploits the opportunities that the market offers and shows strong growth benefits everyone who is involved in its success. In particular, it creates opportunities for the very people who are attuned to the world of the human soul, such as visual artists, writers, theatre directors, actors and ministers of religion.

The philanthropic businessman Jannie Marais first had to make a fortune with the Kimberley Central Diamond Mining Company before he could make the establishment of Stellenbosch University possible.

But the best pronouncement on the relationship between a cause of the soul and the cause of commercial success has to be that of a theologian from Stellenbosch's Theological Seminary, Professor NJ Hofmeyr (1827–1909). He told his nephew Willie Hofmeyr, co-founder and first chair of Nasionale Pers, that the Afrikaans language would only come into its own if it acquired commercial value. Indeed, Willie Hofmeyr led Nasionale Pers in such a way that the company not only offered something of inherent value to readers, but was also able to stand on its own two feet commercially.

This raises a counterquestion one could have posed to Izak de Villiers.

Despite the self-evident value of our success, I still couldn't help thinking about the issue of Naspers's supposed soul and the company's historical commitment to an idealistic cause when preparing a speech for the farewell function that Naspers hosted for me in Cape Town on 6 February 2016.

As mentioned in Chapter 2, I said at the dinner that a big question, one that people asked me in all seriousness, was the following: is Naspers still on the right road? Conservative people tend to associate the expression 'the right road' with Matthew 7:13–14, according to which the broad road leads to hell and the narrow road to heaven. The broad way is the so-called way of the world. But can a company have any significance if it fails to pay regard to the ways of the world?

Yes, I replied to the question about the right road. If one looks at what we were, before 1994 and before the era of digitisation, before the earth-shaking transformation of our society in 1994, then the answer is that we are fully on the right road.

I continued: If we had not embarked on that road with the gravure printing process; with the building of our giant magazine printing plant in 1995; with the establishment of *Die Beeld, Rapport, Beeld* and *You*; with the acquisition of *City Press, Drum* and *True Love*; and if we had not, with M-Net, MTN and MultiChoice, taken the digital road into Africa, across the world, all the way into China, Russia, Brazil – 133 countries – Naspers in its hundredth year would have been a faint shadow of its former strength.

If Naspers had not taken the huge strides required by the surrounding society and global technology trends in good time, we would have been sitting in sackcloth and ashes today in an ever-shrinking little corner, fear-stricken and futureless. Renewal has always been my motivating force and, fortunately, I could drive the renewal with the calibre of colleagues of our group and its boards.

What would have become of our 'soul' or idealism had we failed to adapt timeously to the political, technological and commercial developments of our time and found ourselves unable to determine the course of events? And how could we have gainsaid the justice of the emerging inclusive democracy and sought to maintain South Africa in its state of revolt, oppression and shame without damage to our 'soul'? One could have challenged Izak de Villiers on this point in particular.

But there are some aspects of the historical 'soul' of Naspers that I miss, as is probably the case with older journalists of older media houses the world over. Technology is racing ahead at such breakneck speed today, and the graphosphere of printed matter is so drastically being replaced by the videosphere, that at times I do wonder what has become of our soul as producers of newspapers, magazines and books.

The convivial gathering around the tea urn with the consequent chats, for example, is now a thing of the past.

The 'soul' of an industry that produces newspapers, magazines and books used to involve the clatter of typewriters. It has now become a silent process. The personal computer operates noiselessly, and one spends long periods isolated from direct human contact. Something of the often-impassioned bustle may have been lost.

There could not be much wrong with Naspers's 'soul', it being a company that was at home in the contemporary world and focused on providing value to all concerned. We had achieved enormous success as a company, and were undoubtedly on the right road as far as our adaptation, survival and progress were concerned.

Naspers is now the biggest company on the JSE and in Africa, a giant of a group that employs 67 000 people directly or indirectly. With the opportunities offered by modern technology, the company, founded in 1915, could become a global player. In the original heartland of Nasionale Pers, where it was built up by South Africans of numerous languages, its turnover now makes up only 6 per cent of the company's total trade.

Thanks to digitisation, the Internet and cellphones, the holding company's current CEO can run his office in Amsterdam in the Netherlands. Naspers's financial director is based in Hong Kong. The 'head office' has become an office for a non-executive chair, a person who visits Cape Town periodically. Only two members of the top management team have an office in Cape Town, and they spend about three weeks per month travelling.

Nowadays, it is possible and profitable to do everything this way. The entire modus operandi of newspapers and magazines has undergone a radical shift. Owing to electronics and shift work, one's physical presence at the office is no longer essential. The top team and the board of directors are online 24/7, and communication among them is possible at all times.

The question of Naspers's 'soul', and 'the cause' Nasionale Pers had to advance, fixes one's attention again on the evolution the Pers underwent in the 1970s and 1980s in terms of its political orientation and relationship with the National Party.

The last sensational instance of declaring solidarity with the National Party was the parting of ways between the Nasionale Pers board and its former managing director, Advocate Lang David de Villiers, when the latter promised his support to an independent candidate in the 1987 parliamentary election. His resignation from the board was followed by the resignation of the editor of *Fair Lady*, Dene Smuts. Both of them left because they could not identify with the political road of Nasionale Pers that, in 1987, still strove to live up to its former promises to the National Party.

Izak de Villiers saw this parting of ways in terms of an irreconcilability of souls. He put it like this: 'If I should one day become convinced that my soul is in conflict with the company's soul, I would have only one option. I would have to leave.'

So how *did* matters stand with regard to Nasionale Pers's 'soul' by 1987? The company had by then moved far beyond new employees' having to confirm with their signature on a company form 'that he/she is well-disposed towards the Nationalist aim of the company'.

At the time of the departures of Lang David and Dene, the chair, Piet Cillié, made the following comment, as mentioned earlier: 'You know, if we have to ask everyone at Nasionale Pers whether he is a Nat, we will lose a lot of talent. We will lose some of our best people, because it is always the dissenting man who has brains.'

In other words, by 1987 Nasionale Pers's promises to the National Party no longer really served our professional and business interests, and Piet Cillié acknowledged this albatross around our neck.

On my appointment as managing director of Nasionale Pers in 1984, I inherited the company's commitment to support the National Party. My first Christmas and New Year's message to employees in 1984 still attested to the spirit of a company that was dedicated to a cause: 'Naspers people are always asked: why is your company what it is? The answer is simple: we believe in our people and our people believe in us. The 'cause' still matters and carries the most weight, regardless of how diverse we are.'

But by 1984, the ties between the National Party and papers such as *Rapport* and *Beeld* were almost worn through. Since its founding in 1974, *Beeld* had been no party organ, despite the fact that it still campaigned for the party during elections. As a former editor of *Beeld*, I felt that my soul was ready for the reform that the country and Nasionale Pers required, a shepherd of souls may have said.

As editor of *Die Burger*, Ebbe Dommisse severed the formal bond between *Die Burger* and the Cape National Party in 1990 with the agreement of the party leader, Dawie de Villiers. Both parties felt that mutual detriment was thereby eliminated.

The need for Nasionale Pers to review its political alliances became more and more apparent with our entry into the English-language market. Publications aimed at black readers, in particular, were irreconcilable with outspoken loyalty shown to the government that had enforced apartheid. A formal bond with the NP was prejudicing Nasionale Pers to an increasing extent. As the Pers expanded its operations across the world, its anachronistic association with an old, dying political party in South Africa served only as an obstacle on its path to expansion.

One of the typical questions about the state of Naspers's 'soul' that I was regularly called upon to answer was how Naspers could have expanded, in good conscience, into states such as communist China and the formerly communist Russia.

The counterquestion is why companies such as Microsoft, Volkswagen, General Motors, Maersk, Apple, Philips – just about any multinational company one can think of – operate in countries such as China. As in all countries where Naspers does business, we operate in accordance with the local regulations and laws of the land, and we strive, just like other multinationals, to make a profit, guided by business principles.

In the case of Tencent, we work in partnership with a successful Chinese company. China's economic success has brought about a great degree of personal freedom for a great many of its citizens. This is borne out, for instance, by a recent finding that Chinese from the People's Republic now make up the majority of international tourists.

Citizens' access to information, found effortlessly on the Internet, and their ability to communicate via cellphones, e-mail and digital voice and text messages, are vital aspects of the opening and reform of China itself.

Naspers's main business in China is information and communication services that are delivered digitally. Even though the Internet is censored quite strictly by the Chinese government, Naspers, as a partner within Tencent, still offers communication and information services of great value to hundreds of millions of people. The mobile messaging and social media app WeChat, which is similar to WhatsApp, already has about 900 million users worldwide, but above all in China. These services are used on a voluntary basis, and without cost to the user – in other words, solely because of their inherent value for people. Revenue is generated from optional services such as advertisements and microsales.

How could one even ask whether supplying information and communication services to countries such as China and Russia impairs the 'soul' of Naspers? This is not the case. In fact, providing these services contributes to the new openness of those societies.

When the 'soul' of Naspers is put under the microscope, another question people tend to raise is the shrinking of print media and the shift of journalistic products to the Internet. The decline of print media is a global phenomenon that has forced even internationally renowned magazines such as *Newsweek* to move from print to an online format. So it is not so much Naspers's 'soul' that is at issue here as it is a problem that affects print media worldwide.

At Naspers, too, print media editorial teams have had to be downsized and digital teams strengthened. The experience, expertise and language skills that used to make for quality journalism are no longer always prized to the same extent within the gaudy, evanescent world of instant news, blogs and the often-uncouth opinions of every Tom, Dick and Harry that flash past on one's screen.

The outlook for the 'soul' of journalism is not so gloomy, however, when one focuses on the benefits of digitisation.

With a product such as Netwerk24, for example, Naspers has established a digital news service for Afrikaans users that meets high journalistic standards. It also offers direct access to the digital versions of our print newspapers. In fact, the Internet offers access to the best newspapers and magazines worldwide.

The Internet can be used judiciously. As people become more accustomed to paying for worthwhile media services on the Internet, enormous new opportunities will open up for journalism.

A major benefit not only for readers but also for writers and journalists themselves is digital access to the archives of newspapers and magazines. The search function of print media's digital versions enables subscribers to go far back in history to track down articles or the work of specific writers. This gives a digital subscription a content and value that print media, with the exception of books, could not offer.

The 'soul' of a media organisation such as Naspers is surely also determined by its expertise and its aims or considerations in the production of journalistic products. Specifically as far as South Africa is concerned, quality journalism is one of the few guarantees of the preservation of democracy. Nasionale Pers always had senior editorial staff who could show rookies the ropes. We continue to support the training of competent journalists via journalism departments at universities and other institutions.

The new era has brought with it a certain juniorisation of newsrooms that raises concerns among press people from an earlier era, like me, about the continuity of expert journalism.

But today, we live in a completely new media world. Today, more than a hundred years after its founding in 1915, Naspers is no longer engaged in advancing 'the cause'. Nor is it the print media giant it had been before

1997, when we started with digitisation. The company is now a product of our contemporary age.

Does Naspers still have a soul? As far as my contribution to the formation of Naspers's soul is concerned, if we may stretch the term 'soul' as far as Izak de Villiers does, I take comfort in the flattering words of Rykie van Reenen, arguably the most inspiring journalist of my time. In the 1990s, already incapacitated by the debilitating disease, multiple sclerosis, that would claim her life in 2003, she sent me a note from her bed. An English translation reads:

> Hail, Mr Success! It gives me such delight to witness all of this from afar. I mean to say, this is after all the man who sent me to Dimbaza in those days and who was, in my opinion, the prince of news editors. At first, I thought it was something horrible that had befallen you when you had to become a press boss, and I had great sympathy for you. No need, you are flourishing and expanding – fortunately, I note with a critical eye, at least not around the waist – like only a man who enjoys it would be able to do.

That praise from Rykie now lies in the past. Along with the digital revolution and the new political order in South Africa, Naspers has assumed a new character. Its 'soul' has been transferred.

A lifelong journalist like me, however, can still believe in good, thorough, investigative and fearless journalism within new structures – structures that continue to offer opportunities to us as a media organisation to exercise our freedom of speech with passion and integrity.

CHAPTER 21

Afrikaans in decline

For someone like me who has Afrikaans as his mother tongue and grew up in an Afrikaans family, the Afrikaans language's battle for survival is a depressing experience.

I do not come from a staunch Afrikaner-nationalist background. My dad fought for the Allies, the 'English', in the Second World War. I first discovered the world of reading through English books, thanks to my mother who took me along to the public library in Uitenhage from an early age. But I later started reading the children's magazine *Die Jongspan* and other Afrikaans magazines and books with excitement.

Afrikaans institutions offered me the big opportunities in my life, particularly as far as my career as an Afrikaans journalist is concerned. In Afrikaans, I was able to experience aspects of the country and its people in a way that would have been impossible had I lived only in English. Afrikaans is the language that empowered me.

Nelson Mandela came from a background that was anything but Afrikaans. Yet he studied Afrikaans and Afrikaans literature at university level in prison, evidently with a view to understanding and connecting with his Afrikaans-speaking compatriots, both white and black. His recognition of the value of Afrikaans for millions of its speakers in South Africa forms part of the humanity and wisdom that characterise his legacy.

Afrikaans deserves its status as an official language. In South Africa, only isiZulu and isiXhosa have more mother-tongue speakers than Afrikaans. In many regions of the country, it is the lingua franca, the common language used to communicate across linguistic barriers. According to some estimates, about 15 million people can write and speak Afrikaans, or understand it reasonably well. Afrikaans is deeply rooted in South Africa, unique, and peculiar to the country.

The time when Afrikaans served as a symbol for white Afrikaner nationhood is irrevocably past. Today, white Afrikaners constitute a minority within a large and growing Afrikaans language community. As a language of culture, therefore, Afrikaans still has infinite potential value.

At our arts festivals, Afrikaans flourishes as a creative medium in all genres. Afrikaans developed in South Africa out of the meeting between European, Eastern and indigenous languages, and is celebrated at these festivals as a language that bridges colour or racial differences. The more people from diverse communities have expressed their talents, the more popular our arts festivals have become. This also applies to other Afrikaans fields.

Is there another language in South Africa for which people care so deeply, for which they fight so passionately, and which binds them so strongly to South Africa? This love for Afrikaans makes it painful for me to see how the functions and use of Afrikaans are increasingly being restricted and downscaled today.

Afrikaans is being phased out as an official language at all levels of government. Its formal use is also being curtailed within other institutions such as universities. What lies behind this marginalisation?

One important factor is the advantage it holds for the majority of the country's people to use the international language, English, for all language functions outside of the personal sphere. Over the past century and a half, Afrikaans has been purposely developed and refined for use in all formal and informal contexts: as an academic language, as a language of science, technology, law, officialdom, literature, journalism, the pulpit, and just about any other function or language register imaginable. This is an extraordinary achievement in the history of modern languages.

Because the same effort was not expended on the development of isiZulu or isiXhosa, for example, speakers of those languages mostly used English for further study or other formal purposes. For the rising generation of students, notably black young people, English has therefore become the most advantageous language to use. Universities and other large organisations have adapted themselves to this new dispensation in South Africa.

Moreover, Afrikaans still carries a stigma as 'the language of apartheid'. Rather, Afrikaans was the victim of apartheid because of the Christian-national baggage with which the National Party burdened it. But its negative impression has persisted.

The end result of all these factors is that, more than two decades after our first inclusive democratic election, Afrikaans is being pushed out by the ruling establishment, regardless of the language rights to which it is entitled in terms of our Constitution. The zeal of the NP government has been replaced by the apathy – the antipathy, actually – of the new regime towards Afrikaans. Even in the Western Cape, a largely Afrikaans-speaking province where Afrikaans is one of the three official languages under the DA government, it is swept into a corner.

Digitisation of the media, too, boosts English as the language in which most content can be read worldwide on computers, tablets and smartphones. If one wants to derive full benefit from what is available on the Internet, even German or Italian won't get one everywhere, let alone Afrikaans. The nature of the new media affects the use of languages such as Afrikaans.

Afrikaans radio and television programmes, pop festivals, arts festivals, soapies, songs and popular magazines are continuing unabated, creating a misleading sense that the water is at least still tepid. But the battle for Afrikaans to assert itself as an official language in all spheres has been lost. And a language that is not used officially will go into decline.

By now, nearly all Afrikaners have relatives who have moved to other countries, and these emigrants are walking away from Afrikaans. Afrikaans-medium primary and high schools are still common, but their numbers are dwindling. Coloured Afrikaans speakers now largely contribute to the use and preservation of Afrikaans. Gifted coloured writers, poets, singers and rappers often use extremely colourful varieties of Afrikaans, which carry absolutely no ideological baggage. They are saving Afrikaans with their talent. But as a result of our political history, many coloured creatives do not feel the urge to fortify their mother tongue against English like the older generation of Afrikaans speakers did.

In the industry in which I worked for many years, the Afrikaans print media, sales have fallen drastically. It is not only sales that have declined, but also the depth and scope of articles in the print media. This dilemma is not unique to the Afrikaans media. Worldwide, the loss of revenue caused by the flight of advertising to Facebook and Google has led to cuts in print media editorial staff.[39]

When one points an accusatory finger at the new establishment for its indifference to Afrikaans, however, one's other fingers point back at the old establishment. The complacency and arrogance of the NP government in the first decades of its rule, with the Afrikaner Broederbond as the power behind the throne, created the illusion that Afrikaans was secure for all time, regardless of the demographic realities of South Africa. In 1960, the so-called *Wonder van Afrikaans* (miracle of Afrikaans) was celebrated under the banner of the Afrikaner-nationalist regime, backed by the AB. The conceit was boundless.

Against this backdrop of past abuses, the ATKV and the FAK – as well as the Suid-Afrikaanse Akademie vir Wetenskap en Kuns – battle bravely on. But these organisations, like the Afrikaner Broederbond (now the Afrikanerbond) and the four large Afrikaans Christian denominations, have lost their political sting. Even the idea of a mission of trusteeship over South Africa with which the Broederbond glorified itself has been lost and forgotten.

In the era of Afrikaner self-conceit, I, too, participated in the often-immodest march of Afrikaans as a newspaper editor and, later, leader of our group. All I can say in mitigation is that, from early on in our struggle against the *verkramptes*, we advocated a more open, tolerant and inclusive Afrikaner community in South Africa.

In a speech delivered on 20 June 1991 in Stellenbosch at the annual general meeting of the Akademie, with the topic 'Communication in a transitional stage', I drew attention to a cautionary article by the poet

Dirk Opperman that had appeared in *Die Burger* in 1960. This article spelt out the alternative to the South Africa that we as Afrikaans speakers are experiencing today. It was a world with fewer growth opportunities for Afrikaans than we still have available to us at present.

Opperman referred to Flemish philosopher of culture Max Lamberty's contention that a nation had to develop an attracting force. The Afrikaners seemed to be doing an excellent job of exerting the opposite, namely a strong repelling force, Opperman wrote.

He continued: 'The Afrikaner has constructed his world and strengthened himself, and in the process he has alienated the Englishman, Coloured and Bantu [sic]. This alienation has been accelerated by an urbanisation, or rather a mechanisation, that reinforced impersonal relationships.

'It has also brought about a spiritual alienation, in other words, our cultural world has become impoverished: our children's command of English is worse than ours was and they are less keen to read Dutch and English, the urban Coloured is increasingly speaking less Afrikaans, and we are forcing the native [sic] back to his own language, magazines and books ...'

Opperman's vision of Afrikaners' ultimate destiny was grim: 'But at present the dominant picture of our future is still the one I have painted: within our own ranks and towards outsiders, forces that repel: us from each other, others from us – an expanding universe. The stars move further and further away from each other, they cool down, and in the end each one will come to a standstill in its own self-sufficiency. What fills one with dread about our own future is the vision of this cold, spiritual hell.'

In that speech in 1991, I said that the new South Africa would require exceptional communication abilities to create mutual understanding, overcome suspicion, build consensus and establish peace. Recasting Afrikaans with its image of the language of apartheid as the language of reconciliation would demand much of us. This is still the challenge that faces white Afrikaans speakers in particular: how to free ourselves, in and with our language, from the 'cold hell' of our historical self-isolation. My motto for Nasionale Pers as it had to develop in the 1990s was 'Publish for a more inclusive society'. In other words, step out of the self-isolating communities that apartheid sought to promote.

Ten years earlier, in September 1981, I had stuck my neck out with an article about the future of Afrikaans in the Jewish-sponsored Afrikaans magazine *Buurman*. The title was: 'Is die Afrikaner die dodo van Suid-Afrika?' Was Afrikaans, and the Afrikaner, doomed to extinction, like other species with survival problems?

I pointed out how ironic it was that the more successful Afrikaans became under the political protection of Afrikaner nationalism as a language fit for all purposes, the more talk there was of Afrikaans becoming an endangered species.

A good indication of this irony was the consequences of the homeland policy. South Africa regarded itself as a bilingual country, with Afrikaans and English as official languages with equal status. What would become of Afrikaans in the homelands?

One of the results of the attempt to pin black people down in their own tribal territories was that Afrikaans was ditched in those areas. Every national state/Bantustan/homeland that accepted independence in the NP mould opted for English as the medium of instruction and national language alongside the indigenous language as soon as possible, with the exclusion of Afrikaans.

The image of Afrikaans that homeland citizens had apparently retained was that it was the language of the oppressor: the policeman knocking on your door at night, the official asking you for your pass.

When it comes to the future of Afrikaans, one should recall the words of the poet Dylan Thomas: 'The function of posterity is to look after itself.' It is impossible to predict or to control the future. The future will look after itself. Maybe information and communication technologies will come up with ways of promoting Afrikaans on merit as a language of, inter alia, journalism, science and creative literature, and providing it with opportunities.

The Afrikaans edition of the online encyclopaedia Wikipedia, for example, is the second-largest Wikipedia website in Africa today. Written by Afrikaans speakers in different parts of the world, it is lauded for its excellent quality. Afrikaans novels are increasingly translated into various world languages. Quality does not go under so easily.

What Dylan Thomas said about posterity also applies to the future of a resourceful and dynamic minority group, which Afrikaans speakers have always been. There are still millions of Afrikaans speakers in South Africa, and there is still a large infrastructure of Afrikaans schools.

An upsurge of support for Afrikaans – for instance, a strong increase in the number of Afrikaans singers and songs, and more recently, again, in Afrikaans movies – has manifested itself in the post-apartheid era. Perhaps Afrikaans speakers will be able to look after Afrikaans well in the future, despite the unlikelihood of its ever again becoming a leading language of the South African state as a whole.

With several collaborators, I have tried to conscientise people about the vulnerability – but also the power, value and achievements – of Afrikaans as a medium of self-fulfilment and expression. I took the initiative on behalf of Nasionale Pers of launching the first Afrikaans arts festival, the KKNK, in Oudtshoorn. The intention was to give Afrikaans speakers hope in a new environment in which they would no longer have a dominant voice.

In addition, I initiated the Vriende van Afrikaans (VVA) movement and later the Oorlegplatform (Consultative Platform). The VVA has lived on, thanks to the good work of Christo van der Rheede and now Dr Niel le Roux. The Oorlegplatform is a story in itself.

This baby was born in July 1998 in Sandton amid great enthusiasm. On 2 July 1998, *Die Burger* welcomed the Oorlegplatform in an editorial as a credible umbrella organisation similar to the South African Jewish Board of Deputies. The lack of such a body was the Afrikaners' Achilles heel, the editorial commented, and continued hopefully: 'The Afrikaanse Oorlegplatform is a step in the right direction. But it will take much more than just a consultative platform: establishing and maintaining such an umbrella organisation will require money, time, work and perseverance ... What a challenge with which to conclude the millennium and enter the new century!'

I played a leading role in the establishment of the new movement, which was aimed at co-ordinating the various Afrikaans cultural organisations in a forum that could speak with the power of inclusivity and co-operation. To explain the Oorlegplatform, I referred to a railway station with various platforms where trains move freely to and fro, but which, at the same time, constitutes a junction where passengers encounter one another – in our case, encountering one another for consultation.

Hermann Giliomee planted the idea in my mind after a visit to Belgium, where he had heard of the Flemish phenomenon of an '*overlegplatform*' where different organisations, devoted to the same cause, first reached consensus among themselves before directing a collective request to the government or a municipality.

In his autobiography, Giliomee describes how he started propagating the idea of an Afrikaanse Oorlegplatform (AOP) to act as a pressure group for language rights. He writes: 'Ton Vosloo of Naspers responded to this idea. He was almost the only business leader who expressed himself unequivocally and frequently on the diminishing role of Afrikaans in many facets of public life and the need for an organised response.'

Our core group convened an exploratory meeting in Stellenbosch on 30 November 1996, which about 200 people attended. The audience was representative of all colours and leanings, and the response was generally very positive. The founders were given a mandate to proceed with the formal establishment of an AOP. Thereafter, the ball was largely in my court, as I was able to draw on funds from the Chairman's Fund of Nasionale Pers to take the cause further.

On 28 July 1998, I and 13 others held the AOP's founding meeting in Johannesburg. I asked the meeting to come up with 'an inspiring vision' that could lead the Afrikaans community to 'balanced self-confidence'.

Giliomee recalls in his autobiography that Jakes Gerwel asked: how do we as Afrikaans speakers deal with our past if we want to become a community? Neville Alexander wanted the AOP to create a secretariat that concentrated on mother-tongue education. I closed the meeting with the words: 'We have found something of an overarching and common nature in the discussion that we should work on and refine within the framework of the Constitution.'

This action was followed up by a First Language Summit that took place at Oude Libertas, Stellenbosch, in July 2000. Dr Van Zyl Slabbert joined the ranks of the group. The outcome of the summit was a memorandum that was sent to President Thabo Mbeki. It pointed out the increasing use of English by state structures and the authorities' disregard of the wishes of the majority of South Africans, who preferred to be served by the government in their home languages.

'We would soon discover,' Giliomee writes laconically, 'that government officials were in no hurry to attend to our representations. A request received an acknowledgement of receipt, followed by deafening silence. I referred to it as polite contempt.'

In the end, Van Zyl Slabbert, Giliomee and I got an appointment to see Deputy President Jacob Zuma in January 2001. Mbeki had left changes to the language policy in Zuma's hands.

My memories of the meeting at the ANC headquarters, now Luthuli House, tally with those of Giliomee. He writes: 'At the appointed time Zuma walked into his office and seated himself behind his desk with a broad smile. "Well, gentlemen," he said, "what brings you here to see me? I am just the baggage carrier of the ANC." He made no notes during our meeting and had no one in his office who could keep minutes. After 15 minutes I asked if I could keep minutes of the meeting to send to everyone afterwards.

'A week later I sent my "minutes" to the deputy president's office. There was no acknowledgement of receipt. When I told the story of our visit to Jakes Gerwel, who had been director-general in the office of President Nelson Mandela, he just shook his head and remarked: "That's Jacob Zuma for you."'

Giliomee writes: 'Ton Vosloo and I realised that it was almost impossible for the AOP to function well as a pressure group.'

The jubilations were short-lived, as the AOP baby died a silent death early in the twenty-first century. Afrikaans cultural organisations preferred to keep crowing on their own little dunghills. Perhaps the whole operation had been my fault, in that I had been over-ambitious. Hope had disappointed us.

The history of Hebrew, which was revived to become the national language of Israel after 3 000 years, won't be repeated in South Africa. Still, there are languages such as Welsh, Frisian and Catalan (with 10 million speakers) that have survived well, despite being dominated by the official national language. But do we want to let Afrikaans be degraded to a language that is mainly used for conversing, celebrating, praying or swearing? A local vernacular?

What options do we still have? Is there any hope at all for Afrikaans?

One ray of light is possible initiatives by individuals, affluent capitalists, who love and support Afrikaans, and who would want to provide the means to establish private education institutions, for example. The private Curro schools that initially intended to teach in Afrikaans are now being forced in an English direction by the need for learner numbers. So, there is the need for a materially blessed individual, for whom it is about Afrikaans from A to Z, to come to the fore.

The lesson the past teaches us is that Afrikaans cannot be promoted sustainably if it is promoted on an exclusive basis: through special privileging, or by failing to take the general interest into account. For instance, I have respect for what the trade union Solidarity is doing in many areas, such as the technical training provided to Afrikaans speakers. But its tendency to restrict itself mainly to white Afrikaners frightens coloured people off. And these are the very people on whom the growth of Afrikaans depends today.

I view the situation of Afrikaans at Stellenbosch University in the same way. At a state-subsidised university, there is no longer full scope for separate Afrikaans language and culture as there used to be in the old days. The Maties need to go out of their way to provide access to higher education for disadvantaged coloured students. But to insist on equal tuition time for Afrikaans in modern-day South Africa is ill-considered.

I also have to disagree with my good friend Hermann Giliomee when he seeks a solution in the form of a private Afrikaans Stellenbosch University alongside a state-supported, predominantly English Stellenbosch University. This is an unrealistic idea, as the facilities of the state-supported university cannot accommodate a second university in the same town.

And who has enough money to duplicate all the facilities? A less divisive and exclusive proposal from Giliomee is for departments or institutions to strive towards twin status with Dutch or Flemish institutions. But such arrangements would not really be able to amount to large-scale exchanges and students attending classes at one another's institutions.

Afrikaans simply no longer has the numbers to retain its privileged status of the past, linked to ethnicity. Afrikaners now make up about seven per cent of the population. Within a decade or three, Afrikaners will constitute one per cent of the population. By that time, what need would South Africa have of graduates who have been educated exclusively in Afrikaans?

Jan Rabie writes that Afrikaans is the oxygen he lives on. Great and wonderful literature has been written in Afrikaans. The South African diaspora of the past decades has proved that people who have been educated in Afrikaans can hold their own anywhere in the world and in any company. And that they can accomplish great achievements.

Their fellow Afrikaans speakers will also excel internationally in the future. But they will do so as South Africans who have been freed from the yoke of a race-based political order. They will also be able to do so on the basis of tuition in Afrikaans that did not claim exclusive privileges for this language.

It is the function of posterity to look after itself. The world of Afrikaans is shrinking, says my pessimistic inner voice. But perhaps an inflection point of hope lies ahead, that is still invisible at present. In any case, the final chapter of the history of Afrikaans has not yet been written.

CHAPTER 22

Lighter moments

In my 59-year career as a journalist, editor and business leader, I experienced my fair share of life's sweetness and bitterness. I also had lots of fun and encountered many oddities – some less amusing, others side-splittingly hilarious. And I made some bloopers that make me blush to this day.

The anecdotes I tell or repeat here have not been arranged in any order of importance. I start off with an absurd tale, one that today could have landed the individual concerned in the dock for sexual harassment (and assault!) had he still been alive.

In November 2006, the retired head of Newspapers at Naspers, Jan Prins, sent me a letter describing what had happened to the manager of *Die Volksblad*, Jan Meintjes, when he went to see Bill Troskie, owner of the BMW car dealership in Bloemfontein, about advertisements. Bill was the brother of film and property magnate Boet Troskie. Meintjes described his experience as 'extraordinary'.

The swaggering Bill had begun their conversation by telling Meintjes that he and his brother were 'easily the two richest men in the country'. He invited Jan to lunch and, on a whim, phoned Boet to join them, but Boet had to decline because 'PW' had invited him to a gathering; he apologised

LIGHTER MOMENTS

for not being able to come, but he had to rush off to catch his plane.

Bill had apparently told his brother over the phone: 'Give my regards to old PW.' He told Meintjes it was high time that they invited 'old PW' over for a meal again 'so that we can hear the latest news'.

After the lunch, Jan Meintjes accompanied Bill to his office, where what Meintjes referred to as 'the circus' continued. To impress Jan, Bill summoned his secretary, an elderly woman, and instructed her to tell Meintjes what kind of boss he was. She bragged: 'Sir, there's no one in the whole world who works harder or is a better boss than Mr Troskie.'

Bill called in some of his divisional heads and put the same question to them while they stood in front of his desk. They chorused the same praise.

Then came the cherry on top, as Meintjes wrote to Jan Prins. 'Tell the gentleman what happens on payday if someone messes up during the month.'

The reply: 'If we make mistakes, we get a spanking with a flat hand on our bum.'

Bill boasted that no one in the country could hit harder with the flat hand than himself, seeing that he used to be a boxer. Occasionally, he would get some of the Free State rugby players who worked for him to administer the spankings, 'and if one of the rugby players messes up, I just get some of the other Free State players to do the hitting'.

Then the elderly secretary chipped in: 'Sir, I, too, have been left with a few red marks on my buttocks.'

Meintjes wrote to Prins that he had been so gobsmacked that he just 'humoured' Bill Troskie with 'jislaaik' and 'fantastic'. But when he got home, he told his wife he wanted to get into the shower to wash off the sh—.

Now for another oddity. At *Die Landstem*, where I worked as a reporter from 1958 to 1963, the editorial staff had a copy and language editor by the name of Mr Lotter. Unfortunately, I have forgotten his first name. A quiet, grey-haired man of about 50, he did his work at the monthly magazine *Mense* across the corridor from *Die Landstem*, which was a weekly paper.

Every month, on about the 20th, Lotter would take a few days' leave. He lived in Strand, and we used to wonder what he did with his month-end leave. Eventually, the mystery was solved. In the last week of the month, when the newspaper was at its bulkiest with advertisements, Lotter would take out a full-page ad for a miracle cure that promised to remedy just about any ailment. The ad included a coupon with an address; for a tidy sum that had to be sent via postal order, one could purchase a bottle of the elixir.

The money would flood in. Lotter would take his leave; at home, he and his wife would mix the concoction in a big drum, bottle it and dispatch it to the buyers. Through his sales, he collected enough money to pay for the ad, which he had taken out on credit. He supplemented his salary nicely with the surplus.

In those days, the Medicines Control Council was not such a scrupulous watchdog and Lotter, an unregistered quack, could get away with his tricks.

I still blush when I think of my biggest journalistic blooper. Today, I would surely have been fired for it.

In 1963–1964, the Springbok cricket team was touring Australia. Youngsters such as Graeme Pollock and Eddie Barlow were making a great name for themselves. A brilliant and promising batsman, Peter Carlstein, was a member of the squad; before he had a chance to showcase his talents properly, however, his wife Jackie, three of their four children and their domestic worker died in a car accident near Villiers in 1963.

It was a big story shortly before a long weekend. On top of my day job as political reporter of *Dagbreek en Sondagnuus* in Johannesburg, I was doing freelance work for *Die Landstem*. I then received a request to write a follow-up report on the tragedy. Carlstein was due to leave Australia by plane and would land in Johannesburg on the Friday.

Die Landstem was published on Cape Town on Wednesdays and was available countrywide on Fridays. In anticipation of his scheduled arrival, I wrote a moving report on how the stunned Carlstein landed in Johannesburg and was embraced by his grief-stricken relatives.

Big problem: the plane had engine problems in Perth and failed to

LIGHTER MOMENTS

depart. There was no Friday arrival.

Other papers exploited this blooper, and the guilty paper had to offer some or other lame excuse in its next edition. By that time, Carlstein was back in South Africa, and naturally refused to speak to *Die Landstem*. Mea culpa!

At *Die Landstem*, I also had a lot of fun. It was a paper crammed with human-interest articles. When our Miss South Africa, Penny Coelen, won the Miss World title in London in 1958, our front-page headline was: 'Ons Goue Penny' (Our Golden Penny).

In those days, the paper held the sole rights to the Miss South Africa and Miss World competitions in South Africa. Every year, a member of the editorial team was given a turn to accompany that year's Miss South Africa to London. When my then wife Lorna and I accompanied Yvonne Ficker in 1962, we flew at a price of eighty pounds (then R160) with Trek Airways' four-engine propeller-driven Gold Plate Constellation over three nights, at a speed of just over 400 km/h – first from Johannesburg to Luxembourg, and from there with a smaller plane to London. On our way to Luxembourg, we spent the first night in Windhoek, the next in Kano in Nigeria, and the third in Valletta, Malta.

During the three-day flight we visited the Low Countries, where we socialised, partied with the crew, and went for a swim in Malta. On our return journey, we explored Athens, Cairo and Entebbe. A trip like that was an education in itself.

I got the chance to stay behind in London and conduct interviews with politicians such as Lord Lonsdale, who had business interests in southern Africa, and with leaders in Germany, the Netherlands and Italy. And I went to watch top-class football. Denis Compton, the cricketing hero of my youth, was a football writer at the time, and I was able to meet him in a box at Arsenal Stadium. All thanks to my employer, *Die Landstem*.

Die Landstem could be quite saucy. Springbok rugby captain Hennie Muller was busy at home one Saturday evening in 1953 when his wife Florrie heard the announcement of the team for a test against the Wallabies on the radio. She called out to him with the news. What did *Die Landstem* use as a headline? 'Jy's in! het Florrie gegil.' (You're in! Florrie yelled.)

This paper also introduced several novelties in Afrikaans, and in South Africa. A highly popular column was 'Die Hoekie vir Eensames' (a lonely-hearts column), the precursor of many other copycat columns such as the magazine *Landbouweekblad*'s 'Opsitkers'.

There was also a medical column by 'Dr Welman', the pseudonym of Dr Willempie Steenkamp, one of Cape Town's best-known surgeons. He had a fine sense of humour, and his replies to readers' concerns elicited much reaction.

Every week, Dr Steenkamp received piles of letters, mostly from women. I was then given the job of going through the letters and marking newsworthy passages for 'Dr Welman' to give advice on. Much of the content of the letters was of a sexual nature – frustrated women and disillusioned men.

Editor-in-chief Piet Beukes's personal assistant was Mary MacFarlane, who was in her fifties. She opened all the letters and was the first to read them. The first time she handed me the box of letters, she warned Beukes: 'Ton is too young to read this stuff.'

This letter-reading led to my being put in charge of the paper's letters page. From this flowed a very popular column, 'Oom Lood se Praatjies', in which I published short excerpts from letters (mostly from women) with a light-hearted footnote. The writer of each week's winning letter received a box of chocolates from me. Oom Lood was swamped with letters.

The column was accompanied by a sketch of Oom Lood by the artist Doug Treasure, who would later become well known. The sketch depicted Oom Lood as a kindly, smiling *omie* with a round face and little hair. Oom Lood amassed a huge following.

How did I arrive at the name Oom Lood? It was a play on the lead ('*lood*' in Afrikaans) in the journalist's pencil, but I also knew about a pioneering Afrikaans newspaper writer and owner of the *Albert Gazette* of Burgersdorp in the nineteenth century, Lood Vosloo. And in Somerset

LIGHTER MOMENTS

East, Johannes Arnoldus Vosloo, widely known as Hans Lood, had owned the paper *Het Oosten* and written all its contents.

When I joined *Beeld* later, I started a satirical political column titled 'Lood se Praatjies'. The column poked fun at politicians, and 'Lood' was soon widely read, admired and despised. Columns of this nature are the spice of lively journalism.

Lood the columnist's name is Ton. When I was still under 10 years of age, my pals in Uitenhage thought I was overweight and called me Spekkie. Then one chap said, that's not nice, let's call him Ton. When I got my first byline at the top of a report on the sports page at *Die Oosterlig*, the sports editor, Alex Kellerman, said 'Theunissen Vosloo' was too long for a single column. Let's shorten it, he said. So I ended up being Ton to everyone except my mother.

As a postscript, I was never overweight. I have a photo of our under-13 relay team, the Eastern Province under-13 relay champion in about 1949 or 1950. All four of us had athletic builds.

The most severe reaction to a non-political report of mine related to the 1960 All Blacks tour of South Africa. I travelled with Wilson Whineray's team for part of their tour. On 18 July 1960, they played against Boland in Wellington. The formidable Boland pack included the Springboks Chris Koch and Bertus van der Merwe, as well as a muscular 19-year-old prop, Piet 'Spiere' (Muscles) du Toit. He was the grandfather of the current Springbok lock Pieter-Steph du Toit. From the latter's power and build, it is obvious whose genes he inherited.

Piet scrummed against the All Blacks captain Wilson Whineray, who later became Sir Wilson. With each scrum, he pushed so hard that the All Blacks' backside was forced upwards. Piet was not bulky, but lithe and strong – a farm boy used to throwing bags of wheat weighing close to 100 kg around on the family farm. Doc Danie Craven said he was the most natural prop he had ever coached.

The fitter All Blacks gained the upper hand late in the second half. But their victory was not convincing.

After the match, everyone, the press included, was enjoying a beer in the pavilion. I stood with Whineray and players from both teams. In the presence of both me and Du Toit, Whineray said he would put Du Toit in his place in the tests if he was selected, because Du Toit had scrummed illegally. This was in response to my direct question: what happened between the two of you in the front row?

I made a mental note of his reply as the basis of my report for the following week's edition of *Die Landstem*, which would only appear on the Wednesday.

Referee Piet Calitz then joined our group. Before he could say anything, Whineray brought to his attention that I was a journalist. From that moment on, I said, I would respect the privacy of the conversation. I also mentioned this in my report – as well as the fact that Whineray was mandated to answer official questions, and that he had replied to an official question.

My report became a lead story. Once the paper appeared on the Wednesday morning, the news spread rapidly. It dominated the following week's sports reports in the media.

The All Blacks were playing against the Southern Universities at Newlands that afternoon and, when I arrived at the press gallery box, my colleagues greeted me as if I were a leper.

Before long the All Blacks manager, Tom Pearce, came rushing up to me and said he was throwing me off the tour. I had showed his team in a bad light. If I were to attend receptions to which his team had been invited, he threatened, they would all stay away. His players had been instructed not to talk to me. I had been put into quarantine.

What now? Later that evening I received a call from Doc Craven, president of the South African Rugby Board. 'Pearce can't do anything to you. The planes belong to South African Airways and he has no jurisdiction over our rugby fields. You're coming along on tour.'

Nothing came of Pearce's threats. The South African Rugby Board told Pearce in a friendly fashion that they could not touch me. I was not a

LIGHTER MOMENTS

member of the SARB or the New Zealand team. *Die Landstem* was paying my travel costs.

I went along in the plane to Pretoria, where the All Blacks were due to play against Northern Transvaal on the coming Saturday. I was accompanied by a guest writer, the legendary Bennie Osler, arguably the most famous Springbok fly-half of all time. The two of us sat on our own during the flight, and the All Blacks looked the other way.

In Pretoria, Pearce held a press conference on the Thursday afternoon. He had harsh words to say about me. A week later I wrote: 'I have stood by my standpoint and will stick to it until I am blue in the face.'

In the end, we were able to sort out the matter and shake hands, and the storm in a teacup blew over. The Sunday papers, such as the *Sunday Times*, made a big fuss about the incident.

My final words were: 'The All Blacks are good fellows and one wants to remain friends. Just don't keep on being so touchy when a man who is paid to write does his duty. I am not a PRO for the All Blacks.'

The sudden notoriety, or fame, caught up with me. I went for a haircut in Pretoria. While the barber was scraping my neck with his cut-throat razor, we talked rugby. The All Blacks captain had also had his hair cut there that morning, the barber said, and he was such a nice chap. It's just a pity, the barber added, that some people were trying to cause trouble. 'For instance, take that rubbish *Die Landstem* wrote.'

I muttered: '*Omie*, if only you knew whose neck you have that dangerous knife on right now.' *Die Landstem* acquired one more reader on that occasion.

The following Saturday, the Springboks played in the first test at Ellis Park. I had predicted a Springbok victory – I was one of the few who did – and we ended up beating the All Blacks 13–0. It was a big score if one keeps in mind that a try counted for three points at the time. To me, it was sweet medicine.

Another oddity came my way in December 1963 when I was the political reporter of *Dagbreek en Sondagnuus* and my then wife Lorna the editor of the supplement magazine *Fleur*.

The news spread like wildfire through the corridors: we were getting a Christmas bonus. It would be the first time in the history of Marius Jooste's company that bonuses would be paid.

A day or two before Christmas, we received the bonus: every employee got a huge frozen turkey. Lorna and I found ourselves with two giant turkeys! For months we feasted, doled out portions, and ate reluctantly.

The following year, we got a bonus at Christmas again: this time a frozen chicken each. Presumably the downsized bonus was due to the company's smaller profits. The worst was when it became known that Jooste was a shareholder in the poultry business concerned and had benefited from the higher turnover!

As news editor at *Rapport* in 1975, I received a tipoff that our Miss World, Anneline Kriel, and Mr South Africa, Roy Hilligenn, had posed in the nude for photos somewhere next to the Vaal River. We got hold of the photos. To avoid the newspaper being censored, we published them on the back page with strategically placed stickers. The photos created a scandal.

The story had a sequel in court many years later. The veteran financial journalist Allan Greenblo had written a book on the 'Sun King', Sol Kerzner. Among the topics he covered was the hotel magnate's failed marriage to Anneline, and he wrote about the nude photos. Kerzner appealed to the court to protect his privacy. His application was successful, and Greenblo's book has still not been published.

In my judgement as a journalist, the judge erred in his ruling that suppressed the book.

I am one of the few people who have turned down a business proposition from Kerzner. He had also applied for the pay-television licence that was awarded to M-Net in 1984. When he failed to get it, he appealed to Pik Botha, the minister who was in charge of the SABC at the time. Pik phoned me and asked whether I would be willing to give Sol a hearing. I agreed to see him.

LIGHTER MOMENTS

After a cup of tea, I asked Sol about the purpose of his visit. He said he would like to buy into our licence and become a partner. What kind of stake did he have in mind? I asked. He said about 50 per cent.

My reply was frosty: in other words, he wanted to take control. Was he not aware of the fact that the major condition for the licence was that the shareholders had to own daily papers, and he was not even operating in the newspaper industry? The door stayed closed for him. We remained distant friends.

Hermann Giliomee writes in his autobiography *Historian* that he was the creator of the nickname 'Groot Krokodil' (big crocodile) for PW Botha.

On 15 February 1989, Piet Cillié in his capacity as chair of Nasionale Pers formally congratulated FW de Klerk on his appointment as national leader of the National Party. Attached to his formal congratulations was a handwritten letter in which he apologised to FW for having expressed doubt in an interview with the *Financial Mail* as to whether FW had 'sufficient steel in his teeth' for the position of national leader of such an unruly country. The expression was a play on the Groot Krokodil, De Klerk's predecessor.

Cillié wrote that he had given reporters from *The New York Times*, *The Washington Post* and the *Chicago Tribune* background information about his view of FW's adequacy. The remark about the steel teeth had been put questioningly, he explained to FW, not categorically. His words had found their way into the *Financial Mail,* and that publication gave them a propagandistic slant.

Then Cillié came with a neat sidestep: 'Perhaps the words may nonetheless do more good than bad: "teeth of steel" are not commonly popular after the style of government we have experienced increasingly in the past years.'

From Dr Anton Rupert, I got a gem of a story about what had motivated him in his business career. He told it during a dinner at which I hosted Dr Rupert and his Rembrandt team.

When Rupert still lived in Pretoria, he was, for many years, close to the now-defunct Dagbreekpers that Marius Jooste had established in 1946–1947. He had founded his first company, the Voorbrand-Tabakkorporasie, with the aim of manufacturing cigarettes. He had invested in Jooste's new Sunday paper, *Dagbreek*, and wanted to expand his market.

It the wake of the Second World War, petrol was still in short supply. So, Rupert travelled by train to Cape Town to see Nasionale Pers's head of advertising about adverts in the magazine *Die Huisgenoot*. The ad man, whose name I have forgotten, had a wooden leg. When Rupert walked into his office, the man did not stand up to greet him but remained seated behind his desk on account of his wooden leg. His attitude was frosty. He asked what Rupert wanted.

The answer was that he wanted publicity for his new cigarettes on the coveted back cover of *Die Huisgenoot*. Nasionale Pers's head of advertising replied: 'Mr Rupert, the day you sell more cigarettes than the United Tobacco Company, you can get the back cover of *Die Huisgenoot*.'

And that, Dr Rupert said, had been the challenge that drove him to catch up with the biggest tobacco company in the country and shove it aside. From that day on, he always booked the premium spot – the back covers of prominent magazines – for his cigarette ads. The foundation was laid for his business empire.

CHAPTER 23

The future of Naspers in South Africa

Since its founding in 1915, Naspers has built up a veritable dynasty with its print media. The company serves the reading public with leading newspapers in Afrikaans and English, with regional or community papers, and with more than 50 magazine titles, most of them market leaders. Its publishers are a constant source of good, exciting and stimulating books.

Naspers's print media reflect the political, cultural and intellectual development of the country and the company over a period of more than a hundred years. In this time, Naspers managed, at an early stage and in near-astounding fashion, to conquer territory in markets that have emerged from nascent information technology since the early 1980s. The lifting of sanctions and the opening of the international market after the establishment of an inclusive democracy in South Africa opened an even wider world of commercial opportunities for Naspers.

The downside of this lovely story is that new technology, notably the Internet, exercises a stranglehold over print media worldwide. It also casts a shadow on the future of Naspers's print media. The Internet – where one can read about everything under the sun for free, including the news of the day, if need be, on one's handy smartphone – has radically changed people's reading habits. It has also radically reduced print media sales.

Naspers has become an international media colossus. As a consequence, however, its traditional operations in its home country, South Africa, have declined in financial terms to about six per cent of its international business. This six per cent still makes it a giant in South Africa. But this cannot prevent the difficulties that print media are experiencing in competing with digital media.

The question can rightly be asked: does Naspers, as South Africa knows it – a producer of print media that, inter alia, offers Afrikaans speakers high-quality publications – have a future?

This is an important question. It would be disastrous for the future of Afrikaans if Naspers had to stop, or radically reduce, the production of Afrikaans print media.

But the disappearance or downscaling of print media, whether in Afrikaans, English or other languages, is a matter of even greater public interest: our future as citizens and, more specifically, our freedom in a system dominated by information technology.

Our freedom within a democracy lies first and foremost in our freedom of expression and speech. Above all, freedom of speech means the right to criticise and protest against political abuse of power or any other wrongs effectively. In Dan Sleigh's riveting historical novel *1795*,[40] I read the following words of the American sea captain Potter: 'The true patriot has to tell his government when it is doing wrong. If necessary, he has to shout so loud that the shutters rattle.'

What the print media in South Africa have achieved, and are still able to achieve, is to make the shutters rattle effectively when necessary. The knowledge level, cogency and depth of criticism and protest are also of critical importance to our freedom. The question is whether the digital media can be a substitute for the print media as far as this depth is concerned, and whether they can also effectively reproduce the vigilant role of the traditional print media such as newspapers.

When the rapidly growing content of the Internet hit the print media like a tsunami, one could gradually start to see the ways in which the digital media fail to function as effectively as the print media. The effectiveness of newspapers as watchdogs that monitor the use of political power in a democracy, for instance, is hard to match. Newspapers are, after all, the

THE FUTURE OF NASPERS IN SOUTH AFRICA

kind of media that can blazon a scandalous issue on their front pages, where both the electorate and government leaders cannot fail to see it. The result is that corruption, for example, is mostly highlighted and broadcast by independent newspapers, rather than by television, especially where the latter is subject to a measure of state control.

Newspapers, particularly quality papers that influential people read and which publish articles by authoritative writers, still play a vital political role in virtually every country. They are the appropriate platform for conversations about national affairs between informed and eminent people who seek to assert their influence and who do not wish to use the Internet to reach those concerned, the people who matter.

'Newspapers are a very good medium for analysis, for discussions with subtle distinctions, for instance, a discussion about how we should deal with our economy. The place where you will find the most intelligent conversation is in the newspapers, not on television and least of all on the Internet.' So said Koos Bekker in an interview with Bun Booyens that was published in *Die Burger* on 9 May 2015 and supplemented with video recordings by Netwerk24.

In the 1990s, Bekker had said that 'newspapers are history'. Yet in 2015, he told Booyens: 'If you weaken a society's newspapers, you are weakening the institution through which society talks to itself. This is a huge loss.'

Bekker was also of the view that readers tend to read print articles in a quality paper with greater attention and seriousness than is the case with online articles. 'When I switch from a newspaper to news on the Internet, I read more superficially,' Bekker said during the interview.

Bekker is right in this regard. A big story that is splashed across the front page of a reputable and widely distributed paper, supplemented by thorough commentary on the inside pages, confronts a society and its leaders in a way that the Internet has not yet managed to emulate. One can see the banner headlines of the print media from afar. This is why newspapers continue to play such a major political role worldwide.

In short, freedom of effective expression within a democracy is fundamentally at stake when one talks of newspapers and other print media being discontinued, or even downscaled. The print media are still indispensable in combination with the digital media, where insightful and significant articles are often created today.

What is also at stake is the sphere of our personal lives. In November 1988, *Die Burger* wrote as follows about a newspaper and its readers: 'A successful paper is a member of the family, and can even be an individual conversation partner. At its best it is therefore much more than a source of information, guidance and entertainment. It is a trusted friend whose company one craves, and in the event that it is missing or inaccessible, one is left with a sense of great loss.'

Indeed! This is why faithful readers feel so aggrieved at the attenuation and weakening of their beloved newspapers. The antipode of *Die Burger*'s striking description of the special sphere created by a trusted paper is the phenomenon of addiction to the videosphere, the smartphone and the Internet. This addiction has taken root globally, among young people in particular. At the dining table, in company, while waiting – everywhere, people stand or sit glued to a tiny screen.

And what are they reading on the Internet? The kind of discourse that proliferates here would be unthinkable in a reputable newspaper or book. The often extremist commentary on news events, fuelled by the social media culture of the US, has replaced the considered opinions found on the letters page of a good newspaper or magazine, for instance.

The question remains how to preserve the print media if they are no longer well supported and continue to suffer financial losses.

In its own way, the management of Media24, the subsidiary of Naspers that operates in South Africa, has been addressing the new situation with vigour and with the means available to it. The establishment of Netwerk24 as a platform where readers can access good articles and critical columns online serves as an example. But the big question among experts is still whether we are following the best possible approach.

What has been done in a country such as the US?

The New York Times has retained its print format, but also energetically recruits subscribers for its online product. The reason why someone inside or outside the US would become a digital subscriber to *The New York Times* is to gain access to the quality journalism of the print edition.

A digital subscription to *The New York Times* on the part of, for example, readers from other countries or those from small, remote corners of the US itself is precisely a gesture against the superficial and often unreliable information with which the Internet is swamped.

The problem with *The New York Times*'s approach is that the rise in the number of subscribers to the digital product has not been met with the return of advertising – advertisers have fled to Google and Facebook. *The Washington Post* has a benefactor in the person of Jeff Bezos, the owner of Amazon. He has pumped millions of dollars into both the print and online versions, in the hope of being able to load both products onto Amazon's conveyor belt and sell them.

The point remains: print media are cultural assets with a special value and function in practically every society in the world. They are not a product like bully beef that you simply remove from the conveyor belt once it is no longer making a profit.

Rumours are rife that papers will have to close down within a year or two on account of their losses. But the consequences of doing away with them, specifically in the South African situation where a faction within the ANC seeks to control information and opinions as a result of a craving for power, will be dire. The preservation of quality, critical papers that exercise their right to free speech is of the utmost importance.

One of the cost containment methods that Naspers has employed in recent years is to share editorials among the four sister papers. These papers adapt themselves to their local environments through additional reports. Some of the journalists who used to work at the printed papers have also been transferred to the new digital media. In this way, human capital and money could be saved.

The problem with this, for a journalist and newspaper reader from the heyday of the Afrikaans newspaper industry like me, is that the papers start looking like clones of one another. The input of the editor-in-chief, which in the past could make a big difference to the quality and spirit of the paper, is partially neutralised.

What other possibilities are left to sustain our print media's indispensable contribution to present-day society?

In my days as reporter, editor, executive director and ultimately chair of Naspers, the profits of the Boekhandel group were used to make the founding and running of the daily *Beeld* possible. At the time, *Huisgenoot* with its huge profits could help make the establishment of M-Net possible. Naspers as a group is now making such enormous profits that it is in a position to help out the Media24 group's dailies without any noteworthy sacrifice.

Another possible avenue would be the creation of a trust to ensure the survival of our dailies. An example of this is the Scott Trust that makes it possible for the renowned paper *The Guardian* in the United Kingdom to exist – although, according to my information, the oil in the jar there is also running low. But a trust with shares donated by Naspers and benefactors, if used judiciously, could extend a printed paper's life.

For the political good of the country, the free flow of reliable news and the investigative work of quality journalists are essential. It is also vitally important for Afrikaans that Afrikaans-language print media participate in the debate in and about our society. At present the print media, including the English-language media, enjoy greater freedom than they did before, under National Party rule. But there is a strong faction within the ANC that would like to put the media under government control. For the sake of our country and the strengthening of our democracy, Naspers should think long and hard before it relinquishes the print media as a mouthpiece.

Naspers cannot absolve itself of this responsibility. Newspapers are part of the system of disseminating weighed, verified, balanced information through the media. Along with freedom of speech and freedom under law, this way of dealing with information is the foundation of a true democracy.

Now retired, I shall always watch the fortunes of Naspers, a company I served for so long and with such pleasure.

Notes

1 The name Naspers is used in this book for the group of companies that was known as Nasionale Pers prior to 1998. The new name reflects the transformation of the group's activities over the past 30 or so years. It has become a multinational group that not only focuses on print media. The two names Naspers and Nasionale Pers are both used in this book, depending on the year to which a reference pertains but this rule has not always been strictly observed; it depends on the context and the type of reference.

2 'Lang' (Tall) David because there was another well-known David de Villiers who was also a leader in the Afrikaner community – the latter summarily became Dik (Fat) David to distinguish him from Lang David. Dik David later became co-founder and head of Sasol, and served on the board of Naspers for many years. In fact, there were three of them with the same name and surname who had been fellow students at Stellenbosch University – the aforementioned two and then Dawid, later a theology professor, commonly known as Heilige (Holy) Dawid.

3 De Nationale Pers Beperkt was registered in 1915. In 1921, the company changed its name to Nasionale Pers. This name was changed to Naspers in 1998.

4 Read my column from 1981 at the end of Chapter 6.

5 Read more about Koos Bekker's role in the growth of Naspers in Chapter 5.

6   Koos Bekker's role in the increasing expansion of Naspers's interests is dealt with in Chapter 5.

7   Read in Chapter 4 about how Tencent became an extremely important Naspers asset.

8   ICQ stands for 'I seek you', a program that notifies you when friends and contacts are also online. Among other things, ICQ allows you to chat with them via text or voice contact. OICQ – 'Open ICQ' – refers to an earlier version of this program.

9   Alexa Internet, Inc. is a California-based company that provides commercial web traffic data and analytics. It was founded in 1996 and acquired by Amazon in 1999.

10 Pony Ma, born in 1971, was 27 years old when the company was founded in 1998.

11 IPO stands for 'initial public offering', the first time that the shares of a private company are offered to the public. IPOs are often issued by smaller, younger companies seeking capital to expand.

12 M&A stands for 'mergers and acquisitions'.

13 Rabe, Lizette (ed.). 2015. *Konstante Revolusie – Naspers, Media24 en Oorgange*. Cape Town: Tafelberg.

14 Harber, Anton. 2012. *Gorilla in the Room: Koos Bekker and the Rise and Rise of Naspers*. Johannesburg: Parktown Publishers.

15 These two quotations, and many that follow, are borrowed from the unpublished work *Naspers 100: Chronicle of a company, its country and its world* by Professor Lizette Rabe, head of the journalism department of Stellenbosch University.

16 Giliomee, Hermann. 2016. *Historian*. Cape Town: Tafelberg.

17 At the time, the concept 'liberal' covered an even wider spectrum of meanings in South Africa than in the United States. In the US, liberalists were (and still are) thought of as people who believe in individual freedom, in tolerance of diversity, but also in social commitment and generous welfare-state policies. It is actually liberal socialism that 'liberal' Americans usually have in mind. In a country such as the Netherlands, a liberal inclination is almost the opposite. It suggests a preference for individual freedom of thought, expression and enterprise, a capitalist economy and institutions that arise from private initiative. In the Netherlands, the affluent middle class is associated with a liberal mindset. In conservative circles in South Africa in the era in question, liberalism was associated with dangerous, nonconformist, free

NOTES

thinking – *'andersdenkery'* (dissidence). It was also linked to communism, which in fact comes down to the converse of individual freedom. 'Liberal' assumed a demonising meaning when one was accused of it by an authority figure such as John Vorster.

18   Read more about this in Chapter 10.
19   See Mouton, Alex. 2002. *Voorloper: Die Lewe van Schalk Pienaar*, p. 78. Cape Town: Tafelberg.
20   In 1970, Conrad Sidego became the first coloured journalist to be employed by Nasionale Pers.
21   Rabe, Lizette (ed.). 2007. *Ton van 'n Man*. Cape Town: Tafelberg.
22   Read more about Dene Smuts's resignation in Chapter 12.
23   'Syferfontein' literally means 'sluggish fountain'; the verb *'syfer'* can be translated as ooze, seep or trickle. As a noun, however, a *'syfer'* is a 'figure'. So, 'Syferfontein' could also be understood as 'Figure Fountain'. Today, the scandal would probably have been called something like 'Circulationgate'.
24   Rabe, Lizette (ed.). 2015. *Konstante Revolusie – Naspers, Media24 en Oorgange*. Cape Town: Tafelberg.
25   *Oor Grense Heen* (edited by WD Beukes) was published in 1992, the second publication in the trilogy on Naspers's history for its 75th jubilee. The first was *Sonop in die Suide* (1990) by CFJ Muller, and the third *Boekewêreld* (1992), edited by WD Beukes. The books were published by Nasionale Boekhandel, with editing and design by Tafelberg Publishers.
26   Today, the company belongs to Dr Iqbal Survé's Sekunjalo group.
27   Du Preez, Max. 2013. *A Rumour of Spring*. Cape Town: Zebra Press.
28   The text of the Afrikaans submission is given in the translated format in which it appeared as part of Archbishop Tutu's media statement on the submission. See http://www.justice.gov.za/trc/media/pr/1997/p970926a.htm
29   De Villiers, Dirk and Johanna. 1984. *PW*. Cape Town: Tafelberg.
30   Heard, Tony. 1990. *The Cape of Storms*. Sandton: Ravan Press.
31   Wassenaar, Andreas. 1977. *Assault on Private Enterprise*. Cape Town: Tafelberg.
32   Prinsloo, Daan. 1997. *Stem uit die Wilderness*. Ladismith: Vaandel Uitgewers.

33 On the 'Dawie' column that encouraged Mandela, see also Chapter 9.
34 See Chapter 17 for an account of the day trip on which I accompanied Mandela.
35 Willie Esterhuyse, 2012. *Eindstryd: Geheime Gesprekke en die Einde van Apartheid*. Cape Town: Tafelberg. Also published in English as *Endgame: Secret Talks and the End of Apartheid*.
36 See Part II of Jaap Steyn's excellent biography of NP van Wyk Louw: Steyn, Jaap. 1998. *Van Wyk Louw: 'n Lewensverhaal*. Cape Town: Tafelberg.
37 Barnard, Niël. 2015. *Secret Revolution: Memoirs of a Spy Boss*. Cape Town: Tafelberg.
38 Barnard, Niël. 2017. *Peaceful Revolution: Inside the War Room at the Negotiations*. Cape Town: Tafelberg.
39 See also Chapter 23 about Naspers's perspectives of the future.
40 Sleigh, Dan. 2016. *1795*. Cape Town: Tafelberg.

Prizes, awards and honours

Nieman Fellowship, Harvard University – 1970–1971
FAK award for promotion of Afrikaans culture – 1975
Afrikaanse Handelsinstituut: MS Louw Award for outstanding business leadership in South Africa – 1997
Phil Weber Medal, Naspers – 1992
Businessman of the Year, *Die Burger*/Cape Chamber of Commerce and Industry – 1992
Honorary doctorate in Philosophy, Northwest University – 1994
Marketer of the Year, Marketing Association of South Africa – 1998
Order of the White Rose, Finland's highest civilian decoration, for contributions to trade and culture – 1998
Fellowship Award for contributions to the industry, Print Media SA – 1999
Honorary doctorate in Commerce, Stellenbosch University – 2001
Honorary doctorate in Technologies, Pretoria Technikon – 2002
Frans du Toit Medal for Business Leadership, South African Academy for Arts and Sciences – 2006
Civilian honour for outstanding service in, and significant contributions to, the communications, publishing and business sectors, as well as his work for the preservation and development of Afrikaans, City of Cape Town – 2010
Arts Unlimited honour for service to the arts, Klein Karoo National Arts Festival – 2013
KykNET Fiesta Award for lifetime contribution to the arts in South Africa – 2013
Markus Viljoen Medal for achievement in journalism, South African Academy for Arts and Sciences – 2015
Honorary professorship in Journalism, Stellenbosch University – 2016–2018

Books by the author and contributions to books

Pienaar, Schalk and Vosloo, Ton (ed.). 1975. *Schalk Pienaar: 10 jaar politieke kommentaar.* Cape Town: Tafelberg.
Vosloo, Ton. 1981. 'Sy beeld na buite'. In Smith, Nico J et al. (eds). *Storm-kompas: Opstelle op soek na 'n suiwer koers in die Suid-Afrikaanse konteks van die jare tagtig.* Cape Town: Tafelberg.
Jacobs, Daniel. 2003. *Die Vosloos: Nuttige landsburgers.* Cape Town: Ton Vosloo.

Acknowledgements

In writing this memoir, I tried not to limit my memories to the strictly historical. While writing and finalising *Across Boundaries*, I turned to contemporaries with a wealth of in-depth knowledge of South African journalism for help. I would like to thank Lizette Rabe, Amanda Botha, Tony Heard and Tim du Plessis. I owe them a debt of gratitude for good advice. In the final phase of the project, I received much-appreciated assistance from Etienne Britz and Hannes van Zyl. Their contributions were of enormous value.

My thanks also to the translator of the manuscript, Linde Dietrich.

Jonathan Ball Publishers – notably the founder of the company, Jonathan Ball – guided me supportively and with an expert eye through the process of turning a manuscript into a book. I want to thank the entire team, especially Janita Holtzhausen and Caren van Houwelingen for their professionalism.

In the book I write mainly about my career, and little about my personal life. I had a good marriage with Lorna together with our daughter Nissa. In my ninth decade I rely on the assistance of a team of physicians, but my deepest appreciation goes to my only child: she didn't always have it easy with a father like me. She and my younger sister Joan complete the Vosloo circle. They are loving pillars of support.

In the second phase of my life I have the love and support of Anet, a dynamic, fascinating woman. Being married to her is a treat. We enjoy the art of living to the full, whether it be arts festivals, book launches, music evenings, frequent travels, or socialising with friends. With Anet, I have to run to keep up. Our family include Loren and Jaco, now with Stella and Rita.

I feel privileged to have had a career in the media and all its permutations. To Naspers and its subsidiaries: the company was my heart's home. The little I gave was more than compensated for by the constructive spirit of Naspers and its people. It has made my life's journey a fascinating and joyous one.

To everyone – the companies and people – that crossed my path, I salute you!

Index

3g.QQ.com 52
21 Vianet 54
1795 274

Aardklop 68, 239
Abril 47
Adam Small festival 240
Adams, Marcelle 151
African National Congress (ANC) 27, 40, 44, 69, 74-75, 80-86, 92, 102, 105, 110-111, 117-118, 120, 124, 137, 157, 178, 180, 188, 191, 212, 217, 220, 225-226, 228, 234, 243, 259, 277-278
Afrikaans Consultative Platform (Oorlegplatform) 257-258
Afrikaans Language and Culture Association (ATKV) 91-92, 143, 240, 254
Afrikaans as 'language of the oppressor' 120-121, 256
Afrikaans Literary Society 205
Afrikaans Medium Decree of 1974 120
Afrikanerbond 149, 254
Afrikaner-Broederbond (AB) 8-9, 91, 107, 110, 115, 126, 135-136, 138-142, 145, 149-151, 254
Afrikaner, Die 82, 130
Albert Gazette 266
Alexander, Neville 258
Alibaba 57
Ali, Muhammad 13
Allegro 52
Allen, Fred 12, 213
Altech/Altron 180
Amazon 277
An Adulterer's Prayer 222
Andersen, Roy 237
Anglo American 39, 235
apartheid 21, 74-77, 82, 85, 88, 95, 99, 102-104, 106, 109, 131, 139, 141, 151, 155-156, 162-163, 166, 168, 170-172, 174-175, 177, 180, 190, 211, 224, 228, 247, 253, 255, 257
Apartheid Guns and Money 180
Argus Group 15, 31, 44, 168, 226, *see also* Independent Media

A Rumour of Spring 168
Ashe, Arthur 83
Asof dit gister was (As if it were yesterday) 70
Assault on Private Enterprise 183
Auto & General 236
Azanian People's Organisation (AZAPO) 82, 102

Babylonstoren 61, 71
Bailey, Jim 94, 125
Banana, Canaan 223
Banda, Hastings 106, 108
'Bantustans' (black homelands) 21, 74, 85, 141-142, 163, 256
Barlow, Eddie 264
Barlow Rand 180
Barnard, Fred 88
Barnard, Ian 47
Barnard, Niël 217, 219-221
Barrow, Nic 238
Basson, Jack 19
Basson, Japie 20, 82, 104
Basson, Whitey 19
Beeld, Die (Sunday newspaper) 15, 17, 21, 24, 37, 78-80, 82, 90-99, 104-105, 108, 119, 122-123, 136, 138, 141-145, 189, 202, 205, 244
Beeld (daily newspaper) 24, 26, 37, 80-81, 84, 94, 99-100, 106, 110-111, 113, 119, 121-122, 124-126, 129-131, 138, 141, 145, 147-149, 170-174, 176-177, 179, 186-187, 195-204, 216, 223, 225, 233, 239, 244, 247, 267, 278
Beetge, Anna 6
Beetge, Gert 82, 108, 205
Bekker, Koos ix, 28-30, 32, 35, 43, 46-47, 52-53, 55-56, 60-71, 134, 275
Beukes, Piet 18-19, 82, 266
Beukes, Wiets 112-113, 119, 126, 187, 190
Bezos, Jeff 277
Bezuidenhout, Gert 21
Bible Society 186
Biko, Steve 105
Billiton 235-236

Black Sash 157
Blake, Arthur 15
Blanke Bouwerkersvakbond (white construction workers' union) 108, 205
Blum, Peter 73
Booyens, Bun 238, 275
Boshoff, George 148
Boshoff, Tobie 91
Botha, Amanda 17, 151, 283
Botha, Barry 82
Botha, Elize (academic) 36, 82, 136
Botha, Elize (president's wife) 181
Botha, Fanie 144
Botha, June 28
Botha, Louis 139
Botha, Pik 30-31, 62-63, 81-82, 118, 182, 184, 187, 217, 270
Botha, PW 25, 27, 30, 75, 81, 84, 93, 110-119, 135, 138, 140, 144, 155-158, 160, 182-188, 192, 199, 216, 216-217, 219-221, 224-226, 230, 263, 271
Botha, Saartjie 239
Botha, Stoffel 118
Botma, Piet 130-131, 134, 148
Bourgarel, Roger 213
Bouwer, Alba 169
Brandwag, Hoërskool 7, 9, 10
Brewis, Hannes 1
Breytenbach, Breyten 73, 75, 156
Brink, André P 73, 79
Brookes, Charles 13
Brotherhood of Power: An Exposé of the Secret Afrikaner Broederbond 141
Brown, SED 104
Brutus, Dennis 211
Bruwer, Johan 106
Bruwer, Johannes 106-107
Buitendag, Koos 32, 70, 184
Bureau for State Security 122, 197
Burger, Die 8, 14, 18-19, 21, 24-25, 35, 67, 74-75, 78, 82, 88, 96-97, 103-104, 108, 111-113, 115, 119, 122, 124, 126, 131, 141, 144-145, 147-149, 153, 156, 159, 163, 171, 177, 179, 187, 190, 200, 211, 216-217, 234, 238, 247, 254, 257, 275, 276, 285
Burger, Schalk 15
Burgers, Rieta 28
Buscape 52
Buurman 256

Cable & Wireless 34
Calitz, Piet 268
Canal Plus 47, 53
Cape Argus 168
Cape Philharmonic Orchestra 233, 237
Cape of Storms, The 92, 182
Cape Times, The 18, 91-92, 131, 182, 216
Carlstein, Jackie 264
Carlstein, Peter 264-265
Carter, Jimmy 94, 229
Caxton 145
Celliers, Jan FE 72
censorship 26, 70, 72-73, 88-89, 94, 132, 136, 143, 158, 161, 270
Chen, Charles 49, 51
Chicago Tribune, The 271
China Mobile 51
China Motion Telecom Development Limited 49
China Unicorn 51

Christelike Kultuuraksie 205
Christelike Studentevereniging (CSV) 9
Christiansen, Arthur 129
Cillié, Piet 21, 24-25, 36, 40, 58, 61, 70, 74-79, 82, 96, 104, 106, 108, 112-114, 122-123, 128, 136, 147, 151, 154-155, 158-159, 161, 164-165, 169, 184-187, 192, 194, 246, 271
circulation scandal Perskor *see* press and circulation battle
Slabber, Coenie 147
Citizen, The 94, 110, 216
City Press 37, 94, 124-125, 244
Claassen, George 176
Clark, Mark W 98
Classen, Arthur 19
Clinton, Bill 13, 216
Cluver, Gus 13
Code of Conduct for Nationalist newspapers 123
Codesa 217
Coelen, Penny 265
Coetsee, Kobie 81, 114, 118, 217, 221-222
Coetzee, Blaar 18, 20
Coetzee, George 134
Coetzee, Hubert 40
Colour: Unsolved Problem of the West 76
Combrinck family (Bethulie) 2
Combrinck, Flip 2
Compton, Denis 265
Concerned Social Workers 157
Confucius v
Congress of the People (Cope) 180
Conradie, Campher and Pieterse attorneys 8
Conradie, Frans 8
Conradie, Leo 8
Conradie, Hennie 25, 40, 134
Conservative Party (CP) 110
Cottesloe conference 77-78
Cowley, Clive 15
Craven, Danie 16, 135, 208, 210-211, 213, 267-268
Crompton, Richmal 7
Curro schools 260

Dagbreek en Sondagnuus 21-22, 70, 80, 82, 87-88, 90-91, 94, 98, 108, 144, 207, 210-211, 264, 269, 271
Dagbreekpers 22, 87, 90, 123, 272, *see also* Perskor
Dagbreek Trust 240
Daily Dispatch 30
Daily Express 129
Dakar talks, 1987 74-75
Daling, Marinus 235-236
'Dawie' column 104, 112-114, 126-127, 187, 190
De Beer, Dan 205
De Beer, Sam 20
De Beers 39
De Gaulle, Charles 88
Degenaar, Johan 73
De Kiewiet, CW 88
De Klerk, FW 26, 84, 101, 111-116, 118-119, 126, 140, 145, 170, 184, 188-190, 210, 216-217, 221, 225, 234, 271
De Klerk, Jan 210-211
De Klerk, Marike 216
De Klerk, Willem (Wimpie) 26, 77, 134, 146, 187, 203-204, 210
De Lange, Pieter 36, 82, 114, 127, 136, 149-150
Delius, Tony 16
Democratic Alliance (DA) 180
Denneoord teachers' training college 2

INDEX

Department of Journalism, University of Stellenbosch 68, 148, 176, 241
De Swardt, Salie 134, 148
Detainees' Parents' Support Committee 157
Deutsch, Karl 83
De Villiers, David (Lang David) 23, 25, 36, 98, 104, 124, 132, 144-145, 149, 154-157, 161, 164, 184, 193, 203, 246, 279
De Villiers, David (musical conductor) 151
De Villiers, Dawie 81, 114, 118-119, 184, 246
De Villiers, Dirk 13-14, 16, 82, 91, 142, 169
De Villiers, DP (Dawid Sasol) 113-114, 279
De Villiers, Izak 134, 145, 189, 242-243, 245-246, 250
De Villiers, Tink 150
De Vries, Mike 35
De Wet, Carel 93
De Wet, Johan 171, 173-174, 176
Diamantfees (Diamond festival) 239
Die Vosloos: Nuttige Landsburgers 1
digital era and age 16-17, 33-35, 36, 38, 43-44, 54, 64-66, 68-69, 133, 241, 244, 248-250, 274, 276-277
Dipico, Manne 218
DirectTV 64
D'Oliveira, Basil 212
D'Oliveira, John 15, 92
Dommisse, Ebbe 148, 247
Dönges, Eben 16, 141
dotcom bubble and crash 45, 48-49, 54-55, 65
Drum 37, 94, 125, 132, 179, 244
DStv 34, 53, 69
Du Plessis, Barend 20, 81, 113, 118, 184
Du Plessis, Eddie 146
Du Plessis, Fran 36
Du Plessis, Fred 235
Du Plessis, PG 144
Du Plessis, Tim 166, 170, 172, 175-179, 283
Du Preez, Ben 205
Du Preez, Frik 11
Du Preez, Jas 134
Du Preez, Max 168
Dutch East India Company (Verenigde Oostindische Compagnie, VOC) 2
Du Toit, Hendrik ix
Du Toit, Pieter-Steph 267
Du Toit, Piet 'Spiere' 267-268

Economic Freedom Fighters (EFF) 225
Eefoo 48
Ehlers, Ters 114
Eindstryd – Geheime gesprekke en die einde van apartheid 191
Eksteen, Koedoe 31-32, 186
Electronic Media Network *see* M-Net
Elizabeth, Queen 212
embedded journalism 16
Endgame 191
Enenstein, Craig 36
Engelbrecht, Gideon 25
EP Herald 15, 17
Eseltjiesrus Donkey Sanctuary 240
Esterhuyse, Willie 82, 191

Facebook 49, 254, 277
Federasie van Afrikaanse Kultuurverenigings (FAK, Federation of Afrikaans Cultural Societies) 10, 91, 110, 143, 254, 285
Ferreira, Basil 8

Ficker, Yvonne 18, 265
Fifth Brigade, Zimbabwe 224
FilmNet 34, 43, 56, 64
Financial Mail 61, 271
Financial Times, The 81
Finansies & Tegniek 82
First Language Summit 259
Fischer, Bram 147, 151-152, 156
Five Freedoms Forum 157
Fleur 22, 269
Fourie, Brand 32
Fourie, Jopie 106
Frans Du Toit Medal 283
Frazer, Harry 213
freedom of expression 180, 250, 274, 278
Freemasons 4
Friendstar 49
Friend, The 30
Froneman, Sampie 143

Gandar, Laurence 109
Gerdener, Theo 82
Gerwel, Jakes 191, 258-259
Gibran, Kahlil 145
Giliomee, Hermann 88, 168, 192, 258-261, 271
Golding, Rae 150
Gorilla in the Room: Koos Bekker and the Rise and Rise of Naspers 63-64
Gouws, Piet 148
Graaff, De Villiers 18, 20
graphosphere 66
Greenblo, Allan 270
Greyling, Cas 21
Grobbelaar, Jannie 40
Grobler, Dixie 5
Grobler, Sergeant 5
Groot Verseboek 191
Grosskopf, Johannes 78, 99-100, 147-148, 201
Group Areas Act 126
Guardian, The 81, 278
Gupta family 110

Hancke, Hendrik 197-198
Harber, Anton 63-64
Havenga, Klasie 141
Hawinkels, Hans 47, 49, 53, 56
Heard, Tony 92, 182-183, 283
Hendrickse, Allan 230
Hersov, Basil 180
Herstigte Nasionale Party (HNP) 80, 93, 149, 186
Hertzog, Albert 20, 80, 82, 90, 95-96, 104, 108, 130, 139, 141, 189, 205
Hertzog, JBM 80, 96
Hesse, Hermann 7
Het Jan Marais Nasionale Fonds 240
Heunis, Chris 114-115, 154, 165
Hewitt, FJ 31, 62
Heyns, Kleppies 234
Hilligenn, Roy 270
Historian 88, 271
Hitler's Halt (Despatch) 10
Hobhouse, Emily 71
Hoekie vir Eensames, Die 266
Hofmeyr, NJ 243
Hofmeyr, Willie 96-97, 169, 234, 243
Holomisa, Bantu 180
Holzapfel, Johann 148

Home Box Office (HBO) 29
Hoofstad 82, 96, 99, 143-144, 148
Horwood, Owen 184, 212
Hudson Institute 83
Huisgenoot (*Die*) 15, 22, 159, 177, 217, 272, 278
Hultzer, John 8
Human, Koos 134, 136, 169
Human & Rousseau 134
Huntington, Samuel 83

IDG Technology Venture Investments 49
Independent Media Group 44, 168
Information Scandal 94, 110, 199, 212, 224, 229
Innibos festival 239
Insig 177
Internet Plus 55
Investec ix

Jacobs, Daniel Malan 2
Jaekel, Heinie 25, 134
Jessop, Tom 92
Jeugbond 93, 207-208
Jewish Board of Deputies 257
Jews for Social Justice 157
Jodac 157
Jongspan, Die 8, 251
Jonker, Abraham 18
Jonker, Ingrid 18, 73, 191
Jonker, Lourens 36
Jonkmanskas 136
Jooste, Marius 22, 70, 90, 96, 98-99, 111, 123, 143-144, 146, 149, 201-204, 270, 272
Joseph policy of Naspers 40
Justice and Peace Commission, Roman Catholic Church 157

Kabila, Laurent 216
Kahn, Herman 83
Kaunda, Kenneth 107-108
Keet, Bennie 76
Kellerman, Alex 15, 267
Kemp, Franz 15, 146
Kemp, Reinet Louw 17
Kennis-legger 171-172
Kerzner, Sol 62-63, 270
Keys, Derek 236
Kimberley Central Diamond Mining Company 243
Kinghorn, Jane 28
King Kong 6
Kisbey-Green, Gillian 69, 134
Klein Karoo Nasionale Kunstefees (Klein Karoo National Arts Festival, KKNK) 238-240, 257
Kleurkrisis en die Weste, Die 76
Klopper, Henning 183
Koch, Adrienne 221-222
Koch, Chris 267
Koekemoer, Martin 188
Koen, AJ 90
Koornhof, Piet 30, 62, 144, 151
Kotzé, Adri 176
Kriel, Anneline 199, 270
Kriel, Hernus 233
Krige, Uys 18, 73
KRIT 238
Krog, Antjie 73, 159-160
Kroniek van 'n koerantman 126
Kruger, Elsa 17

Kruger, Jimmy 89, 122, 131
Kruger, Paul 11
Kruger, Peet 176, 179
Krynauw, Dr 6
KykNET 68, 238, 286

La Grange, Flip 136, 144
Laingsburg flood 199
Lamberty, Max 255
Landman, Ruda 179
Landbouweekblad 15, 266
Landstem, Die 17-18, 22, 80, 83, 98, 144, 263-266, 268-269
Langley, Tom 21, 95
Lategan, Esther 154, 157, 161-162
Laubscher, Twakkies 146
Lau, Martin 51
Leadership 184-185, 193
Leipoldt, C Louis 72
Lekota, Mosiuoa 180
Leon, Sonny 230
Le Roux, Dawie 20
Le Roux, Niel 257
Leroux, Etienne 73
Liberale Nasionalisme 76
Liberty Life 237
Li, Eric 47
Li, Richard 50
Lojale Verset 76
loyal resistance within Afrikaans media and by Afrikaners 73-75, 77, 104, 139, 168-173
Lonsdale, Lord 265
Loskopdam speech by HF Verwoerd on sports policy 89, 108, 207-210, 211-213
Lotter, Mr 263-264
Louw, Ben 15
Louw, Eli 117
Louw, Elretha 17
Louw, Kobus 210
Louw, Murray 40-41
Louw, NP van Wyk 73-76, 169, 205-206
Lubner, Bertie 180
LW Hiemstra Trust 240

Machel, Graça 217
MacFarlane, Mary 266
Macmillan, Harold 77
Macsteel 180
'Magic of the Book, The' 7
Maibowang 48
Mail.ru 47, 52, 58
Ma, Jack 57
Malan, DF 96, 103, 140-141, 234
Malan, Magnus 113, 118
Malan, Recht 40, 58
Malan, Wynand 20
Malema, Julius 21
Malherbe, Jeff 36, 136, 168
Mandela, Nelson 34, 40, 80, 101, 126-127, 160, 188-191, 211, 215-222, 226, 251, 259
Mandela, Winnie 157, 190
Maoris 108, 208-210, 213
Ma, Pony (Ma Huateng) 49-51, 56-57, 68, 280
Marais, Andrew 238
Marais, Ben 76
Marais, Eugène N 73-74
Marais, Jaap 20, 82, 139, 189, 213

INDEX

Marais, Jannie 243
Marais, Piet 154, 165
Marais, Piet (Weskus) 20, 82, 232
Marais, Willie 20
Maree, Gaffie 95
Maree, Willie 89
Matjila, Daniel 44-45
Mazzini, Giuseppe 133
Mbeki, Thabo 189, 191, 259
M-Cell 218
McFarlane, RJ (Mac) 19, 183
Media24 44, 57, 134, 179, 191, 238-239, 276, 278
Medicines Control Council 264
Mehl, Reverend 217
Meijers, Neville 49
Meintjes, Jan 262-263
Meiring, Karen 238
Meng my wyn 9
Mense 18, 22
Menzies, Robert 90
MER (ME Rothmann) 169
Mervis, Joel 98, 109
Meyer, Piet 32, 110-111
Middleton, Norman 230
MIH Asia 47, 53
Millin, Philip 97
Minipot, invention of 202
Minnie, Derek 16
Minnie, Derick 16
M-Net 31-37, 41, 43, 60-62, 65, 68, 125, 135, 183, 187, 217, 238, 244, 270, 278
Mocke, SI 205
Modise, Joe 219
Moolman, Terry 145
Motlana, Nthato 34
Motsepe, Patrice 237
Mouton, Jannie 70
MTN 33-34, 37, 43, 244
Mugabe, Robert 223-230
Muir College 9
Mulder, Connie 21, 110-11, 183
Muller, CFJ 128
Muller, Florrie 266
Muller, Hennie 266
Muller, Hilgard 11, 107
Muller, Piet 148
MultiChoice 35, 37, 43, 64-65, 137, 244
Multiply 52
MWEB 43, 218
My land van hoop 77
MySpace 49

NAIL 34
Napoleon Bonaparte 133
Nasionale Boekhandel 25, 134, 278
Nasionale Koerante 18, 25, 92, 126, 134, 175, 177, 184, 186, 190, 192, 262-263
Nasionale Tydskrifte 15, 25
Naspers (Nasionale Pers) ix, 21, 23-39, 43-48, 50-61, 63-71, 83, 103, 129, 133-134, 137, 145, 161, 166-167, 170, 176, 180, 190-191, 217-218, 231-234, 236-240, 242-250, 258, 262, 273-279, 283, 285
Naspers 100: Chronicle of a company, its people, its country and its world 33
Natal Witness 30
National Council against Communism 205
National Education Union of SA 157

National Intelligence Service 219
National Party (NP) 10, 16, 20, 24-25, 27, 31, 36, 58, 67, 72-76, 79-80, 84-85, 87, 91, 93-95, 98, 101-105, 108-114, 116, 118-124, 131, 138, 140-142, 145, 147, 149, 151, 154-156, 163, 165, 171-173, 175-176, 180, 185-186, 204, 207, 212, 217, 224, 234, 246-247, 253-254, 256, 271, 278
National Union of South African Students (NUSAS) 105, 157
Naudé, Beyers 27, 73, 77-78, 139, 156
Naudé, Jurie 25, 134, 158
Neethling, Piet 114
Nel, Daan de Wet 143
Netease 49, 54
Netwerk24 249, 275, 276
New National Party (NNP) 234
Newspaper Press Union 135, 233
Newsweek 248
New York Times, The 81, 271, 276-277
Niemann, Keppies 115
Nkomo, Joshua 224, 229
Nöffke, Carl 146, 203
Nokwe, Duma 228
Norval, Jim 4
Norval, Luther 6
Norval, Martie 6

Ofsowitz, Solly 5
Oggendblad 96, 99, 143, 148
OICQ 49
Old Mutual 11
OLX 52
Olympics rugby club 2
Oom Lood se Praatjies (Lood se Praatjies) 266-267
Oor Grense Heen 167
Oosten, Het 267
Oosterlig, Die 4, 8, 13-17, 82, 267
Oppenheimer, Harry 18
Opperman, DJ (Dirk) 78, 169, 254-255
Opperman, Dumpie 145
Opsitkers 266
O'Reilly, Tony 44, 168
Osler, Bennie 269
Ossewabrandwag 151, 183
Otto, Chris 70

Pacak, Steve 69
PaiPai 52
Pakendorf, Harald 143
Palm, Calvyn 134
Pan Africanist Congress (PAC) 92, 102, 105, 226
pay television ix, 29, 31, 62, 65, 125, 133, 187, 231, 270
Pay TV 47-48, 53-54
PCCW Ventures 49, 54-55
Pearce, Tom 268-269
Peil 29
Perold, Sakkie 144
Perskor 13, 31-33, 44, 70, 80, 83, 87, 90-91, 95-96, 98-99, 109, 111, 123, 142-149, 183-185, 193, 195, 200-204
press and circulation battle, Afrikaans 80, 89-100, 109, 142-149, 183-185, 196-197, 200-204
press freedom 109
PG Glass 180
Philip, Prince 232
Phil Weber award/medal 56, 283
Phuthuma Nathi 43-44, 137

Pienaar, Anet *see* Vosloo, Anet
Pienaar, Hetta *see* Vosloo, Hester
Pienaar, Schalk 15, 19, 21, 74-78, 91, 93, 95, 99, 108, 122-123, 136, 142-143, 145, 147, 159, 169, 189, 195, 204
Pienaar, Wynand (Bunny) 2, 6
Pieterse, André 32
Pieterse, Gideon (Giep) 8, 13
Plaatje, Sol 109
Platter, Erica 158
Platter, John 158
Pollock, Graeme 264
Population Registration Act 126
Potgieter, AP 205
Potgieter, Denzil 167, 170
Pratt, David 87
Pretoria News 13
Prins, Jan 18, 25, 29, 134
Prins, Pieter 61
Prinsloo, Daan 184
Prinsloo, Koos 136
Prophet, The 145
Progressive Party 20, 75, 84, 109, 183
Protter, David 196-198, 200
Public Investment Corporation (PIC) 44
PW 181

Qoboza, Percy 94, 121-122, 131-132
QQ 52, 53
QQ.com 52
QQ Games 52
Qwelane, Jon 124
Qzone 52

Rabe, Lizette 33, 68, 172-173, 283
Rabie, Jan 73, 261
Rabin, Yitshak 197
Radio Sonder Grense 238
Rand Daily Mail 94, 109, 124
Raphaely, Jane 28, 157, 160
Rapport 24, 80, 83, 98-99, 106, 111-112, 114-115, 119, 121, 134, 138, 144-147, 149, 171, 177, 179, 187, 189, 191, 197, 204, 216-217, 239, 242-244, 247, 270
Rapportryers, Junior 143, 189
Rautenbach, Renée 8
Rebellion 1914 106, 139
referendum, 1983 156-157
referendum, 1992 27, 36, 102-103, 139, 157
Reservation of Separate Amenities Act 126
Rembrandt 39, 271
Retief-Meiring, Martie 148
Rex Collings Publishers 141
Reyneke, Karools 203
Rheeder, Benjamin 17
Rheeder, Margaret 17
Rhoodie, Eschel 110
Richard, Dirk 70, 143, 146, 210
Richemont 39, 47
Ries, Alf 92, 112-115, 220
Roelofse, Koos 204
Rooi Jan books 9
Roos, Karen 28, 71
Rossouw, Arrie 176, 179
Rousseau, Gawie 134
Roux, Antonie 52, 55-56
Roux, Jannie 114, 184
Rupert, Anton 82, 104, 232, 271-272
Rupert, Johann 43, 180

Samson, Eric 180
Sanlam 11, 70-71, 180, 183, 233-237
Santam 234, 236-237
SA Observer 104
Sarie 28, 159, 172, 177, 179, 242
Sauer, Paul 20
Savimbi, Jonas 216
Scheffler, Andre 217
Schmidt, Louis 11
Schoeman, Beaumont 82
Schoeman, Ben 98, 123, 144, 213
Scientific and Industrial Research Council (CSIR) 31, 62
Scott Trust 278
Searle, Charles 47, 53, 56
Secret Revolution: Memoirs of a Spy Boss 219
Sekunjalo consortium 44
separate freedoms 21
separate voters' roll 75-76
Serfontein, Hennie 81, 141
Sewe dae by die Silbersteins 205
Sharpeville tragedy 77, 104, 211
Shaw, Gerald 92
Sibiya, Khulu 124-125
Slabbert, Frederik van Zyl 73-75, 84, 172, 192, 237, 259
Sleigh, Dan 274
Small, Adam 73, 109, 240
Smit, Cora 198
Smit, Flip 82, 142
Smit, Robert 198
Smith, Arthur 18
Smith, Gerald 4
Smith, Ian 84, 224, 229
Smuts, Dene 28, 134, 157-161, 246
Smuts, Jan 18, 82, 96, 103, 151
Socrates 123
Solidarity 260
Sonn, Franklin 215-216, 219
Sonop in die Suide: geboorte en groei van die Nasionale Pers 1915-1948 128
Sorour, Mark 47, 53, 67
SoSo 52
South African Associated Newspapers 18
South African Non-Racial Olympic Committee (SANROC) 211
South African Press Association (SAPA) 19, 177
South West African People's Organisation (SWAPO) 81, 84, 86
Southey family (Steynsburg) 2
Sowetan 216
Soweto youth uprising 120-121, 124-125, 199
Sparks, Allister 20, 109
Spies family 6
Sportscn 48
Starcke, Anne 28
Star, The 89, 92, 97, 208, 216
Steenekamp, James 5
Steenekamp, Sarah 5, 7, 9-10
Steenkamp, Willempie 266
Steyl, Jack 91, 207
Steyn, Jaap 206
Steyn, Nora 124
Steyn, Pierre 235
Steytler, Jan 20
Stofberg, Cobus 47, 56, 69-71
Stroebel, Frans 232
Strooidak en toring 243

292

INDEX

Strijdom, JG (Hans) 21, 75, 95, 97, 104, 140-141, 199
Strydom, Barend 199
Strydom, Hans 140
South African Breweries 39
South African Communist Party (SACP) 105, 147, 151
Southern African Nature Foundation 232
South African Rugby Board 16, 209, 268
South African Broadcasting Corporation (SABC) 23, 29-32, 62, 65, 91, 110-111, 183-184, 186, 194, 215, 270
Suid-Afrikaanse Akademie vir Wetenskap en Kuns (South African Academy for Arts and Sciences) 15, 91, 110, 136, 143, 206, 254
Suid-Afrika – Waarheen? 'n Bydrae tot die bespreking van ons rasseprobleem 76
Suiderstem, Die 18
Sunday Times 22, 98, 109, 269
Super Afrikaners: Inside the Afrikaner Broederbond, The 140-141
SuperSport 35, 43
Survé, Iqbal 44, 281
Suzman, Helen 20, 182-183
Swart, Freek 146
Syferfontein 149, 195, 200, 204, 281, *see also* press and circulation battle

Tambo, Oliver 226
Taswell, HL 83
Tencent 43, 46-59, 65, 68, 248, 280
Tencent Research Institute 51
Tenpay 52
Terre'Blanche, Eugéne 159
Terreblanche, Mof 40
Theunissen, Roelf 148
Thomas, Dylan 256-257
Thomas, James 89, *see also* Kruger, Jimmy
Time 16, 88, 219
Times Media group 31
Timol, Ahmed 105
Tom.com 50
Transvaler, Die 12-13, 19, 78, 96-99, 141-142, 146, 148-149, 195, 200-204
Treasure, Doug 266
Trek Airways 265
Treurnicht, Andries 21, 82, 96, 110-111, 121, 139, 143-144, 159
Tricameral Parliament 111, 156, 230
Trollip, Alf 212
Troskie, Bill 262-263
Troskie, Boet 262
Trouw 81, 131
True Love 37, 94, 125, 244
Tsafendas, Dimitri 91-92, 182
Tuin van Digters poetry festival 239
Tutu, Desmond 167, 176-177, 178

UBC Pay TV business 53
Ubuntu-Botho 237
UDI declaration 84
Uitenhage Chronicle, The 1, 9
Uitenhage Times, The 1, 9
United Democratic Front (UDF) 111, 157
United Democratic Movement 180
United Party (UP) 10, 18, 20, 82, 93-94, 96, 109, 187
United Tobacco Company 272
Uys, Cornelius (Boet) 15

Vaderland Beleggings 98

Vaderland, Die 19, 70, 78, 82, 90, 96, 98-99, 141, 146, 148, 200, 203
Van Aswegen, Attie 9
Van Breda, Alex 20
Van Breda, Michelle 179
Van den Bergh, Lang Hendrik 122, 126, 197
Van der Elst, Jacques 15
Van der Merwe, Bertus 267
Van der Merwe, Billy 136
Van der Merwe, Daan 21, 95
Van der Merwe, HA 9
Van der Merwe, Jac 56
Van der Merwe, Johnny 6
Van der Merwe, Koos 196
Van der Merwe, Lorna 17 *see also* Vosloo, Lorna
Van der Merwe, Nak 144
Van der Rheede, Christo 257
Van der Ross, Ben 36
Van der Schyff, Jack 12
Van der Schyff, Manie 148, 233
Van der Vyver, Marita 196
Van der Vyver, William 134
Van der Walt, Désirée 198
Van der Westhuizen, Christi 176
Van Deventer, Hennie 81, 126-127, 134, 148, 177, 196
Van Dijk, Bob 52, 56
Van Heerden, Neil 36, 82, 239
Van Heerden, Willem (Wollie) 22, 32, 184
Van Niekerk, Danie 134, 136, 169, 191
Van Reenen, Rykie 78, 82, 88, 91, 143, 146, 159, 169, 205, 250
Van Rensburg, Hans 151
Van Rooy, JC 140
Van Schalkwyk, Marthinus 234
Van Schoor, AM 146
Van Vollenhoven, Tom 11
Van Vuuren, Hennie 179-180
Van Walsem, Bob 112, 114, 148
Van Wyk, Chris 57-58
Van Zyl, Boetie 36, 236
Van Zyl, Dorothea 239
Van Zyl, Hannes 148, 283
Van Zyl, Johan 71, 237
Veg 82, 108, 136
Venter, Bill 180
verlig/verkramp concept and battle 20, 26-29, 36, 74, 77-78, 80, 84, 93-95, 98-99, 102-104, 106, 108, 111, 119, 122, 124, 138, 141, 143, 145-147, 149, 156, 157, 160, 169, 170, 189, 195, 201-204, 206-207, 213, 243
Vermaak, Leon 236
Vernon, Raymond 83
Verwoerd, Betsie 89
Verwoerd, Hendrik 20-21, 44, 74, 77-79, 82, 87-92, 95-98, 104-108, 140-142, 182, 188, 207-209, 211-213
VIA channel 68
videosphere 66, 245, 276
Viljoen, Christo 65, 149
Viviers, Jack 114-115, 125, 146, 148, 196
Vivo 58
Vodacom 33
Volksblad (Die) 19, 24, 30, 96, 108, 113-114, 119, 124, 126, 148, 171, 177, 239, 262
Volkwyn, Jim 47
Voorbrand-Tabakkorporasie 272
Voortrekkers youth movement 10, 143
Vorster, John 15, 76, 79-80, 92-95, 98, 104-108, 110, 122-123, 131, 140, 142-144, 188, 199, 212-213, 222-225,

293

227, 229-230, 281
Vorster, Koot 76-77
Vosslöhs 2
Vosloo, Andries 16
Vosloo, Anet (wife of author) v, 190, 238-239, 283
Vosloo, Hester (Hetta) Jacoba Combrinck (mother of author) 1, 4, 6-8, 11, 107, 251, 267
Vosloo, Jacobus Johannes Vermaak (father of author) 1-2, 251
Vosloo, Jan (grandfather of author) 2
Vosloo, Jan (forefather) 2
Vosloo, Joanna Jacoba (Joan, sister of author) 2, 5-7, 283
Vosloo, Johannes Arnoldus (Hans Lood) 267
Vosloo, Lood 266
Vosloo, Lorna (wife of author) 17-18, 22, 113, 265, 269-270, 285
Vosloo, Nissa (daughter of author) 22, 202, 283
Vosloo, Ton
birth 2; youth 2-10; exposure to books and love of reading 6-7, 9, 137, 251; as clerk, Department of Forestry 1, 10-12; as reporter at *Die Landstem* 17-18, 21, 80, 82, 98, 144, 263-266, 268-269; as parliamentary and political reporter 17-21, 29, 87-88, 99, 105, 129, 142, 146, 190, 208-209, 219; as Nieman Fellow at Harvard University 20, 28, 82-83, 94, 99, 121, 146, 283; as news editor of *Rapport* 99, 146-147, 250, 270; on the future of Afrikaans 251-261; and the Truth and Reconciliation Commission (TRC) 26, 127, 167-180; on the independence, loyal resistance and conflict of interest of journalists 8-9, 15, 72-74, 76-77, 94-95, 122-123, 125, 136, 139, 154-156, 161-166, 169-171, 190-191, 193-194, 247, 267-269; 'Ton's Ten Lessons for Life' 137; and the resignation of Dene Smuts and 'Ton of bricks' 134, 157-161, 246; on the resignation of Lang David de Villiers as chair of Naspers Board 154-157, 161-166, 246; and listing of Naspers on Johannesburg Stock Exchange 39-42, 44, 56, 69, 231; prizes, awards, honours 285; and view of Naspers on the Dakar talks of 1987 74-75; retirement ix, 69, 145, 241, 278; as managing director (executive head) of Naspers ix, 20, 22-40, 83, 94, 128, 173, 247; and column on negotiations with ANC 26, 80-81, 83-86; difference of opinion with Koos Bekker on centenary publication of Naspers 68-70; as editor of *Beeld* 21, 24, 80-88, 129-132, 200-205, 222, 233; prosecution and conviction under the Prison's Act 106; cooperation and agreement with Percy Qoboza of *The World* 121-122; as initiator of the Vriende vir Afrikaans 257; as initiator of the Afrikaanse Oorlegplatform 257; and appointment of and working with blacks and black journalists 121-125, 130-131; role in directional change of Afrikaans media at Naspers 125, 127; on the role of leadership in a company 128-137; on inclusiveness and South Africanism 132-133; as chair of Sanlam 181, 233-237; on the 'soul' of Naspers 242-250; on digitalisation of the media 16, 32-33, 36, 42-43, 64, 244, 248-250, 274-277; working with NP van Wyk Louw against far-rightwingers 206-207; as member and chair of the World Wide Fund for Nature (WWF South Africa) 232; as member of the National Parks Board (SANParks) 233; invitation to become leader of New National Party (NNP) in Western Cape 234; on Naspers ties with and doing business in communist China and Russia 247-248
Vosloo, Wynand Frederick (Freddie, brother of author) 2-6
Vriende van Afrikaans 257
Vryheidsparty 180

Truth and Reconciliation Commission (TRC) 27, 127, 166-174, 176, 178-179
Truth and Reconciliation Commission submission by Naspers journalists 172-179
Wallerstein, David 49
Waring, Frank 212, 222
Waring, Joyce 222
Washington Post, The 271, 277
Washington Star 110
Wassenaar, Andreas 183
Weber, Phil 35, 40, 56, 58, 75, 83, 98, 123, 136, 144-145, 169
WeChat 52, 57, 248
Weekblad, Die 19
Weg 238
Weideman, Esmaré 179
Weiss, Detlev 143, 205
Weiss, Hymne 143, 205
'Weiss Squad' 143, 205
Welgemoed, Piet 33
Welkom Yizani empowerment scheme 44
Welman medical column 266
Wentzel, Tos 19
Wepener, Willem 80, 83, 99, 113, 145, 147, 169, 187
WhatsApp 248
Wheatfields 221 70
Whineray, Wilson 18, 267-268
Wiese, Christo 180
Wiese, Eric 40, 106, 134
Wilkins, Ivor 140
Willers, Willie 198
Winer, Ada 6
Winer, hoofkonstabel 3, 5
Winer, Paul 3, 6
Winer, Trevor 3, 6
white *baasskap* (domination) 20, 75, 95, 140-142
Woord en Daad 77
Woordfees 239
World Association of Newspapers 233
World Council of Churches 77
World, The 89, 94-95, 121-122, 131-132
World Wide Fund for Nature (WWF South Africa) 232-233, 237
Worrall, Denis 154, 158, 160-161

Xu, Daniel 51

You 37, 177
Young, Andrew 229
Young Christian Students 157
Yu, Han 86

Zaayman, Bart 108
ZANU 224
ZAPU 224
Zhang, Tony 49, 51
Zuma, Jacob 189, 191, 259

www.ingramcontent.com/pod-product-compliance
Lightning Source LLC
Chambersburg PA
CBHW060832190426
43197CB00039B/2560